The Laws of Trading

The Laws of Trading

A TRADER'S GUIDE TO BETTER DECISION-MAKING FOR EVERYONE

Agustin Lebron

WILEY

Library of Congress Cataloging-in-Publication Data:

Names: Lebron, Agustin, 1976- author.
Title: The laws of trading: a trader's guide to better decision-making for everyone / Agustin Lebron.
Description: Hoboken, New Jersey: John Wiley & Sons, Inc., [2019] | Includes bibliographical references and index. |
Identifiers: LCCN 2019008179 (print) | LCCN 2019010385 (ebook) | ISBN 9781119574194 (Adobe PDF) | ISBN 9781119574200 (ePub) | ISBN 9781119574217 (hardback)
Subjects: LCSH: Investment analysis. | Investments—Decision making.
Classification: LCC HG4529 (ebook) | LCC HG4529 .L43 2019 (print) | DDC 332.6401/9—dc23
LC record available at https://lccn.loc.gov/2019008179

Contents

Acknowledgments   vii

Foreword by Aaron Brown   ix

Introduction   xiii

Chapter 1   **Motivation**   1
        Know why you are doing a trade before you trade.   1

Chapter 2   **Adverse Selection**   21
        You're never happy with the amount you traded.   22

Chapter 3   **Risk**   41
        Take only the risks you're being paid to take. Hedge the others.   41

Chapter 4   **Liquidity**   71
        Put on a risk using the most liquid instrument for that risk.   72

Chapter 5   **Edge**   93
        If you can't explain your edge in five minutes, you don't have a very good one.   95

Chapter 6   **Models**   115
        The model expresses the edge.   115

Chapter 7   **Costs and Capacity**   141
        If you think your costs are negligible relative to your edge, you're wrong
            about at least one of them.   142

Chapter 8   **Possibility**   167
        Just because something has never happened doesn't mean it can't.   171

Chapter 9   **Alignment**   197
                   Working to align everyone's interests is time well spent.   198

Chapter 10   **Technology**   217
                   If you don't master technology and data, you're losing to someone who does.   220

Chapter 11   **Adaptation**   239
                   If you're not getting better, you're getting worse.   240

Notes   261

Index   271

Acknowledgments

First and foremost, I want to thank the people, past and present, of Jane Street. When I walked in the door in 2008 I honestly didn't know what to expect, other than something new and challenging. That I got, but what I didn't imagine was how much I'd learn over the next six years. I learned plenty about finance and trading of course, but the most important things I learned were a way of thinking about the world, and about how to attack difficult problems. It was a wonderful place of work, and I hope y'all find this book worthy of the high intellectual and ethical standards that have come to characterize the firm.

My editor Bill Falloon was presented to me as a "prince of editors" and indeed the words proved prophetic. You took a chance on an unknown writer and guided me through the often-confusing process of bringing a book to life.

Many thanks also go to Aaron Brown, whose kind help and advice was always freely given and immensely useful. This book wouldn't be what it is without your help.

A quarter-century of arguing over email with "the chumps" was perhaps the greatest preparation I could ever get for having to write convincingly and concisely.

Most importantly I want to thank my family. My parents, who feel more than ever like old friends. To my wife Ana Paula. This book started its weird life in the kitchen of your parents' house, and I know you've had to put up with a lot of lonely evenings as I worked on this sometimes-quixotic project. Eduardo and Mateo, you'll write your own books too someday. And yes, you'll probably get to use a computer.

Foreword by Aaron Brown

As old and as true as the sky

Both laws and trading are older than human history, and older than humans. Back in 1894, Rudyard Kipling documented the laws he observed among wolves in the jungles of India. Four of Agustin's eleven laws can be found among Kipling's first six stanzas.

> **The Law for the Wolves—Rudyard Kipling (1865–1936)**
>
> Now this is the law of the jungle, as old and as true as the sky,
>
>> And the wolf that shall keep it may prosper, but the wolf that shall break it must die.
>
> As the creeper that girdles the tree trunk, the law runneth forward and back;
>
>> For the strength of the pack is the wolf, and the strength of the wolf is the pack. *Law 9*
>
> Wash daily from nose tip to tail tip; drink deeply, but never too deep; *Law 2*
>
>> And remember the night is for hunting and forget not the day is for sleep.
>
> The jackal may follow the tiger, but, cub, when thy whiskers are grown,
>
>> Remember the wolf is a hunter—go forth and get food of thy own. *Law 1*
>
> Keep peace with the lords of the jungle, the tiger, the panther, the bear;
>
>> And trouble not Hathi the Silent, and mock not the boar in his lair.

When pack meets with pack in the jungle, and neither will go from the trail,

> Lie down till the leaders have spoken; it may be fair words shall prevail. *Law 3*

Jungles are places of sparse natural resources and the densest and most diverse life of any ecosystem. Everyone knows there is a law of the jungle and agrees what it is. Deserts are places of sparse natural resources and sparse life. "Law of the desert" is a less familiar term with many different meanings. We don't have a common "Law of the forest," "Law of the prairie," or well-known laws for any other environment.

Not only did you know that there's a law of the jungle, you also knew that it has a lot of overlap with the laws of trading. But why? Laws become important when a dense and diverse population competes aggressively for scarce resources. Deserts don't need as many laws because there are fewer individuals and species to interact. When there is plenty for everyone, there are fewer conflicts to resolve.

But laws of the jungle and trading were not made by humans or wolves. They are the product of evolution. "The wolf that shall break it must die." "The trader that shall break it must fail and find other work, usually going on CNBC to give trading advice to others." These are not traffic laws with fines for those who break them and are caught by humans. They are not Newton's laws of motion woven into the fabric of nature. These are laws because everything contrary to them no longer exists.

Another way to express the same idea is that the jungle and the trading market only exist due to their laws. Without the law of the jungle, the jungle would be a desert. Without the laws of trading, financial markets would be replaced by what John Law described as the "State of Barter" back in 1705 (Money and Trade Considered With a Proposal for Supplying the Nation with Money):

> *This State of Barter was inconvenient, and disadvantageous.*
> *1. He who desir'd to Barter would not always find People who wanted the Goods he had, and had such Goods as he desir'd in Exchange.*
> *2. Contracts taken payable in Goods were uncertain, for Goods of the same kind differ'd in value.*
> *3. There was no measure by which the Proportion of Value Goods had to one another could be known.*

In this State of Barter there was little Trade, and few Arts-men. The People depended on the Landed-men. The Landed-men labour'd only so much of the Land as serv'd the occasions of their Families, to barter for such necessaries as their Land did not produce; and to lay up for Seed and bad Years. What remain'd was unlabour'd; or gifted on condition of Vassalage, and other Services.

The Losses and Difficulties that attended Barter, would force the Landed-men to a greater consumption of the Goods of their own Product, and a lesser Consumption of other Goods; or to supply themselves, they would turn the Land to the product of the several Goods they had occasion for; tho only proper to produce of one kind. So, much of the Land uas unlabour'd, what was labour'd was not employ'd to that by which it would have turn'd to most Advantage, nor the People to the Labour they were most fit for.

Agustin makes similar points in more modern language when he defines financial markets as places with standardized products, many and heterogeneous participants, and low transaction costs. People can try to create these qualities, and they often do, but they fail unless they attract traders who know the law. Traders make markets, markets don't make traders.

While the laws of the jungle and trading can seem harsh to outsiders, Agustin reminds us that they are essential to prosperity. We may enjoy the austere beauty of the desert, but if we want the planet to support many billions of diverse people in comfort and freedom, we need the hyperefficient use of sparse resources we find only in jungles and financial markets. We may have romantic feelings about simple, self-sufficient villages of organic farmers and craftspeople organized for mutual support, but that lifestyle is profligate in resources, something only the richest 0.1% or so of the population could ever afford.

I would add only one thing to the excellent advice in this book. Agustin is a trader to the core of his being, and insists his laws are valid for all kinds of decisions outside financial markets. I agree with him that the laws of trading apply everywhere, but if you're not actually trading or in a jungle, there are other laws that can apply as well.

Consider his example of choosing whether or not to jaywalk. Some trading laws are useful, such as Law 7: "If your costs seem negligible compared to your edge, you're wrong about at least one of them;" Law 4: "Put on a risk using the most liquid instrument for that risk;" Law 3: "Take only the risks you're paid to take. Hedge the others." One of the costs of jaywalking is constantly monitoring traffic for opportunities which may eat up more attention—missing out on productive thinking time or tripping over obstructions in the sidewalk—than your average time savings are worth. If you are going to jaywalk, choosing a liquid opportunity (such as one with a median strip that allows you to change your mind halfway across the road) is smarter than an illiquid one. Make sure that a successful jaywalk will actually save you time and not, for example, just get you sooner to a place to wait for the same traffic light or underground train.

But there's a reason we have traffic laws. You must consider those as well. "Look both ways before crossing the street;" "Wait for the light;" "Cross at the crosswalk;" "Keep to the right except to pass;" not only help keep you safe; they help all traffic flow as quickly and safely as possible. When you jaywalk, you may or may not be making a good trade of survival for prosperity, but you also should ask if your strategy would make you and everyone else less safe and fast if universally adopted.

The laws of trading are all you need in places of dense competition where efficiency is of great importance. Outside those domains the same ideas apply, but don't forget there are other laws as well. Not just the kind that can put you in jail, but the ones that guide you to treat others as you would have them treat you.

I predict this book will quickly become a minor classic. By that I mean a book that will not hit the bestseller lists, but that as you go through life you will find that it has been read by most interesting people you meet who care about trading, risk-taking, economics or decision-making; and that you will recommend it enthusiastically to the rest. Minor classics are short, clear, easy-to-read distillations of centuries of experience filtered through the logical brain of expert practitioners.

> *Now these are the Laws of the Jungle, and many and mighty are they;*
> *But the head and the hoof of the Law and the haunch and the hump is*
> *— Obey!*

Introduction

It's Monday February 24th, 2014. A trader at this point in my life, my job is to buy and sell securities on financial markets around the world, and to do that profitably. Markets in London open at 8am, so that's when my trading day starts. Today is going to be an interesting day, since on Saturday the Ukrainian parliament decided to remove its president from office. Trading is always busy after big news like this happens. And yet if I think carefully, I can count ten different trades that I did before markets even opened:

1. I got out of bed and went to work. 6am is early, but I traded away a bit more sleep (and a relaxing day off) in exchange for the wages I'm going to be paid for my work.
2. I wore the heavier jacket. It would have been nice to find the thinner one in this unseasonably warm weather, but the risk of rooting around in the closet and waking up my wife was too great. I traded some comfort on the way to work in exchange for a smoother home life.
3. On the walk to the Underground station, I got a notification that the old golf clubs I had put up on eBay had finally sold. I'd rather have the extra money than a backup set of old irons anyway.
4. When I saw a gap in the traffic I decided to jaywalk in the middle of the block, saving myself somewhere between 2 and 30 seconds of waiting at the corner for the light. I bought those seconds with (a) the small risk of injury or death if I had misjudged the gap, and (b) the even smaller risk of getting a ticket.
5. I swiped my Oyster card at the station, exchanging some hard-earned money for the right to board the Underground to work. It's entirely too far to walk, and taking a cab would be more expensive and likely slower too.
6. As the train came, I noted how full it was. I like to position myself so that I board the car that will be closest to the

escalator at the arrival station. But this time, the train was busy enough that I probably wasn't going to get a seat if I boarded the optimal car. I moved one car over, trading those precious jaywalking seconds for a higher chance at getting a seat.

7. A few stops from my destination, a woman with a *Baby on board* lapel button got on. I saw another man start to move, but I got up faster. I won the trade, giving up my comfortable seat in exchange for a smile, a warm feeling, and the social approval of a few random strangers.

8. Since it was the last Monday of the month, it was my turn to get coffee for my trading desk. The purchase was obviously a trade, but the fact that I bought coffee when I don't even like it is another one. Better to create and maintain a good esprit de corps, even if it means a small delay and a small expense for some smelly liquid I won't be drinking.

9. As we were setting up the systems for the day, my junior asked if we could confirm the vacation schedule. We can't both be out on a trading day, so we traded a couple of vacation days back and forth until we were both happier with the result than before.

10. At 7:57am, I noticed that I would like to go to the bathroom before markets opened. But I judged the chance of missing the first few seconds of the opening was too high, so I traded away some small avoidance of discomfort in exchange for guaranteeing being at my desk as the opening bell rang.

So, there you have it. Ten trades, all done before any of the thousands of trades that constitute my "real" job as a trader. I bet you could come up with a similar list of decisions evaluating risk and reward. And that makes you a trader as well.

What Is Trading?

Trading is the act of buying or selling, and it's everywhere. Straight-out trading has been occurring since before the beginning of recorded human history, across continents and cultures. It comes naturally to us and we start at an early age. Even children barely able to talk are able to negotiate complex futures trades with their siblings, ensuring a steady supply of just the right Legos for their creations.

All of our relationships involve trading at some level, even if that trade isn't monetary in nature. As you saw in my walk to work, we sometimes trade our time, our comfort, even our sleep in exchange for other things of value. You may not keep an explicit ledger of those trades, or even realize you're making them, but you are. And when a relationship becomes too one-sided, like a friend who never calls or a cousin who always needs a favor, your trading instincts kick in and you reevaluate the social trades you're making. The laws of trading apply to these implicit exchanges just as much as they do to the trades I make in financial markets every day.

Now, if trading is so common, then what's so special about trading on financial markets specifically? It is worth remembering that these sorts of markets are a relatively recent invention. Government debt began to trade in Venice in the thirteenth century, and common stock began to trade in Amsterdam in the seventeenth century. Commodity futures markets also organized themselves around the same time and, as it turned out, the innovations embedded in these markets were so useful that the ideas quickly spread. This eventually gave us the present-day smorgasbord of organized financial markets, and the influence of these markets keeps growing, even today. In the past 10 years, the world has seen a great deal of innovation in business models such as Google, Uber, and Airbnb, based largely on the ideas that have been driving financial markets forward for the last half-century.

Yet for many people, possibly including you, financial markets often seem impenetrable and opaque. For one, finance people in suits like to act important just like anybody else. Add the tendency to overuse jargon (bulls, bears, shorts, and longs) and it's clear that trading deserves some of its reputation for impenetrability. But this flies in the face of the fact that we're all natural-born traders, so there's no good reason for it!

The 11 laws of trading I present in this book are distilled from my own experience learning from and working with some incredibly sharp minds. The laws themselves aren't exactly my own invention. Versions of some of them can be found in the great works of literature, from *Macbeth* to *Alice in Wonderland*. I had a vague sense of them even before I started trading, and you may read them in the table of contents and say, "I know that!" This trader is willing to bet that you don't, not really. Learn from my experiences as a trader, from my many mistakes and occasional successes. In so doing, you'll learn to apply these laws successfully in finance or anywhere else. Even walking across the street.

Why Study Trading?

Considering the universal role of trading in human affairs, it's shocking how easily it's misunderstood. Even educated people can be seduced by the view that trading is a zero-sum game, where one person's win is their counterparty's loss. But in order to have functional markets in the long run, the opposite of this assumption must happen. If trades were a zero-sum pursuit, over time markets would wither and die. In fact, in nearly every trade that takes place in modern financial markets, *both* parties to the trade are better off for having made it. Pension funds invest in stocks by trading with market makers. Farmers hedge their crop risk by trading futures against speculators. And both sides are happy to have done the trade.

Over 240 years ago Adam Smith published *The Wealth of Nations*, a study that describes, in great detail and with piercing clarity, the ways in which trade makes both parties better off. The majority of his examples center on labor markets, and how specialization and division of labor emerge from trade between people. But the principle that trading makes *both* parties better off applies much more broadly. Trading, in this very persuasive view, is the key mechanism through which countries' economies grow and people prosper.

And yet, though trade-as-engine-of-progress is as close to scientific fact as is possible in the social sciences, the myth of the zero-sum trade persists. This belief is actually reinforced every time there is a financial crisis, which, according to many, once again "proves" that financial markets are "a drain" on our modern societies. Incredibly, this happens despite the fact that everyone knows buying and selling food (so that we don't all have to grow our own wheat, for example) is good for the world. This may be obvious to a large portion of the population, but time and again I hear that it is "obvious" that the securitization of mortgages, for example, is bad for the world. This misguided view is apparently compelling to many, so it's necessary and important for us to understand more thoroughly how trading actually happens, especially in financial markets, and to reconnect again with the great benefits that result.

I see trading as practically a human universal and a powerful force for good. But one of the arguments of this book is that trading, especially on financial markets, is an activity where you can develop useful mental tools for dealing with a wide variety of situations. The abilities to perceive the competitive world accurately, to understand risk and uncertainty, and to register both our motivations and those of the people around us, are critically important for making good rational decisions and hence profitable trades. As you will see, these mental tools, forged in the competitive fire of financial markets, help us make good decisions in all other areas of life. From buying a new car to finding a new job, the principles behind good trading teach us how to make better decisions in all sorts of situations.

What Are Financial Markets?

Financial markets are the different sorts of markets you hear about when you turn on CNBC: stock[1] (or shares, or equity) markets, commodities[2] markets, foreign exchange, and many others. We can and do talk generically about the process of trading, generalizing across most financial markets, because these markets have certain common characteristics, as follows, in roughly decreasing order of universality:

1. *Standardized products*: Let's consider the market for shares of Apple Inc. (denoted by the symbol AAPL), which relies on the fact that all AAPL shares are the same. This is unlike the market for used cars, for example. Everyone agrees on what "1 share of AAPL" means, and there is no chance of either buying a particularly good share or getting stuck with a bad share. The interchangeable nature of stock shares is in fact a property of all products that trade on financial markets worldwide.[3] A case in point: the crude oil price that you read about refers to a very specific kind of crude oil that's delivered at a very specific time and place. Everyone[4] has agreed to trade crude oil under those specific conditions, and this standardization is a key reason that financial markets are as liquid (goods quickly bought or sold) and pervasive (quickly spreading) as they are. Liquidity will be discussed extensively in Chapter 4.

2. *Many participants*: At any given time during market hours, there are probably a dozen entities willing to buy AAPL shares, and another dozen or so willing to sell AAPL shares.

If one looks at the totality of trades over a given day, there are probably thousands of different individual entities who transacted in AAPL. This high availability of trading partners (counterparties) is another defining characteristic of financial markets.

3. *Heterogeneous participants*: Classifying participants into categories by organization (retail[5] investor, pension fund,[6] hedge fund,[7] investment bank,[8] market maker,[9] etc.) or by function (investor,[10] speculator,[11] hedger,[12] indexer[13]), you find there is an immense variety of people who are active in financial markets. While this is less true in more uncommon products such as institution-to-institution swaps,[14] for example, it's still much truer than in the market for a new car. In that market, if you want to buy a new Honda you *must* buy it from one of a small number of local Honda dealers. The seller is the same, or virtually the same, and the buyers are nearly all people who want to buy a Honda to drive themselves.

4. *Low transaction costs*: The ease and low cost with which investors, even retail ones, can trade in financial markets is phenomenal, and it's improving all the time. Buying $500,000 of the SPY ETF[15] would cost a sophisticated investor less than $20 in fees and spreads, and a retail investor not significantly more than that. Compare that to the process of buying an equivalently priced house, with its seemingly endless agent fees, escrow fees, legal fees, and significant time cost. Buying a car is little better, in percentage terms. Think of the dealer fees and the hassle of having to repeatedly state you don't want the rust-proofing. In fact, buying half a million dollars of SPY probably costs less than buying a hammer at Home Depot, once you factor in all the costs: time, taxes, store profit, gas to get you to the store, and so on. Lesser-known products such as options do carry higher trading costs, but even these costs are quite low when compared to their high-volatility competitors. Betting on good AAPL earnings by buying some upside call options (more on this later) is significantly cheaper, and until very recently considerably more legal, than going to a bookie and betting on your team to win the Super Bowl.

While not all of the above characteristics are true of *all* financial markets, they're general enough that the rare exceptions will be noted when they're relevant.

Vested Interests

In most of the developed world, operating in markets like the ones described above is straightforward, even for people with no prior knowledge of trading. It takes less than 15 minutes to open an account at a retail brokerage,[16] and around a day to fund it. Once funded, a few clicks on a website are all that separate a fresh-faced investor from a shiny new position in any of thousands of possible financial products.

But which products? Buy? Sell? What price? These are not easy questions, and they're not made any easier by the firehose of data and opinion sprayed out by financial markets every day. Remember the saying "A fool and his money are soon parted"? Well, predictably, this overload of information has given rise to a huge industry of professionals who make it their business to usher us through the maze of financial markets.

Many, if not most, of these helpers are well-meaning professionals who genuinely try to help their customers. Still, they do have an incentive to make the world of investments and trading seem more complicated than it actually is. These facilitators come in a few broad categories:

1. *Investment manager*: Managers take on many forms. Most visible to the retail investor are (a) the portfolio managers of the actively managed mutual fund into which retirement savings are frequently invested, and (b) the personal investment advisers who banks and brokerage firms provide for retail clients. Creating a cloud of complexity helps hide the fact that the vast majority of these investment managers provide no value. In fact, their value is almost universally negative value once you subtract the inevitable and often hard-to-find fees (Malkiel, 2012).

2. *Broker*: Since the advent of online and low-cost retail brokerages (E-Trade and the like) most people no longer deal with a human whose job title is "broker." Nevertheless, the economics are the same as ever: the more you trade, the more they make. It's certainly not clear how retail clients get value from up-to-the-millisecond trade data, research, phone calls, so-called robo-advisers, and ever-changing trade recommendations. Naturally, people will trade more than they otherwise would, and in this way pay more broker fees than they probably should.

3. *Financial press*: Shouty CNBC analysts love to "explain" the world of trading by providing a meaningless narrative (after the fact, of course) behind the random movements in the prices of securities. Human brains are suckers for a narrative (Taleb, 2007). This keeps people watching and keeps advertisers, such as the aforementioned brokerage houses, happy.

One of the main arguments of this book is that these segments of the financial world mostly provide a *disservice* to the retail investor to the extent that considerable attention is paid to them. Of course, willful overcomplication isn't exclusively a phenomenon of the financial world. Wherever there is opportunity for someone to filter information as well as an incentive for them to do so, it pays to be wary. Are real estate agents always acting in your best interests? What are the downsides of that one-year gym membership contract? How can you get a good deal on health insurance?

This book will provide you a set of tools and ways of thinking that will help you identify poor arguments, cut through overcomplication, and ferret out hidden self-interest. What makes trading such a wonderful world in which to learn these tools is not just how intrinsically useful they are while trading, but also how frequently you need to use them. Once you know how to use them well, these mental tools will help you outside the world of trading and financial markets, in all those situations where we have to make good, reasoned decisions.

Who This Book Is For

I hope that the examples, arguments, and analysis in this book will appeal to a wide variety of readers:

- Those interested in a career in trading, or more broadly in finance. It is exceedingly difficult for outsiders to get a good sense of what goes on in investment banks and trading houses. That is why lifting the veil should help prospective traders understand if this is a career for them.
- Interested outsiders, for the same reasons as above. Much ink has flowed recently on subjects surrounding trading, and the vast majority of the writing has been done by people who are clueless about what goes on in the trenches.

- Retail investors, whose need for reliable information about financial markets is the greatest. Almost always, the most useful trading tip for retail investors is "do less," and this book aims to explain why (a) that's so difficult and yet (b) so critical.
- People whose job it is to make rational decisions. Management, broadly considered, is the job of making good decisions under uncertainty. The ideas and techniques in this book can help people think about those decisions more clearly and powerfully.
- People who work in trading-adjacent markets, whose numbers have exploded in the last decade. Areas as diverse as advertising, power generation, and even the new gig economy require a good knowledge and understanding of trading concepts in order to be navigated safely and profitably.
- Rationalists, and indeed anyone interested in the process of making rational decisions. Since decision-making is the essence of trading, financial markets are the most competitive cauldron in which to test ideas about how to make decisions.
- People who make financial decisions (i.e. virtually anyone). The world of trading provides a clean venue in which to learn about quite universal thought processes useful in any financial decision. Whether it's buying a car or a house, figuring out where to live, or looking for a job, the world of trading has much to say about how to think about important decisions.

What This Book Will Not Do for You, and What It Will

This book will not teach you specific trades that make money, nor will it teach you how to create such trades, at least not directly. Moreover, it will not teach you about specific trades that don't make money! It will become clear that any book that purports to provide this sort of specific information (a) doesn't, and even if it did, (b) wouldn't be particularly valuable over the long term. What I'm after is a set of ideas that lets us figure out if and how a trade makes money. This allows us to go for the trades that do make money, and not so much for the ones that don't.

Understanding the world of trading, and how to think about it, provides a valuable set of mental tools that have far-reaching applications. Anyone who loves markets and understands the way in which they make the world a better place should want to see the tenets that underpin it spread more broadly. There is a lot of inefficiency in the world, and there are many people who earn a living without providing much value in return. Hopefully this book will help you learn how to spot these inefficiencies wherever they may lie and, to use a technical term, to arbitrage[17] them out. A succession of small improvements can make the world a better place.

Why Laws?

Ideas and tools are only useful if they're available when needed. This book is organized around the principle that remembering a few pithy laws and key points makes it easier to keep these tools accessible in daily life.

Thus, the goal of this book is to present a few simple, memorable laws based on observed and documented facts that help us think about trading. As I've said, trading ends up serving as a useful case study for a wide range of decision-making processes that, at some point in our lives, we all have to engage in. Thinking about these laws of trading, and internalizing their lessons, will help us think about all sorts of decisions. Carrying around this mental utility belt of ideas, always at the ready, will make you a formidable trader and decision maker.

I'll begin the story with the most important person involved in the trades you do: yourself. It turns out that understanding your own motivations, and how they affect your actions, is more difficult and confusing than you could ever believe.

References

Malkiel, B. (2012). *A Random Walk Down Wall Street*, 10th ed. New York: W. W. Norton & Company.
Taleb, N. (2007). *The Black Swan*. New York: Random House.

1

Motivation

> Know why you are doing a trade before you trade.

Why Are You Trading?

David, a well-to-do dentist, is settling into his home office on a Friday morning. He usually takes Fridays off from work. In the morning, he likes to trade stocks and in the afternoon he plays golf. David has CNBC on the TV in the corner as he settles in to read the *Wall Street Journal* and FT Alphaville. He mostly likes to bet on quarterly corporate earnings announcements, usually by trading short-dated options.

David's wife, Rachel, comes into the home office:

Rachel: "Going to pick up some things at the supermarket. Want anything? How are things going by the way?"

David: "Good, earnings season is heating up. Got a good feeling about some of these picks I've made."

Rachel: "How have you been doing so far this earnings season?"

David: "I made a couple of good calls yesterday. Decent. Nothing like that awesome streak from last year, but pretty good."

Rachel: "So you're making money?"

David: "Look, there's a lot of variance so it's hard to say for sure. What I do know is that when I get in the zone, like I did those couple of weeks a year ago, I make all the correct calls. It's like Neo from the Matrix."

Rachel: "Neo traded options?"
David: "No he didn't. But when he got in the groove, time slowed
          down and he couldn't miss. That's how it feels when you're
          trading and you're feeling it. Like you almost can't lose."
Rachel: "Can't lose? I thought there was a lot of variance."
David: "Ah, you just don't get trading ... "

Shouldn't This Chapter Be Short?

If people were perfectly rational, profit-maximizing, highly capitalized[1] entities, this chapter would be quite short. "Why are you trading?" *To make money.* But the real world is more complicated.

Even if we were perfectly rational profit maximizers, there would still be very good reasons to trade other than "to make money." For example, when you buy home insurance you know (and in fact hope) that the expected value[2] of that transaction is negative. However, you buy the insurance anyway because it decreases the risk of a huge loss if your home ever goes up in flames. You are said to be *hedging* your home-loss risk, and it's perfectly rational to do so. When we cover this idea in detail in Chapter 3, you will learn that the quantity you want to maximize is not profit but *utility*, a sort of risk-adjusted notion of wealth. So, are people who trade in financial markets motivated by utility?

In a trivial sense, anyone can answer yes after the fact. Much like a child who trips and falls and says, "I meant to do that," utility is what we claim it is. But humans are complicated, and *perceived* utility comes in many forms that differ from *actual* utility. In fact, as described in great detail in various recent works (especially Daniel Kahneman's *Thinking Fast and Slow*), humans are an unreconstructed bag of cognitive biases that cloud our judgment of utility. There is a whole field of social science called behavioral economics that seeks to identify and understand all the ways in which we fail to behave as perfectly rational decision makers. And it turns out that by and large we humans are quite poor decision makers:

- We underestimate small probabilities sometimes (the chance of getting hung up in traffic and arriving late to an appointment) and overestimate them other times (the chance of dying in a plane crash).

- We consistently overestimate our knowledge (a cognitive blind spot known as the Dunning-Kruger effect) and abilities (well over half of surveyed people think they're better-than-average drivers).
- When suitably framed, we consistently say that A *and* B occurring is somehow more likely than A only occurring. When we do this, we're violating a basic principle of logic without even noticing it.[3]

Many of our motivations, our sources of utility, aren't even *about* profit or risk-adjusted profit. This is obviously true in general, but it's even true within the narrower world of trading. We really do need to examine these trading motivations in detail, since they surface most clearly in the world of financial markets but they can also appear in other trading-like contexts. This fact alone should make the following classification of human foibles useful even if you've never dabbled in financial markets. Let's take a tour of the irrationality that characterizes the human mind and the sometimes-odd places it finds utility.

Greed and Fear

Greed and fear are the famous emotions of trading, and of financial markets in general. Recall Gordon Gecko in the movie *Wall Street*, or the Duke brothers in *Trading Places*, and how they were motivated by greed and fear. Many books have been written about these emotions, and how they relate to trading: how to mitigate their effects, how to use these emotions positively, how the induced herd-like behaviors affect the markets themselves, and many other aspects. There are books and articles that purport to teach amateurs how to "think like a pro" with respect to these subjects, and hence trade profitably. Without casting aspersions on specific works, almost all of these books are worse than worthless: they focus you on the *wrong thing*.

The plain fact is that almost no professional traders think of their work in terms of greed and fear. The profitable trades they've developed, the systems they've built to trade them, and the social environment in which they work are all designed to make these emotions fade into the background. In a highly underappreciated paper from over a decade ago (Lo, Repin, & Steenbarger, 2005), the authors study a population of traders, and correlate their results to their emotional states and personality types. The results show clearly that the traders whose emotional reactions were the most intense were the least-successful ones. It didn't matter whether the emotions were positive or negative, it was the fact that these emotions weren't being modulated. Interestingly, the paper also shows that there was no apparent correlation between personality type and success at trading. Thus, the stereotype of the loud, hard-charging, aggressive trader is not borne out in the data. All personality types can be successful, in principle.

Other studies of the emotional reactions to risk taking are found in *The Hour Between Dog and Wolf* (Coates, 2013). The story is similar: to the extent that trading and risk taking cause emotional reactions, those reactions generally obscure clear thinking in those high-pressure situations. This is not to say, however, that there is no place for emotion in trading. It's that the specific emotional reactions need to be trained, just like every other aspect of your approach, and greed and fear just aren't terribly useful.

In my own case, I know that I tend more toward the fear end of the spectrum. When I was first starting out in trading, I didn't have any real trading authority. I did what senior traders told me to do, learning as I went. But eventually, I got the opportunity to make my first real trading decisions. That first time I decided to buy those upside call options in Deutsche Bank, I knew intellectually that it was a good decision. But that didn't entirely inoculate me from the fear that I had either misjudged the situation or that the trade would go against me by random luck. There isn't much you can do about that latter situation, but tell that to your amygdala (the grey matter inside your head that experiences emotions) while it's happening. Over time, as I got feedback and validation that I was making good decisions, I managed to retrain my emotional reactions into more useful forms.

Boredom

Greed and fear are, in the world of trading, two extremes of the same emotional continuum. They are emotions related to high activity: winning or losing. Something's happening. But along another axis, we know that the level of activity in financial markets varies greatly. And most of the time, in modern financial markets, not much of anything is happening.

Quick, go Google "trading boredom." If your results are anything like mine, the top few results will be articles on amateur trading blogs and websites that try to give people tips on avoiding boredom. Evidently, this is a common problem among amateur traders, as well it should be. People frequently claim they're getting into trading because they want to make money, but in fact the reason is much closer to: "it gives me something to do," like our friend David at the beginning of the chapter. And often, there really isn't anything to do. The average amateur trader, no matter how prepared or sharp, is not going to find very many obviously profitable trades to do (assuming they're not fooling themselves). The result is long stretches of doing nothing, which is certainly not what they signed up for. The prevalence of articles trying to help amateur traders "deal with boredom" is all the evidence we need that many people indeed get into trading to avoid boredom.

Boredom is probably what brought David to trading in the first place. Trading certainly gave him something to do on those free Fridays, and he sunk his teeth into it. He read reports, created spreadsheets, looked at historical data, and slowly built up an earnings-based options-trading strategy. The problem was, most of the time the data told him to do nothing. Edge—your technical or strategy advantage over others in the trading arena–is hard to find, after all. The boredom returned, and so David started dabbling in other sorts of trading. He wanted a feeling that comes with putting money in play. That feeling is frequently known as the Zone.

The Zone

In the excellent book *Addiction by Design* (Schüll, 2012), Natasha Schüll takes the reader into the world of video poker and slot machines. She describes the manner in which these machines are designed to take advantage of the predilections and desires of problem gamblers. This subpopulation is targeted specifically because compulsive gamblers are by far the most profitable segment of the gambling public.

Particularly interesting is her description of the exact value that is the utility that problem gamblers derive from these machines, especially considering the often significant personal cost of their addictions. She describes in minute detail the fact that these problem gamblers aren't necessarily seeking wins, exactly. What they're looking for is a feeling, a sensation of transcendence that playing these slot machines provides. The most common name for this feeling, one where time itself seems to melt away, is "the zone." Consider Katrina, on page 135 of the book:

> The best scenario is when the free spins have been coming around regularly and perhaps normal game play has been good as well. ... This is where it particularly feeds into the zone where you can play for quite some time. ... You can just relax and "lose" yourself.

There are many other similar reports in the book. This zone that ensnares problem gamblers can also appeal to traders, especially active day traders. When caught in the zone, the goal of active trading isn't to make money. Rather the motivation is the process itself of making decisions and living in the world of price movements and charts, escaping normal life. Of course, many books and marketers exploit this desire to enter the zone. Consider the highly popular book *Trading in the Zone* (Douglas, 2000). The following passage from the preface is particularly telling:

> While this may sound complicated, it all boils down to learning to believe that: (1) you don't need to know what's going to happen next to make money; (2) anything can happen; and (3) every moment is unique, meaning every edge and outcome is truly a unique experience. The trade either works or it doesn't. In any case, you wait for the next edge to appear and go through the process again and again.

Couldn't such a paragraph have just as easily been written about "successful" slot machine play? It's clear that the focus is not at all on making money, but rather on getting the feeling of making decisions and then ignoring the results. What's important for our friend David at the beginning of the chapter is entering the zone of day trading. Profits really are secondary.

Risk Seeking

We live in an uncertain world. Whether it's winning the lottery or having a tornado flatten one's house, uncertainty rules our lives. Even everyday activities carry uncertainty: will I get a ticket if I park in the fire lane for five minutes? Will I meet the woman of my dreams if I stay in the library an hour longer?

You can think of every single action we take as a decision made to shape an uncertain future. So how do you make these hundreds of decisions a day? Do you carefully weigh all the costs, benefits, and risks[4]? Of course not. Most of the time, you make largely automatic decisions because if you didn't, you'd be paralyzed by this careful weighing process. Behavioral economists call this automatic decision-making process "System 1" and the more deliberative process "System 2." What concerns us in this section is how our System 1 works, and how it automatically assesses risks and rewards. It turns out that we all carry deep within us a surprisingly well-defined taste or preference for risk, which we'll call our risk-tolerance setpoint.

In a study by John Grable and Abed Rabbani of the University of Georgia (Grable, 2014), the authors examine the question of whether risk tolerance is a broad-based disposition, robust across many domains, or whether it's domain specific. Using a large panel dataset from the National Longitudinal Survey of Youth in 2010, they discovered that indeed people's risk-tolerance is quite robust across domains. A single "risk-tolerance" factor explains the majority of variation for a variety of behaviors, from everyday risky situations such as smoking to financial and occupational decision-making.

So, if indeed you have a well-defined risk-tolerance setpoint, an interesting question presents itself: what if the life you lead has a dramatically different risk profile than the one with which you're comfortable? What happens to you, and to your decisions?

Taking a page from biology, we can theorize a sort of risk homeostasis process. If Janine's life has more risk than she'd like, then she'll avoid additional risky situations in order to seek stability and certainty, even if those situations are advantageous. If Leroy's circumstances are overly stable and riskless, we should expect him to seek out risky situations in order to get closer to his natural risk-tolerance setpoint. My own risk setpoint was exposed when I started trading. Before my career as a trader, back when I was an engineer, I played a lot of online poker. I was good at it, and it evidently filled a need for some randomness in my otherwise stable life. Almost to the day that I started my job as a trader, my desire to play cards for money evaporated. My regular job had plenty of randomness for me, and

I certainly didn't need any more. I had found my risk setpoint in a different manner.

You may argue that's just me, but the best screenwriters in Hollywood certainly believe in risk setpoints. Classic caper movies, such as *Ocean's Eleven* and *The Italian Job,* start with the lead character having just been released from prison. Free from their incredibly boring prison existences, Danny Ocean and Charlie Croker, respectively, immediately set about plotting their next heist. Far from setting them on the straight and narrow, their prison experiences push them strongly back in the direction of action, of getting closer to their risk-tolerance setpoints. The reason you believe in these characters and that you empathize with them (aside from their matinee good looks) is that you instinctively understand that the high-risk lifestyle is fundamental to who they are.

You may now argue that that's fiction. But real life provides plenty of similar examples. In the documentary film *Free Solo,* for example, we follow Alex Honnold as he attempts to scale the 3000-foot-tall granite wall known as El Capitan in Yosemite National Park, California. Rock climbing is already risky enough that most life insurance policies consider it a disqualifying factor. But Honnold goes a giant step further: he scales these massive walls with no ropes or other aids. One wrong move and he would inevitably fall to his death, as many of his fellow free solo climbers have done. What rational person could bring themselves to take such extreme risks? The film provides us some answers: an MRI scan of Honnold's brain shows no activation in his amygdala, the fear center. Honnold is, to all appearances, virtually incapable of feeling the sort of fear that would make our System 1 scream to stop a risky activity like free soloing El Capitan. Yet Honnold has no death wish. He states, believably, that he'd much rather avoid dying. It's just that the only times he feels alive enough to be worthy of the term is when he's taking life-threatening risks. You can't argue with your setpoint.

This fact is not lost on the various financial intermediaries we learned about in the introduction. The financial services industry, at least at the retail level, clearly markets itself to affluent people with exactly the sort of language that will appeal to people motivated to seek financial risks. Our friend David at the beginning of the chapter, comfortable but somewhat bored in his comfortable life, is trying to increase the amount of uncertainty in it.

It should come as little surprise that trading in high-volatility stocks can be an excellent way of exposing yourself to financial risks. While the advertised and perceived goal of trading may be about finding good trades and making money, given what I've learned about risk-tolerance setpoints, it's just as likely to be about finding ways to put money in play, to expose yourself to profits and losses.

Wanting a Big Score

We've established that different people's tolerance of risk varies and that it varies in consistent ways. But people's perceptions of the value of a trade vary in equally interesting ways. Consider lotteries. Why are lotteries as popular as they are? They pull in an exceedingly large amount of money, by some estimates as much as $70 billion per year (Thompson, 2015) in the US alone. What is it about their structure that makes them so incredibly attractive?

Consider a bet where you are asked to flip 8 fair coins. If they all come up heads, you win $255 and otherwise you lose $1. Would you take this bet? What about paying $1 up front to play the following game: flip 8 coins and if they all come up heads, you win $256.

If you're like most adults in modern Western society, the second game *sounds* more attractive than the first, in spite of the fact that they're identical in every respect except the wording of the game. By changing the description of a bet, I can change your intuitive (or heuristic, System 1) perceptions of its attractiveness. Behavioral economists have, over the last 30 years, studied in great detail the ways in which the wording of uncertain outcomes affects perceptions. But again, the manner in which the financial industry markets itself to retail consumers shows they understand these effects quite well too.

In the above two examples, you can calculate that your expected profit in the games is zero. Your losses in the majority of cases (when at least one tail comes up) exactly counteract the very rare win when all heads come up so that on average you make no money playing this game. But if I can formulate the game so that the big rare win is more mentally salient than the small costs incurred to play, I will get many people interested in playing the game. And if I can increase the cost to play by a small amount (say $1.10), then I've created a game that's actually profitable for me, the seller of the game, as well as attractive (though a losing proposition) to the buyer.

Lotteries are so successful at hacking the human brain's risk perceptions that governments typically claim a monopoly on the right to run them! But financial products with highly asymmetric payoffs like those of lotteries also exist. The most common of these, at least in the US, are options, especially out-of-the-money options. These products have the payoff of small lottery tickets: they cost relatively little, most of the time they expire worthless, but every so often they win. When they do, the payoff can sometimes be a multiple of their original purchase price. For example, let's say Amazon is trading at $2,000. Earnings are coming up, and you bet that they're going to be bad. So, you purchase a $1,800 strike put (the right to sell), for around $16. Most of the time, Amazon will not drop below $1,800 upon earnings, and the put will expire worthless. But if Amazon drops to $1,700, then you've made a profit of $100 − $16 = $84! It's perhaps no surprise that deep out of the money options (such as the above) are consistently more expensive than their historical probabilities would indicate they should be.

All of these products prey on the buyer's desire for a large payoff without exposing herself to a large loss. By hiding the probabilities of the various outcomes, and by emphasizing the rare win, you are induced to lose a small amount of money. Aggregated across millions of people and repeat buys, this can be a very profitable business for the seller. As the old poker saying goes: *You can shear a sheep many times, but you can skin it only once.*

Intellectual Validation

Financial markets are some of the most competitive environments on Earth. What's more, the winners and losers are determined with piercing clarity: whoever made the money won the contest. Couple these characteristics with the already mentioned low barrier to entry, and one should expect a large number of aspirants to the throne of King of Trading.

In the same way that competitive sports appeal to the more athletic among us, trading appeals to the intellectually competitive. Being able to win at trading implies, in the popular imagination, having a sharp mind, good instincts, and a strong desire to win. The world of trading provides a compelling arena in which to test one's wits.

In fact, even a quick perusal of academic literature shows all manner of scientists, mathematicians, economists, and psychologists writing papers purporting to show how to beat some market or other. Invariably, the theories and techniques of the source discipline are applied to financial markets, and attempts are made to show those techniques can be used to make money trading. In the great majority of cases, these papers exhibit fatal flaws, ones which means they do not contain actual profitable trading strategies. From a distance, this should come as no surprise: if some obscure technique known only to a few algebraic geometers were capable of producing a trading profit, why would these geometers give it away to the world in exchange for a mere citation count?

Using trading as a means of intellectual validation isn't restricted to academics, of course. In the same way that poker players find stimulation from playing games above their bankroll and skill level, people who do not have the capital, skills, or information to compete in financial markets try to do so anyway. Their primary motivation is not to make money, but rather to test themselves. If they make money then that means they've successfully tested themselves, but in any case, the former is a secondary consideration compared to the latter.

> If I'm being perfectly honest, intellectual validation motivates me more than I'd like to admit. I enjoy reading mathematics and machine learning papers, and I enjoy thinking about ways to apply these ideas to trading. I'd tell myself that this was an important part of my job, and it was. But a lot of the motivation, perhaps too much of it, was finding a cool mathematical technique to apply to financial markets. It was about the math, not the trade.

Why Does Motivation Matter?

You may have noticed that a common thread runs through the above list. By and large, these motivations privilege a feeling or emotion, and the goal of trading becomes obtaining or satisfying that feeling. We can't say categorically that people are wrong for having these motivations. But, to the extent that they are unaware that the true reason for our trading *isn't* to maximize profit, they're setting themselves up to be exploited by others who (a) do care about maximizing profit, and (b) know them better than they know themselves. Self-knowledge, Aristotle tells us, is the most important kind of knowledge.

As you've already seen, the world is full of people with varying degrees of scruples about exploiting human frailty for profit. By being aware of your own weak spots, you can more easily navigate these dangerous waters. Let's now restate the rule at the beginning of this chapter.

Know why you are doing a trade before you trade.

You can now see why such an obvious-seeming rule can be so difficult to follow. As you've seen, "knowing why" can be fraught with danger and self-deception because of who "you" is. Thus, the first way in which we should think about the rule is less as a rule about trading and more as a rule about self-awareness. Does David the dentist really understand enough about himself to realize that, deep down, his trading isn't about maximizing profit?

Make Peace with Your Motivations, or Change Them

Let's say you've done a careful mental and emotional inventory and find that much of your motivation for trading in financial markets comes not from a profit motive, but from something else. Typically, this something else is a desire to achieve or change a particular feeling or emotional state. What do you do then?

Certainly, the least difficult avenue is to simply proceed as if nothing had changed. There is no rule that says that the trades you do must be made for financial gain. Maybe you're trading because it's fun, and the losses (in expected value) that you suffer are payment for your entertainment. If this is the case, I hope to convince you there are cheaper and more effective ways to get those results. Besides, no one ever said you *had* to do unprofitable trades in order to get your entertainment!

If you're like many successful traders, accepting this state of affairs is intolerable. You feel you're being exploited by the clever marketing strategies of financial services firms large and small. You feel you're being duped into believing you're making good trading decisions while all the time they're the ones making the money! For you, the rest of this chapter will serve as a guide to structuring your trading in order to avoid the pitfalls of unknown or nonconscious motivations. It will also show you the way to maximize the value of following our rule.

The Role of "You"

Protecting Ourselves

If you do want to avoid the sort of hazards triggered by your unawareness of the nature of motivation as described above, how do you go about it? You might be tempted to think that, if the most common ways of going astray revolve around your feelings and emotions, then you must surely strive to eliminate them. Call it Star Trek-itis, an inflammation of the desire to become Spock or Data. Unfortunately, for humans this is much easier said than done. Not only that, but emotions can be a useful guide in trading. Therefore, as you'll soon see, ignoring them can be just as dangerous as falling under their spell.

So what is to be done? We can find a path forward by seeing that the problem with the motivations we examined wasn't that they were informed by feeling and emotion, but rather that those emotional states were end goals in themselves. In a very important sense, trading isn't *about* feelings, even if those feelings can be useful in trading. A pithier way of stating this is: *trading isn't about you.*

That being the case, the question remains: what is trading about? Fundamentally, it's about the relationship between you and the rest of the world. Trading to maximize profitability isn't about you, fundamentally. It's about finding and exploiting a profitable edge, and as we will see in Chapter 5, these edges come from things that specifically and in particular you know and can act upon *that others cannot.* The only "you" that matters is how you relate to the others against whom you're competing. The best protection against bad motivations comes from an honest assessment about the nature of your edge, and this requires deep self-knowledge but also, critically, deep knowledge about the markets in which you're trading.

Making "You" Small

In 2009, the computer scientist and entrepreneur Paul Graham wrote an insightful short note entitled *Keep Your Identity Small*

(Graham, 2009). In it, he theorizes that the reason discussions about religion or politics quickly become useless is because these areas deal directly with notions of personal identity. In subjects where self-identification and self-labeling become important, we lose the ability to think rationally about the matter at hand. We become preoccupied with protecting and justifying "me" and the discussion stops being a productive one. While his analysis centers on the difficulty of having useful discussions about religion or politics, the point made about the dangers of an expansive notion of "me" has much broader applicability.

In the context of trading, having a large self-image (in the sense of maintaining many labels to describe yourself) creates similar difficulties for rational decision-making. The more statements of the form "I am the kind of person who ... " you feel you must satisfy, the more ways the market and its participants can attack you and get your money.

Caring about the Right Things

So how do you make your self-image small? How do you make yourself care about the right things? You could, through sheer force of will, change your motivations. However, evidence from many experiments shows this is extremely unlikely to work over the long term. Our willpower is a finite quantity that is difficult to maintain over time. Fortunately, researchers have discovered at least one way to make long-term changes in our behavior: the mechanism of precommitment (Crockett, 2013). Precommitment and habit have been extensively studied in the social sciences, and these techniques have been shown to be capable of effecting significant changes in behavior.

In his book *The Power of Habit* (Duhigg, 2012), Charles Duhigg shows the ways in which we can change our behavior by precommitting and forming a habit that forces the desired behavior to emerge. For example, suppose you want to stop raiding the cookie jar for a midafternoon snack. You need to create a habit that prevents or forestalls such an act. You could, perhaps, set an alarm for a time slightly before your usual trip to the kitchen, and when the alarm sounds you eat a banana you've already set out beside your desk. By creating a new desirable habit to replace the old undesirable one, you've changed your behavior without having to rely on willpower alone.

So how does this apply to trading? The idea is to create structural habits that strongly encourage good decision-making processes during trading. This means establishing an intellectual culture that fosters the right sort of mindset about trading. I will have much to say about this in Chapters 5, 9, and 11, but for now we can simply say that the crux of it is sociology.

Having a set of people with whom you can talk about your trading ideas, creating a systematic process for evaluating them, making plans, and evaluating those plans, all of these are ideas that are fundamentally social and cultural. If you're successful in creating such a culture, the desirable habits become automatic and the day-to-day decision-making inherent in trading becomes the sort of process you want.

Precommitment and Hindsight

Why does the rule tell us you should have your reasons sorted out before you do a trade? If you can retrospectively show that your decision was a good one, surely that's good enough?

Given what we now know about the human mind, it should be obvious that it's not. Hindsight bias is among the most significant and hard-to-eliminate biases to which we're subject. Also known as the knew-it-all-along symptom, hindsight bias makes you believe that, after something has occurred, you could have predicted it or did in fact predict it. Indeed, you get this clear impression quite frequently, despite your having no reasonable basis for making one prediction or another.

The most powerful protection against hindsight bias is, perhaps not coincidentally, precommitment. If you explicitly record your beliefs before an event occurs (in this case, a trade), you have made it more difficult to backfill a convenient story after the fact. This record doesn't have to be particularly strong in order for it to help protect you against hindsight bias. A simple note jotted down on a piece of paper, a statement to a colleague about your thought process, all of these serve in your brain as markers of beliefs *at the time*. The rule tells you to take advantage of this, to actually use it to your advantage. Again, one of the best ways to avoid fooling yourself about your previous beliefs and motivations is to set them down in writing at that time. After all, it's hard to argue with a piece of paper.

The most powerful way to leverage precommitment is to make it structural. Structural precommitment is culture. It's a habit of writing things down, of making conditional plans and decision trees to describe your future actions. It's precommitment that's so ingrained it becomes the default action. This habit can be personal, but it can also be encoded in the culture of an organization. This is what lets you analyze your thought processes in a less-biased manner, and to improve them over time.

Self-Knowledge and Precommitment in Other Contexts

We can extend the insights of the rule about trading into many other contexts where we need to make rational decisions.

Buying a New Car

Aside from buying a house, few purchasing decisions are as nerve-wracking as that of buying a new car. You could in fact argue that buying a car is more stressful. After all, each house is unique so it's harder to conclusively establish whether you underpaid or overpaid for the house. However, cars are (ideally) undifferentiated from each other. If someone else paid less for the same car, they clearly got a better deal. Dealerships remain, in spite of some progress, places that are structured to extract as much from the consumer as possible. Even internet sales divisions aren't immune to these characteristics. So how can you use the rule to help you?

- *Self-knowledge.* How motivated are you to buy on that day? How much time do you have, how patient can you be? Could you change your mind about details of the car? How do you want to approach the conversation with the dealer? Is your inclination to be friendly, or to be adversarial? You should think about these and many other questions before you enter the dealership. Dealers are trained to understand these tendencies and to exploit them to their advantage.
- *Precommitment.* How knowledgeable are you about the buying process? In fact, most car purchases can be regarded as

about a dozen possible purchases: the car itself, after-market accessories, extended warranties, service plans, rustproofing, paint treatment, insurance, and just about anything else related to the car. Have you already studied these items and made decisions about which ones you want? With this knowledge, you can precommit to buying only the things you actually do want, instead of having to make a decision at the time. Write down the decisions you've made and bring that paper to the dealership. When in doubt, refer to the paper!

Navigating the Job Market

Looking for a job and accepting possible offers is fraught with peril, and having good self-knowledge is the first step in making good decisions about the jobs you seek and accept. The most important piece of self-knowledge you need, unsurprisingly, concerns your own motivations: what is it that you look for in a rewarding job? Is it money? Prestige? A good work environment? Interesting work? Many people can endure a bad job for good pay, but others feel that an interesting job with good co-workers is non-negotiable, even if the pay isn't as good.

It's at least a little surprising that, given the importance nearly all of us attach to our job, there is so little practical and tailored help available to help you when shaping and planning your careers. Yes, high schools and universities do have career guidance programs, but given the ratio of supply to demand, in practice they generally provide little value. Fortunately, a good (and humorous) guide can be found at the Wait But Why website (Urban, 2018). Though quite long, the guide takes you through the process of truly understanding yourself and your motivations, especially as they relate to jobs and careers (I encourage you to have a look).

Once you are in the process of finding a job and accepting offers, self-knowledge continues to be important, but perhaps just as important is a small dose of precommitment. Suppose you know that, in order to be happy and satisfied, you will require a certain minimum salary and, perhaps, a minimal level of status or seniority. You then ask yourself what you would do if you received the job offer but it didn't contain those minima. What are you going to do? You might be sorely tempted to accept the offer anyway, under the "a bird in the hand is worth two in the bush" philosophy. Yet if you know that the absence of those non-negotiables will lead, over the longer term, to unhappiness and disappointment, perhaps the right thing is to hold out for them. You can precommit yourself: if the offer doesn't have certain must-have characteristics, you will decline (or negotiate to obtain them).

The same precommitment process is important during the job search itself. If you know yourself well enough to understand that having a good personal rapport with your boss is important to you, you can precommit yourself to that. If a job offer comes in with good salary and other benefits, but you know you won't be able to get along with your boss, then the right answer is to decline. Precommitment helps you clarify your understanding of yourself and clarify your priorities. This leads to better decisions over the long term.

Precommitment for Self-Improvement

Sometimes precommitment can seem like a magic wand to get us more of what we want, and other times it can make us miserable and yet not get the results desired. How can you tell which of the two you'll get in some specific situation?

Consider the website stickk.com. The idea behind the site is that you register your goals with the site (for example, to lose weight or to finish writing a book). You commit that if you fail to meet your goals, you'll accept a financial loss (such as giving $5 to charity, or to the campaign of a hated politician). Furthermore, your friends and relatives, or even strangers, will be notified of your failure to meet the goal. The question is: does this sort of precommitment work?

It seems the answer is "it depends." Specifically, it depends on how much you dislike the loss you'd incur compared to the difficulty of meeting your goal. If the stick isn't big enough, the rational thing to do is still to shirk our goal. However, making the stick big and painful enough may well just make your life miserable. You're forcing yourself to do something because of an external motivator, as opposed to an internal one. As you'll see later in the book, evidence shows that this can be useful for stretches of time, but over the long term, external motivators may actually be counterproductive. As with all things, precommitment is a tool to be used judiciously if it's to maintain its usefulness.

Summary and Looking Ahead

- The most important knowledge is self-knowledge. Be aware of your tendencies, your flaws, your blind spots, as well as your strengths.
- Don't rely on your willpower to ensure you make good decisions. Create a structure that encourages the right sort of decision-making processes and they will become habitual.
- Precommit to courses of action that you want to take. Make the wrong path hard to walk.

In the next chapter, we'll actually dive into trading: what's it about, and how does it actually work? As we'll see, things can get pretty hairy pretty quickly, and it all has to do with information. Who has it, and how much of it do they have?

References

Coates, J. (2013). *The Hour Between Dog and Wolf: How Risk-Taking Transforms Us, Body and Mind.* Penguin Books.

Douglas, M. (2000). *Trading in the Zone.* Prentice Hall Press.

Duhigg, C. (2012). *The Power of Habit: Why We Do What We Do in Life and Business.* Random House.

Grable, J. E. (2014). "Risk Tolerance across Life Domains: Evidence from a Sample of Older Adults." *Journal of Financial Counseling and Planning* 25, Issue 2.

Graham, P. (2009). Keep Your Identity Small. Retrieved from http://www.paulgraham.com/identity.html.

Kahneman, D. (2011). *Thinking Fast and Slow.* Farrar, Strauss & Giroux.

Lo, A. W., Repin, D. V., & Steenbarger, B. N. (2005). "Fear and Greed in Financial Markets: A Clinical Study of Day-Traders." *American Economic Review*, pp. 352–359.

Molly J. Crockett, B. R. (2013, July 24). "Restricting Temptations: Neural Mechanisms of Precommitment." *Neuron* 79, Issue 2, p. 391–401. Retrieved from https://www.cell.com/neuron/fulltext/S0896-6273(13)00448-0.

Schüll, N. (2012). *Addiction by Design.* Princeton University Press.

Thompson, D. (2015, May 11). "Lotteries: America's $70 Billion Shame." *Atlantic* Retrieved from https://www.theatlantic.com/business/archive/2015/05/lotteries-americas-70-billion-shame/392870/.

Urban, T. (2018, 04 11). How to Pick a Career (That Actually Fits You). Wait But Why. Retrieved from https://waitbutwhy.com/2018/04/picking-career.html.

CHAPTER 2

Adverse Selection

Imagine you're walking down the street in midtown Manhattan, and a man stops you. He's holding a large glass jar full of coins. He has the following proposition for you: "Give me a bid for this jar of coins. If I like it, I'll sell you the jar and its contents." You think about the proposition. The man hands you the jar, lets you look at it from every angle, and you even shake it a little bit. Your best guess is that it contains $220 in coins. You're not too sure about this guess, so you decide to play it safe. "I'll bid $160." Now ask yourself how you'd react to either of his responses:

- "No sale," he says. Assuming the man is a rational person, he must think the jar has more than $160 in coins in it and he'd take a loss if he were to sell it to you. You're sad you didn't manage to buy the jar.
- The man thinks about it, then says "Sold!" Again, assuming he's acting rationally, the man believes the jar contains less than $160 in coins, so he's making a profit selling it to you. You're sad you paid $160 for the jar.

The key reason you're glum, no matter the outcome, is that *the jar seller knows more about the coins in the jar than you do*. In this transaction, you were "adversely selected against" because there is an asymmetry of information. He probably counted the coins before he put them in the jar! Most importantly, your skills at estimating coins in jars is completely irrelevant when the person you're trading with *knows* the value, right down to the last penny. You could be great at coin-jar-estimating or terrible at it, but it wouldn't matter. Whatever price you say, either: (a) you bought a jar, in which case you wish you hadn't, or (b) you bought no jar, in which case you wish you had bought one.

We quickly arrive at the second law of trading:

> You're never happy with the amount you traded.

An Information Theoretic View of Trading

The above scenario is clearly an extreme example of information asymmetry. Your counterparty knows the exact value of what's being traded, and you don't. Of course, most real-world situations aren't nearly as extreme. But the insights we draw from the example apply in many other situations. Notice:

- Your knowledge on an absolute scale doesn't matter. All that matters is your knowledge *relative* to that of the person with whom you're trading. Remember the old poker saying: "It doesn't matter if you're the 9th greatest player in the world when players 1 through 8 are sitting at your table."
- The act of trading (or not) teaches you (and anyone else who's paying attention) something you didn't know before.

In fact, this second property of the scenario generalizes into a powerful way to view trading. Consider another, more realistic thought experiment, drawn from my own experiences as a trader:

You are a market maker[1] in South African mining companies. Through years of effort and continual improvement, you have built a trading model for the company Veldt Resources. You walk into work one day, ready to set up your trading for the day. It's a stock that doesn't trade much, and usually there are only two market makers: you and another (we'll call her Jo). She's sharp, and she competes well to trade against customer orders that come in.

Your model has Veldt valued at 54.35 ZAR (South African rand). You're going to start quoting[2] the stock, so you're about to turn on your machine making a market 54.25 – 54.45 (1000x).

Before you turn on, you check the current market and notice that Jo has already turned on and she's making her market 53.50 – 54.00 (2000x). If you were to turn on your machine, your market would cross her market, and you would buy 1000 shares from her for 54.00.

You now need to make a decision. Whose model do you believe more, yours or Jo's? If you believe yours, you should turn on your machine, trade at 54.00, and expect to make money. If you believe Jo's model, you should adjust your own model parameters to match her market and turn on, making a similar market to hers.

What to do? As with many dichotomies, this is a false one. And as with many decision processes, Bayesian reasoning lights the way. A few comments about Bayesian reasoning, which might be useful before we move on.

A Holy War among Statisticians

Back in the late nineteenth century, an imperious Victorian gentleman named Francis Galton was busy founding the field of modern statistics. Chief among the tenets of the fledgling field, at least as far as Galton was concerned, was the importance and primacy of data. The prevailing scientific paradigm of the day relied fairly heavily on theory, and that theory was frequently little more than opinion or collective agreement.[3] Galton, rightly exasperated with this approach, sought to build mathematical tools to let the data speak for itself. The field of "frequentist" statistics was born.

Unbeknownst to him, a century earlier a little-known clergyman named Reverend Thomas Bayes had sowed the seeds of a somewhat competing approach. It took a while for others to pick up on those obscure ideas, so by the early twentieth century frequentist statistics was the dominant mode of statistical analysis.

It was not, however, without its problems. Imagine you get a stack of pennies from the bank, and you pick one out at random. You decide to flip it a few times to see how often heads will come up. Say you flip it 10 times, and by chance 3 heads come up. Your frequentist statistician friend will tell you that the likeliest long-term probability of heads, denoted P(heads), is 30% with some well-defined error bars on that estimate.

By the mid-twentieth century, a heretic band of Bayesian statisticians began to loudly shout "That's insane! Coins are well-known to have a P(heads) of almost exactly 50%! You just happened to flip 3 heads out of 10 on that coin by chance, but I bet over the long term its P(heads) is much closer to 50% than 30%!"

The frequentists would respond, "But the 10 flips are all you know about *this particular coin*. That's your data. Period."

The academic war would rage, for a few decades at least. And while frequentists statistics still has its place in certain niche applications, Bayesian reasoning has carried the day in nearly all the fields that matter, especially in trading. So strong is the influence of this little-known reverend that the tomb of Thomas Bayes, located in a nondescript cemetery in central London, has become something of a place of pilgrimage for the more mathematically inclined traders across the City. For readers interested in learning more, there is a gentle though long introduction available at (Yudkowsky, 2008), with a more technical treatment.

Having Beliefs and Updating Them

Getting back to our story, how do you use Bayesian reasoning to integrate your beliefs with those of your competitor? Jo presumably believes Veldt is worth around 53.75 (the average of her bid and offer). But how confident is she in her belief? The width of her market can give you a clue. It's 0.50 ZAR, whereas yours was going to be 0.20 ZAR wide. All other things equal, you should think that Jo only has 40% (0.20/0.50) of the confidence in her fair value as you do in yours.

On some absolute scale of confidence, you can say you had a belief-strength of 100 in your fair value of 54.35 (before seeing Jo's market), and Jo has a belief-strength of 40 in her fair value of 53.75 (before seeing yours). And it turns out the weighted average of these two beliefs is quite a reasonable way to combine them: 100/140 * 54.35 + 40/140 * 53.75 = 54.18. Your updated fair value, having seen Jo's market, is thus 54.18 ZAR.

This procedure is a quick, heuristic, and reduced version of Bayesian belief-updating, and a good reference on the subject is A.L. Barker's 1995 paper (Barker, 1995).

Using Our Updated Beliefs

After updating, you now believe that the stock is worth 54.18. Assuming your trading costs, risk limits, and return requirements are satisfied, buying 1000 shares for 54.00 is a good trade. Naively, you might just put out a 54.00 bid for 1000 shares, trade with half the 2000 share offer, and hope to collect your expected-value ZAR.

In practice, however, you might be able to make even more. If Jo is making a 0.50 wide market, maybe she'd be willing to sell lower than 54.00. It's conceivable that if you put out a 53.90 bid for 1000 shares, Jo will sell at that price, and you collect an extra 100 ZAR!

Of course, Jo could react differently. She could see your bid and use that information to change her market, in much the same way you did before turning on. These are difficult decisions, ones where experience with the product and the market make a big difference in being able to eke out a little extra edge. Let's play it safe however and pay 54.00 for 1000 shares.

After the Trade

You trade, and Jo reacts by immediately canceling her market. This is not an uncommon occurrence in illiquid stocks, especially in emerging markets, so you're not too surprised. You wait a couple of minutes, mentally visualizing Jo in front of her six monitors, evaluating her trade and her model.

Finally, she turns back on. Her new market is 53.50 – 54.05 (10000x)! You reason that Jo has seen that someone (you) disagrees with her valuation of the stock. Jo is a good Bayesian like you, and so she has incorporated that information into her model and updated her beliefs about the fair value of the stock. Her updated belief is that she now wants to sell even more stock, at a marginally higher price. Clearly, she almost entirely discounts the information you've communicated to her with your trade.

How should you react? It seems fairly clear that, assuming Jo is not a crazy or incompetent market maker (usually a fair assumption), your trade was a bad one. You bought 1000 shares, when in retrospect, you would have wanted to buy much less, probably zero.

Imagine instead that Jo had turned back on with a market of 54.00 – 54.50 (1000x). Her reaction now clearly indicates the information you gave her with your trade is valuable, and she has adjusted her beliefs accordingly. Your trade was probably a good one. Don't you wish you had bought all 2000 shares on offer?

No matter what Jo's reaction is, you will be unhappy with your trade. Note that Jo will be unhappy too, since retrospectively she should have either made her initial market bigger or smaller. Welcome to the joyous world of trading!

It's All Bayes, All the Way Down

This process of belief-updating happens billions of times a day in the hundreds of thousands of markets that trade. A market is a distributed aggregator and integrator of information. Everyone who participates contributes their private beliefs and knowledge, and the information that results (trades and prices) constitute some of the most reliable sorts of information our society produces.

Markets and Society

It's easy to underestimate the value that markets provide to the world. Naively, you might think that the only people who care about the price of Veldt Resources are the people who trade (or want to trade) the stock. But this is a myopic view of the value of market prices.

The fundamental problem of economics is, essentially, to determine the appropriate allocation of scarce resources in order to produce economic outputs. These resources can take many forms: labor, land, capital, even technology. In order to solve the allocation problem, the world needs information: how valuable are each of the above inputs, and how valuable are the resulting outputs?

Unfortunately, the necessary information is diffuse and broadly distributed, so the normal hierarchical means of aggregating this information don't work very well. In fact, the economic history of the late twentieth century is largely the history of distributed information-gathering (market economies) outcompeting hierarchical information-gathering (command economies).

Thus, we now begin to see market prices for what they truly are: the most reliable public signal about what everything is worth. Now, reasonable people can and do disagree about how accurate these prices are. But the point is that (a) having everyone mostly agree on a price has enormous benefits, and (b) this is the best we've got anyway. Consider these situations:

- A rubber manufacturer needs to decide whether to expand, maintain, or contract its capacity. The prices of the raw materials and the finished rubber are critical in this decision.

- An Iowa farmer considers whether to plant soy or wheat this spring. The market prices for each commodity (and their yields on his land) are the most important inputs to his decision.
- A student considers whether to study petroleum engineering or botany. She is indifferent to either choice, and believes she would be just as good at either. The market prices for each occupation are an important consideration for deciding which subject to study. Let's now say she isn't indifferent: she'd rather study botany. How much more would the petroleum career have to pay for her to consider switching?

Note that the progression of examples puts us further and further away from the actual markets in which the relevant products trade. The rubber manufacturer buys his inputs and sells his output directly in the markets in question. The farmer does too, though perhaps with a layer of intermediation (a cooperative, for example). As for the student, in all likelihood she won't even begin to enter in the job market for another four years, and her average tenure in the market will be measured in decades. The existence of a credible price signal (in the form of publicly available salaries) allows her to make informed decisions that will affect the rest of her life.

A Paradox: Why Does Anyone Trade at All?

There is a famous paradox about trading that goes something like this: if markets are so efficient, why does anyone trade? Of course, it's not much of a paradox since we know markets aren't completely efficient, but even so, they're pretty efficient most of the time. Why do things trade as much as they do?

I believe our hypothetical Veldt scenario points us to the answer. The financial products that are commonly traded are highly complex instruments. No one has a monopoly on the information that defines their fair values. At best, people can specialize in certain sorts of information. For example:

- An investor like Warren Buffett is good at knowing about business fundamentals.

- A market maker is good at knowing about supply and demand for a given instrument, but different market makers see different pieces of the supply/demand picture.
- An activist investor knows what pressure they can bring to bear on boards and executives to change a company's practices.

The only way we can aggregate these disparate kinds of information is through trading. Heterogeneous beliefs, reasonable disagreement, and Bayesian updating of beliefs is how we find out, all of us together as best we can, how much things are worth.

Special Trades

The Veldt example in the previous section is an everyday occurrence. The job of being a market maker is very much to engage in that sort of Bayesian updating. It's what you might call a *normal* trade, one for which carefully built models and systems are made to operate.

Now imagine that Veldt has decided to pay a large dividend, say 5.20 ZAR. Unfortunately, you don't know when the stock goes ex-dividend on the exchange. When a stock pays a dividend, there is a well-defined date at which all stock holders of record are entitled to receive that dividend. The ex-dividend date of a stock is the first date at which buyers of the stock are no longer entitled to the dividend that the company has now just paid.

Either the stock you buy today is entitled to receive that 5.20 dividend, or not. An uncertainty of 10% in the value of a stock is, in modern markets, enormous. Let's say that you make 500 ZAR per day trading Veldt by trading 25,000 shares and making 0.02 ZAR per share traded. Now that you have dividend uncertainty, trading those 25,000 shares either makes or loses on the order of 5 ZAR per share; 125,000 ZAR profit or loss on some small South African mining stock is a lot. The dividend uncertainty has made this a *special* trade.

Special trades feel and behave very differently from normal trades. The quality of your finely tuned models doesn't matter. The quality of your trading systems doesn't matter. All that matters is whether or not you're right about the dividend status of the stock.

You check your Bloomberg terminal,[4] and it states that the stock is ex-dividend. Jo is making a market, which clearly implies that she doesn't believe the stock is ex-dividend. As far as you're concerned, her markets are too high by about 5 ZAR! Maybe she made a mistake and overlooked this recently announced dividend. After all, South African mining companies aren't always paragons of corporate communications, not even large ones. So you sell as much as you can, and Jo turns off. After a while, Jo turns back on, making almost the same market. Ecstatic, you sell some more. She turns off again, this time for 20 minutes. You can see she's worried, and she's trying to figure out what's going on.

Eventually she turns back on, *again* making a similar market. Like a good Bayesian, you start to get worried. But you have a checklist for just such "uh oh" situations. And sure enough, you see you missed a step. You start to feel the cold sweat you know is coming. Instead of Jo having incinerated hundreds of thousands of ZAR, you might have. Jo might have just paid attention to that extra bit of detail, you didn't, and that has made all the difference.

You start calling people: Bloomberg, your broker, that South African buddy you met at a party, anyone that can get you some reliable information. Everything's inconsistent, nothing makes sense. A stay of execution comes fifteen minutes later when you see a notice on Bloomberg: Veldt put out a notice confirming it is indeed ex-dividend.

You hurry back to the market, but Jo has already turned off. She won't be turning back on in Veldt for a while. Maybe forever. But who did the good trades? You're the one collecting the ZAR, evidently, but it's a bit hard to chalk that up to good trading. Special trades are a high-stakes game of higher-order reasoning, except sometimes you're not even aware you're playing.

Keeping Your Head When Others Are Losing Theirs

Special trades require a skill set that can be quite different from that needed in normal trading. By definition, these trades are out of the ordinary; they're trades for which the usual rules, the usual procedures, and recent experience are of little use. Special trades require a blend of what might seem like polar opposites: both caution and aggressiveness, both intuition and rational analysis, both quickness and deliberation. Profitably balancing between the extremes is something that only the most skilled human traders can do.

For this reason, most trading firms codify rules that approximately say, "If anything is the least bit weird or unusual, turn the machines off." This is because not even well-designed trading systems are good at assessing information for which there is little or no precedent.

Some firms doubt their human traders can do much better in these situations; in fact, so reliant are their business models on automation and efficiency that traders are also discouraged from trading when the markets display unusual behaviors. For many firms, this is likely to be a good policy.

Thus, even though special trading situations are among the most stressful and risky, they're also frequently the most profitable for those who can manage to keep their wits about them. When markets are behaving erratically—for example, during a correction or crash—market dynamics change dramatically.

There is a lesson here that applies much more broadly, well outside the world of trading. Most of the time, your life is fairly routine: you go to work, you come home, every day much like the next. And yet every so often, crises occur. In the trading world these come in the form of periodic financial crises, but our lives contain them as well: a layoff, a health emergency, a natural disaster, or any number of other rare but significant events. You're generally unprepared for these events, and the usual reaction to this lack of preparation is inaction. You don't know what to do, so you do nothing in order to avoid doing the wrong thing. This is a safe policy, but the story of special trades shows there is another option: recognize that this is a special situation. *The normal rules do not apply.* If you remove yourself from your usual routine, if you think hard and clearly about the specific situation, maybe you can do something good. Perhaps even great. Others will be paralyzed by inaction, but perhaps you won't be. Crises *can* be opportunities.

Adverse Selection in Other Financial Markets

As you've seen already, the essence of trading is being fairly unhappy about the trades you do and don't do. There are particular markets, however, where being unhappy is pretty much a constant state of affairs.

IPOs

When a privately owned company wants to become a publicly owned company, one with shares trading on public exchanges, it must go through an Initial Public Offering (IPO) process. The details of the process are rather complex, but fundamentally the company decides to issue public shares for some fraction of the company's equity and hires an investment bank to *place* the shares with interested buyers.

At this initial stage, as if on cue, adverse selection appears. This is due to the very fact that the IPO is taking place. Indeed, taking into consideration that company insiders have decided that this is a good time to sell portions of the company, it's likely that those insiders know more about the future prospects and value of the company than prospective IPO buyers. Clearly this is a situation where, given that insiders want to sell, buyers should be wary of buying from them considering the asymmetry of knowledge about the company.

The second step at which adverse selection occurs is during the placement of the new shares. The investment bank attempts to place the shares by first estimating how much each share should be worth, then calling up its clients and asking them how many shares they'd want at that price. If the bank sees that not many people are interested at a given price, they can lower the proposed IPO price, whereas if there seems to be a significant demand, they can raise the proposed price.

The investment bank's fees are essentially paid by the company going public, thus their incentives should be to make the company happy.[5] However, since the investment bank also wants more IPO business, the best way to get that business is to have an exciting IPO history to market to future clients. Between the original adverse selection and this fact, the investment banks tend to want to underprice a company at least a little bit. This ensures that the first day of trading sees a decent price increase and favorable news coverage for the newly listed stock. The buyers of the IPO shares should be happy about this, of course. Besides that, one would think the companies going public would be unhappy, since they forewent the additional capital they could have received. Yet apparently being able to ring the opening bell at the NYSE and appearing on financial news channels would seem suitably to quell these sorts of concerns.

So, we've established that IPOs are typically underpriced by the investment bank. Thus, if you're the one receiving the call from the investment bank asking if you want to buy shares, your answer will likely be yes! Not only that, but you'll want as much as you can get. Your fellow investors will know these facts about IPOs too, and in all likelihood the demand will outstrip supply. Say that 5 million shares will be offered, and that 10 people are being offered the shares. It is entirely possible that to secure your 1/10 of the shares on offer, you may need to tell the bank you're willing to buy 2 million shares, which they then pro-rate back down to 500,000.

Note that we've said IPOs are *typically* underpriced, as measured by the day-1 rise in the stock price. However, this is not universally true. Some companies go public but the investing public shows little if any interest. Perhaps there are doubts about the company's business prospects or its management. In those situations, the investment bank will have to work hard to secure investors. This is where the skill of an investment banker really pays off for the company that hired it, if it manages to IPO a bad stock at an impressive-seeming price.

This ends up being the biggest adverse selection involved in IPOs. For super-hot high-demand IPOs, you're going to be very happy if your eventual allocation of shares ends up being even a small slice of the issued stock. You bid for 2 million shares, you get 200,000, and though you're happy to have gotten even that much, you'll be sad you didn't get more. Now consider how you feel those other times when you find out you received your full 2-million-share request. This means that almost no one else was interested in the issue, which means you're left holding 2 million shares of what's likely a dog of a company. What's more, since you're an IPO investor, you're locked out from selling the shares for 90 to 180 days. Six months can be a long time in the world of trading.

Rights Issues

Publicly traded companies can raise additional capital in a number of ways. They can obtain bank loans, they can issue bonds, they can issue preferred shares, and they can issue additional common shares. They can also do what's known as a *rights issue*, an option that is particularly popular in Europe and parts of Asia.

In a rights issue, every shareholder is given rights to purchase additional shares. In order to induce shareholders to exercise these rights, the price at which the additional shares are sold is typically below the price at which the stock is currently trading. These rights are also typically tradeable in the open market. Let's look at an example.

Foo Corp is currently trading at $40 and has 10 million total shares outstanding. They are looking to raise an additional $20 million. With the help of the ever-present investment bank, they decide to issue 1 million new shares at a strike price of $20. They therefore issue a rights prospectus detailing the following: every share of stock gets one right. Ownership of 10 rights entitles someone to buy 1 new share of stock for $20.

A question now arises: how much is one right worth? You might naively say $2,[6] but it turns out that's not quite right. Consider that once the rights issue finishes, the company will have 11 million shares of stock, which the world should value at $40 * 10 million + $20 * 1 million = $420 million. Consequently, each *new share* of stock is worth $38.18. Since 10 rights entitle the holder to 1 new share for a price of $20, each right is worth ($38.18 − $20) / 10 = $1.82.

This means that, when the new rights begin trading in the open market, and the original shares go ex-rights (in the same way shares go ex-dividend), all other things being equal the rights should trade at $1.82 and the stock should trade at $38.18, again assuming the rights issue is successful. But what does it mean for a rights issue to be unsuccessful?

When companies raise additional capital, it can be for many reasons. Funding a new and capital-intensive business is a common reason, but other reasons exist too. In the case of European banks after the 2008–2009 crisis, the reason was often basically "our debts are too big, we need more cash." And sometimes the reason isn't especially clear, even after reading the rights issue documentation. As we've been discussing, the adverse selection question is simple: how much do you know relative to your competitors?

By and large, market makers aren't in the business of minutely parsing the business prospects of the companies they trade. In these cases, the people trading against the market makers probably know, at least on average, more about the company and what they're actually going to do with this cash infusion. If they judge that it's a good idea, the market makers will find themselves short the rights, having sold them to interested parties. If everyone on average thinks it's a bad idea to give the company more capital, the market makers will end up holding a lot of rights.

Market makers are not in the business of holding large positions in anything, and so they'll flip out their positions, likely at a loss.

The price pressure of these activities will tell the tale of whether the rights issue is a good one or not, but either way the market maker is likely to be left licking their wounds. It's not fun to be trading when you're the last one to find out the important information. In fact, due to technical reasons, bad rights issues can end up entirely breaking the arbitrage relationship between the stock and the rights. Again, market makers aren't generally the first to find out about these things.

An Extra Special Rights Issue

Rights issues all have the same broad mechanics, but the specific details of each rights issue differ enough that it's difficult to establish good universal strategies for trading them. Among the important aspects are the minute details of the issue, as specified in the rights issue master prospectus. This is a long, technical document that is the definitive source for information about the rights issue. Or so you'd expect.

In late 2009 and early 2010, rights issues were very much in fashion for European banks. The European Central Bank (ECB) had decreed that banks needed more equity capital, and rights issues were seen as the most prudent way of obtaining it. And so it was that an unnamed large Greek bank came out with a prospectus detailing that every share would be entitled to one right, and each right would entitle the holder to two new shares at some reasonable discount.

On the first day of trading for the rights, markets open and appear to be off in price. By the very standard calculation in the previous section, the rights should be worth 2.50, and yet the electronic market in them is 1.20 – 1.30, in reasonable size. Jeff decides to buy as much as he can, and predictably the market maker turns off his machine immediately. Jeff expects the market maker to realize his mistake: the market would have been perfectly reasonable if each old share gave *two* rights, and each right gave *one* new share. The market maker must have misread the prospectus.

Since he expects the market maker to have realized his mistake and to turn back on making a market around 2.50, imagine Jeff's shock when he sees the market maker turn back on making the same 1.20 – 1.30

market! Panic sets in as Jeff rereads and gets his co-workers to reread the prospectus again. And yet Jeff is correct: the prospectus *clearly* states one old share gives *one* right, each right gives *two* new shares. In desperation, Jeff calls his Greek broker and simply asks "what is the deal with these rights?" Ever solicitous, the broker promises to move heaven and earth to find out.

Two hours go by with Jeff unable to reach the Greek broker. Finally, a call comes in. The Greek broker spoke with certain mysterious Greek entities, and it has been determined that there was a typo in the prospectus. Although the prospectus *clearly* states the terms, and although the prospectus is the *only* definitive legal document detailing the terms of the rights issue, apparently the published prospectus was wrong. The rights issue was in fact one old share for two rights, each right gives one new share.

In a remarkable coincidence, it turns out that the market maker with whom Jeff had traded was *also* the same investment bank who underwrote the rights issue for the Greek bank, and who wrote the typo-filled prospectus. The upshot from this series of events is that Jeff discovered another source of adverse selection aptly summed up in a sports metaphor: "The goalposts have moved." The takeaway: do not trade a contract with someone who can apparently retroactively change the terms of the contract to suit them.

Adverse Selection in Everyday Life

The law about never being happy with the size of a trade may not seem like it bears much relevance to situations outside trading, but you'll see that it does indeed. The rule is a way of describing the phenomenon of adverse selection, and this phenomenon occurs in very nearly every environment where people trade and negotiate with one another. The classic example of adverse selection in everyday life concerns the market for used cars, as famously described in George Akerlof's Nobel Prize–winning work (Akerlof, 1970). However, adverse selection appears in many other situations, and each one teaches something a bit new about how to deal with it.

eBay and the Winner's Curse

Perhaps the most obvious place where adverse selection predominates is in eBay-style auctions. In these auctions, the eventual buyer of an item is the person who bid the highest for it. That is, she beat out all the other bidders for the right to purchase the item. This is a classic situation where the winner's curse appears. The winner's curse is a well-known game theoretic phenomenon where, under very broad assumptions, the winner of a multi-bidder auction is extremely likely to have overpaid for the item.

The basic idea is that there is uncertainty about the true fair value of an item. Every bidder has a different estimate of the value, and absent any other knowledge we expect the mean of these estimates to be close to the true value. The winner of the auction is the person with the highest estimate, and so is likely to have paid more than the fair value for the item. So how do you combat this phenomenon?

The answer is to underbid. The bid should reflect not your estimate about the fair value of the item, but rather your estimate *conditional on having won the auction*. In this way you can, on average, avoid overpaying in these auctions. But a new problem presents itself: how can you generate these new conditional estimates?

You need to estimate a variety of factors: at the very least we need to estimate the number of other bidders and your (and their) uncertainty as to the value of the item. The issue is that buyers on eBay (and similar auction sites) are heterogeneous. For instance, some people spend a lot of their time gaining knowledge and experience in these auctions. For this reason, they will have much better estimates about these sorts of parameters than infrequent bidders. Thus, even if an inexperienced bidder attempts to account for the winner's curse, the mere fact of having won an auction against more-experienced bidders likely means they still overpaid.

This insight about eBay auctions generalizes, as we saw in our original rights issue discussion. Information asymmetry matters not only when it's between buyer and seller, but also when it exists *among* diverse participants on the same side (whether buying or selling). It's typically the case that when thinking about adverse selection, you're likelier to worry about the person you're potentially trading against. But you need to think about the equally important questions regarding the pool of people with whom you're competing to do the trade.

Store Sales and Specials

Retailers frequently announce sales of their merchandise. The goal is to clear their old inventory in order to have room to bring in new inventory that will sell at a higher margin. But what do we make of this old inventory that is being marked down? How good a deal is it?

Consider that the old inventory was once new inventory. Some portion of it got sold at full retail price. Presumably, the fraction that got sold was the most attractive portion, so therefore the remaining inventory that did not get sold is less attractive. Perhaps the remaining colors of the clothes are less appealing and the sizes less standard; perhaps they look fine but end up feeling itchy when you put them on. At any rate, these clothes didn't sell for various reasons, and they're now discounted for those reasons. But is it a good deal?

The insight from the eBay example fully applies here. Who am I competing against? What is my relative level of skill at identifying good discounted clothing deals? If, like me, you shop for clothes only on pain of death, then you should consider yourself unlikely to find a good deal in the clearance rack. If, on the other hand, clothes shopping is your personal hobby, then your knowledge of relative values allows you to find good deals in these situations.

This example leads us to another insight about adverse selection: specialize! If the competition between fellow buyers (or sellers) is a defining characteristic in doing good trades, as it often is, then it's important to gain and maintain expertise in the markets you're trading. Don't try to do good trades in a variety of markets. You're unlikely to gain enough expertise to overcome the experts in the fields. Better to pick a few choice markets and become an expert yourself.

Job Market

Adverse selection in the job market appears on the side of both the employer and the prospective employee. Employees are looking for the most attractive job they can find, while employers are looking for the best candidate for the job.

Prospective employees are subject to various selection pressures, not all of them adverse:

- Given that the company is looking to hire employees, things can't be going all *that* badly for the firm. This could have a positive selection effect, for once. Nevertheless, maybe the company is hiring because people are leaving and they're having trouble finding hires. It's a double-edged sword.

- The job description is likely to be embellished, at least a little bit, especially for less-attractive jobs.
- The interviewers in a company are typically better-than-average employees since they're the ones the company chooses to represent them to potential hires. Thus, the applicant sees a rosy picture of the quality of her future co-workers.
- Employees typically only seek out new jobs every few years or so. As a result, their skill at job finding is lower than the companies' skill at candidate finding. This asymmetry of skill and knowledge works in the companies' favor.

Employers, however, suffer significantly greater adverse selection, since in the end the employee is the one making the final decision of either accepting or rejecting a job offer:

- When hiring people with prior experience, the applicant pool skews in the direction of lower-quality workers. This is because good workers will be preferentially incentivized to remain with their current employers. On average, therefore, people with prior experience looking for jobs aren't as good as those who have jobs (Greenwald, 1986).
- The process of interviewing to decide whom to hire is an imperfect one. Companies will therefore not be able to sufficiently distinguish between good and bad workers, meaning they will tend to squeeze offered wages toward the average. This is advantageous for less competent workers, who, for the most part, will be the ones looking for work, and disadvantageous for good workers, who will be driven away from the job market by the lower-than-deserved wages on offer.
- Potential employees will select the best offer from all the ones available to them. Good workers will have a large pool of available offers, and will pick the best one. If a given employer isn't universally known as the most desirable one, then it's fair to say that a worker who accepts an employer's job offer does so because she couldn't get a better one elsewhere.

How should job seekers protect themselves against these issues? The most important thing you can do is to practice job seeking and interviewing. Even when holding a job and with no desire to move, wise and foresighted workers will apply to jobs every so often just to keep their interviewing skills sharp. Also, when actively looking for a job, you should apply to more jobs than just the ones in which you're truly interested. Try to schedule the applications so that they progress in increasing order of attractiveness. That way, by the time the process begins with the desirable jobs, you've got some recent interviewing experience under your belt.

Finally, remember that the job interview is the most useful diagnostic of what the position you're applying for is actually like. Think about the skills and abilities you were asked to demonstrate during your interview. Are those the skills you'd like to have to use in your job? Look at your interviewers and try to assess them honestly. Would these people be ones you'd want to work with? Would slightly worse versions of them still be people you'd work with? If your interviewers didn't impress you, your future co-workers won't either.

Insurance

One of the few situations where adverse selection can work in favor of the average person are insurance markets. In these markets, insurers are much less differentiated among themselves than the people they're attempting to insure. The asymmetry of information operates in the opposite direction from the typical scenario. This is because insurance buyers know more about themselves, their specific personal situations, than do the insurers. Since insurance buyers will typically obtain multiple quotes, they can essentially auction themselves off to the various insurers and let *them* suffer the winner's curse of being selected as the lowest-cost provider.

Of course, insurers are skilled at this game too. Why are insurance contracts so complex, opaque, and difficult to understand? This is not a mistake; it's a feature. By making the details of the insurance provided as arcane and difficult to compare as possible, insurers protect themselves by adding randomness to the public's selections. Since most people seeking insurance aren't experts in the details of the contracts being offered, the asymmetry of information gets redressed through these tactics aimed at hiding the true nature of the contracts.

Summary and Looking Ahead

- Adverse selection rules the world of trading. You'll never be truly happy with the trades you did. The best you can do is to be mildly unhappy and accept that this is a fundamental aspect of the job.
- Adverse selection between buyer and seller is important, but equally important is knowledge asymmetry between varied fellow buyers, or fellow sellers.
- Combat adverse selection by specializing. Become an expert in your markets, and don't frequently stray from them.
- If you're forced to do trades in an unfamiliar market, then trade them using mechanisms with little price or size discrimination. This will minimize your disadvantage.

We've done a lot of heavy lifting in the first two chapters. You understand your own motivations, your place in the world, and you've begun to look at what fundamentally characterizes the act of trading. You now have enough foundation to tackle perhaps the most misunderstood idea in trading: risk. To quote George Costanza's voice-doppelganger in the *Seinfeld* episode "The Fatigues": "In order to manage risk we must first understand risk. How do you spot risk? How do you avoid risk; and what makes it ... so risky?"

References

Barker, D. B. (Nov 1995). Bayesian Estimation and the Kalman Filter. *Computers and Mathematics with Applications* 30, Issue 10, pp. 55–77.

Akerlof, G. (1970). The Market for Lemons: Quality Uncertainty and the Market Mechanism. *Quarterly Journal of Economics* 84, No. 3, pp. 488–500.

Greenwald, B. C. (1986). Adverse Selection in the Labour Market. *Review of Economic Studies* 53, No 3, pp. 325–347.

Yudkowsky, E. (2008). Retrieved from http://yudkowsky.net/rational/bayes.

CHAPTER

3

Risk

A risk analyst comes into the office of the chief risk officer. It's the fall of 2008, and high above the streets of midtown Manhattan, inside one of the many crystal cathedrals of finance, things don't look good.

"Sir, the extra stress tests you asked me to run show a problem. We might be on the hook for a $12 billion loss if things keep moving like they have the last couple of days."

"How is this possible? Where's our hedge?"

"We're hedged according to the original scenarios. But some of the new ones show some hedges breaking down."

"Which scenarios exactly?"

"The ones where the junk spread[1] doesn't blow out. Everything just keeps tanking."

"I can see the headlines now: storied investment bank goes belly up because the good, safe, AAA-rated debt is actually just as bad as the junk debt."

"That's the picture right now sir."

"Okay, thanks. I'm calling the CEO; he has to bring in the board again. We need to find more capital. Somehow, from somewhere . . . ."

> Take only the risks you're being paid to take. Hedge the others.

What Do We Mean by Capital?

In order to tell the story of risk, I first need to define some useful concepts. Often the problem with talking about trading and finance ideas is that we use regular English words, but it turns out people have subtly different definitions for those words. What do we mean by risk? Capital? Hedging? Without spending a little time defining terms, we end up talking past each other. And if you've never had someone explain what these important-sounding words mean, all the better! The next time your investment advisers suggest you trade some more to "hedge" your portfolio, you'll know what they mean. And you'll be able to tell if it's something you should even be doing.

Self-Financing Portfolios

In the first book of the Bible, Genesis, we learn that in the beginning there was nothing. Similarly, modern cosmology tells that the whole universe emerged from a singular Big Bang. Less grandiosely, I will begin the story of risk in the same way. Let's imagine that you begin with no money, no securities, nothing of any value other than the ability to act. What sorts of things could you do with no money, in this hypothetical world?

Since you own nothing, in order to buy something (like a share of stock) you need to sell an equal value of something else. In this case the "something else" is money, since financial markets don't generally operate on the barter system.[2] Of course, you didn't *have* any money to sell, so you borrow some money in order to be able to sell it. Buying a share of stock means you need to borrow the money to do so. The combination of the purchased asset (a share of stock in this case) and the liability you incurred (borrowing the money to buy it) is known as a *self-financing portfolio*. That's just a fancy way of saying, "All the transactions at the time net out to zero."

Why is this important? It's because in order to evaluate a trade, you can't do it in isolation. Is, say, buying IBM shares a good trade? It depends on many factors, among them the cost of the money used to buy the shares. Borrowing cash at an interest rate of 150% per year, as opposed to borrowing it at 0.1% per year, makes a big difference. If you had started out with some cash already, instead of a self-financing portfolio where you're forced to borrow it, then things would actually get more complicated, not less. For one, you'd have to think about everything else you might possibly do with that cash. In a high-interest-rate world, for example, perhaps lending that cash is a better trade than buying IBM stock.

Thinking about trades as self-financing portfolios lets you account for the value of the money you're using to do the trades. If you already have cash to begin with, then thinking in this way allows you to properly consider the *opportunity cost* of the trades you didn't and won't do with the money. All those missed opportunities have some value (whether positive or negative) and this approach lets you value them properly.

Collateral and Capital

If buying IBM is the trade you want to do, then the self-financing principle tells you to think *as though* you must borrow the cash to do so. One share of IBM costs $187.50 to buy, so you borrow $187.50 for, let's say, one month. One month from now, you will repay $187.55 to your lender, for an effective annual interest rate of 0.32%. Your trade will make money if you sell IBM for more than $187.55 one month from now (ignoring costs, dividends, or other corporate actions).

Now let's say IBM announces bad earnings tomorrow, and stock drops to $171.20. Your position has lost $16.30. You're sad that your trade went against you, but remember that your trades are self-financing: in the beginning you had nothing. You're already destitute. The person who will bear this loss is the one who lent you the money! One month from now, IBM will be trading near $171.20, and when you sell the share you won't be able to fully repay the $187.55 you owe. You can't get blood from a stone (a bankrupt trader), and so the lender will end up with the short end of the stick.

For this reason, lenders demand *collateral* when lending. If you're borrowing to buy shares and the lender is a US-regulated broker-dealer, US Federal Reserve Board Regulation T (Reg T) requires the lender to demand at least 50% of the value of the stock purchase as collateral or *margin*. That is, in order to borrow $187.50 to buy IBM, the buyer will have to deposit $93.75 in an account accessible to the lender. This collateral posted to the lender cushions losses for the lender in the event the trade goes against you, the borrower.[3] Of course, if IBM goes below $93.75 overnight then the lender takes your collateral, but they're still on the hook for at least some loss. And *this* is the true reason you need capital (money) when you trade.

Collateral needs (or *capital requirements*) are important considerations. So, in addition to evaluating a self-financing trade by thinking
of its expected value (i.e. taking into account the cost of money), you
must also evaluate how much collateral (or margin, or capital) the
trade will consume. Money pledged to collateralize one trade cannot be used to collateralize a different trade, so you must evaluate
trades relative to each other: their expected value *and* their capital
consumed.

Being Right and Losing Anyway

Now that I've gotten some definitions out of the way, let me introduce
you to Ethel, our star trader for this chapter. Some years ago, Ethel
started a small hedge fund (Persephone Investments) that focuses on
stock picking. That is, the edges that Persephone attempts to find and
trade involve buying stocks that are undervalued, selling those that
are overvalued, and waiting for the broader market to subsequently
converge on Ethel's view of their value. It's a good business: she's
made her clients money in the last few years, and Persephone's assets
under management (AUM) have increased steadily in that time.

It's October 2007, and Persephone has identified XYZ Corp as
a promising company. For a variety of fundamental reasons, Ethel
believes that XYZ shares are undervalued by around 15%, and so she
decides to put on a big trade buying a stake in XYZ. Unfortunately
for her, October 2007 is a decidedly bad time to buy equities, and
over the next 18 months the S&P 500 (and hence the US market in
general) loses nearly half its value.

It turns out that XYZ had done significantly better than the
broader market over that time, having only lost 30% of its value.
Sadly, this fact is cold comfort to our young fund manager, whose
investors have by now lost patience with the fund's persistent losses.
These investors have withdrawn their investment in Persephone,
and this withdrawal has forced the liquidation of the fund. Ethel
was right about XYZ, but she lost everything anyway. What could she
have done differently?

Before I get to that, it's worth noting that this idea of "you were
right but still lost" isn't restricted to financial markets. You took the
subway home from work instead of a taxi, but there was a signaling
failure on the line and you got stuck for an hour. You decided against

buying insurance for your mobile phone, but a day later your dog knocked it off the table and broke it. You got a great deal on a house in Malibu, but then wildfire season came and your house happened to be in the path of a fire that burned it down. You made the right call in expected-value terms, but nonetheless lost because of other random occurrences. Some of these random occurrences are unavoidable, but as you'll see with Ethel, some of them can be accounted for. This accounting-for is known as *hedging*.

Risk and Hedging

Ethel's thesis was that XYZ was an undervalued company, and the way she acted on that belief was to buy shares of XYZ. But what does "XYZ is an undervalued company" mean? A reasonable interpretation is that she believes XYZ's share price will outperform the average company as people come to recognize its cheapness over time. That is, a cheapness that's relative to other companies' averageness. While buying XYZ does expose her to that risk factor (XYZ as compared to the average company), it also exposes her to the risk of the whole market moving against her (down, in this case). It turns out that she was right about XYZ, but the broader-market risk she took on overwhelmed her correct call on XYZ's outperformance.

It's not that Persephone was undercapitalized for the trades she wanted to do, exactly. It's that her capitalization is part of a feedback loop that, for better or worse, takes into account how well she has been doing. I will examine this feedback loop at greater length in Chapter 4.

Let's wind the clock back for Ethel and Persephone. For one, they could have significantly improved the risk profile of her trade by *hedging* the market risk. Let's look at this idea in detail. As Ethel buys XYZ shares in October 2007, she could also sell an appropriate amount of broad market futures (or ETFs). That way, she can establish a portfolio that is less exposed to the movements of the market:

- If XYZ goes up 1% and the market also goes up 1%, Ethel wins on her XYZ position and loses on her market position. These cancel out, and Ethel makes no money. This is true anytime XYZ moves in tandem with the market.

- If XYZ moves up more than the market, Ethel makes money. This is true no matter the market move. If XYZ is up 10% and the market is up 8%, she wins. If XYZ is down 10% and the market is down 12%, she still wins.
- The opposite is true if XYZ is down more than the market, using the same reasoning.

Hedging her market risk has given Ethel an exposure to exactly the risk she thought she could make money by taking. By hedging out her exposure to risks that she has no incentive to take, Ethel shows the value of following this chapter's rule. We will return later to the story of Ethel and XYZ, but first I need to answer what should be a nagging question by now: what do we mean by risk?

What Is Risk?

It's time to define our last big term for the chapter: risk. Everyone has strongly held opinions on what's a reasonable risk and what's not. Remember Alex Honnold, the climber from Chapter 1, scaling almost a mile of sheer rock alone and without ropes, for the fun and challenge of it. In the financial world also, people debate what are reasonable risks and what are not, and this too is unsurprising. Financial markets are complex systems, with lots of feedback mechanisms and connections to the physical and social world. It would be pretty unlikely for there to be some clean, universally applicable understanding of risk that you can use to analyze all trading. There exists a wide variety of risk measures, and each of them has its strengths and weaknesses.

The important thing to keep in mind, even before examining the idea of risk in detail, is that it's a mistake to rely on one specific view or measure of risk. Standard deviation, max drawdown, skewness, tail exponent, value-at-risk, all of these technical risk measures can be useful. But none are useful to the exclusion of the others, and relying on only one or a few measures is itself an important risk factor. By relying on some specific measure, the decisions that result will tend to optimize for the weaknesses of the risk measure. This phenomenon, one with broad applicability, has come to be known as Goodhart's Law. This law is usually formulated as: "When a measure becomes a target, it ceases to be a good measure." That sounds quite abstract, so let's make it concrete by examining one of the most popular risk metrics: value-at-risk (VaR).

VaR and the Mismeasure of Risk

Value-at-risk is a risk measure that became popular in the aftermath of the 1987 market crash. VaR attempts to model the probability that losses in a portfolio exceed some number. More properly, for a given probability level and time horizon, VaR reports the minimum value of a loss that can be expected with that probability over that time horizon.

For example, let's say that a portfolio's one-day 1% VaR is $11 million. This means that the VaR methodology estimates that a loss of at least $11 million dollars over the next day will occur with a probability of 1%. If risk managers had already decided that the maximum one-day 1% VaR is only allowed to be $10 million (the VaR limit), then the portfolio is said to be in a "VaR break."

The intent of the VaR metric is to alert risk managers to the minimal loss (or downside risk) of a given portfolio. However, many proponents of VaR have claimed that the benefit of calculating VaR isn't really to produce the exact numbers, but rather it's the exercise, or process, of coming up with the numbers that is the most valuable aspect. For firms and organizations that had hitherto never used a structured risk management process, this is almost definitely true. Nonetheless, the story of risk measures is the story of the misuse of risk measures, and VaR has become a sort of poster child for these kinds of stories.

Let's think about the information that VaR is providing. The result of a VaR analysis is a minimum loss number (for a given time horizon and probability). But you are surely more interested in just about any other loss metric. A risk manager would rather know what the maximum possible loss could be. Or failing that, what is the average possible loss. Or failing that, the median possible loss. Any of these measures is much more instructive about the risk of a position than the minimum possible loss. Consider a portfolio that loses exactly $1 million with probability 1%. This represents a VaR of $1 million. Now consider a portfolio that loses $1 million with probability 0.9%, and $100 million with probability 0.1%. The 1% VaR of this portfolio is *also* $1m. And yet the second portfolio is, by any reasonable judgment, much riskier than the first.

It's easy to conclude from this illustration that VaR is a fatally flawed risk measure and should not be used, but that would be the wrong conclusion to draw. As I said at the outset, every risk measure has strengths and weaknesses and I have merely identified one of VaR's biggest weaknesses. The problem arises when VaR (or any risk measure) is used to the exclusion of other risk measures. This is because every risk measure can be gamed, and if the motivation exists to game it, it shall be gamed.

Gaming the Measure

Xin is a trader at a large investment bank. His desk has a strict $5 million one-day 5% VaR risk limit, and let's assume the bank's risk managers only care to look at the VaR reports as a risk measure. Let's also assume that Xin's compensation is tied very strongly to his annual profit-and-loss (P&L), and that he doesn't have any other incentives (such as an equity stake in his firm, or other cultural or institutional reputational risk) at play.

Xin has found himself a client whose trade he wants to facilitate. The client wants to buy a $25 million stake in a biotech firm. This biotech is going to announce the results of a drug trial tomorrow. The stock is currently trading at $10. If the announcement is positive, the stock will likely go above $25, and if it's negative, the stock will drop to around $5. In practice, biotech drug announcements are never this clearly bimodal (i.e. having two clear outcomes, good and bad), and so there is some uncertainty around these numbers. Nevertheless, the pricing of the stock indicates that the market believes the news will be good with a probability of around 25%.[4]

In order to be compensated for the risk, Xin will want to sell the stock to his client at a premium, and he will also want to hedge his risk. For example, he could offer the stock at $10.10, believing he can buy back 80% of the stock paying an average of $10.02. That way, he makes $0.08 on $20 million of stock (a profit of around $160,000) and will be left with the risk on the $5 million of stock he couldn't manage to buy back (with an EV of $50,000 on that portion). Unfortunately, if the stock does indeed go to $25, he will be left with a loss of approximately $7.5 million (losing 150% on his short sale of $5 million of stock). This certainly breaks Xin's $5 million one-day 5% VaR limit. Of course, he could just scale down the trade in order to stay within the limit, but what self-respecting trader would leave any client unhappy, as well as $50,000 of clean profit lying on the table?

Fortunately, Xin's desk quant Ashok has an idea. Positive news on the drug trial is likely to bring the price to $25, but there's a large range of possibilities there. Ashok tells Xin to propose the following contract to the client: if the stock price goes above $20 but below $30, the client is capped out at $20. If the price goes above $30, the client gets double the profit otherwise due. In fact, studying the probabilities, Ashok thinks Xin can probably sell this extra contract for an additional $0.01 per share. Analyst consensus is that the probability of the stock going above $30 is no more than 2%. Let's ponder this rather complex contract:

- *If the news is bad, and the stock moves to $5:* This happens 75% of the time, and the bank makes the original $160,000, the $50,000 on the contract, plus the profit on the short sale of the stock he couldn't buy back ($5.10 x 500,000 shares = $2.55m) for a total of $2.76 million profit.
- *If the news is good, and the stock goes to between $20 and $30:* This happens 24% of the time, and the bank makes the $210,000 but loses on the short sale (capped at $20): ($10.10 − $20) x 500,000 shares = −$4.95 million, for a total of $4.74 million loss.
- *If the news is good, and the stock goes above $30:* This happens 1% of the time, and the bank loses *at least* ($30 − $10.1) x 500,000 shares x 2 = $19.9 million loss on the unhedged shares, making the loss in this case $19.9 million − $0.21 million = $19.69 million loss.

In EV terms, the trade is still very good for the bank: EV of this trade works out to $586,000!

Through a bit of financial alchemy, Xin and Ashok have constructed a trade that (a) sounds more attractive to the customer (b) significantly increases the bank's profit on the trade, and (c) brings the trade under the risk limit. No wonder such intelligent people get paid as much as they do! The client agrees to the extra contract and they do the trade. And most of the time (98% of the time) the trade works perfectly and everyone receives their bonuses for a job well done. When that happens, it can be difficult to remember that they avoided the 1 in 50 chance of losing around $20 million dollars and perhaps much more!

It's worth repeating that it's too easy to blame the VaR risk measure for encouraging the sort of risk metric gaming illustrated here. Doing so would be much like shooting the messenger. In the narrow context of risk, the problem was the overreliance on one particular risk measure. The broader problem, as you'll see in detail in Chapter 9, was a trading culture where Xin's and Ashok's incentives are separated from the incentives of the investment bank.

What Sorts of Risks Are There?

So far in this chapter I've been talking about risk as though all that mattered were market risk. But more fundamentally, you need to ask, "What sorts of risks is my portfolio/position/trade subject to?" Financial risks come in various forms, not just market risk, and some are more obvious than others. As a trader I've taken my share of risks, and here are some broad categories:

1. *Market risk:* The most well-known financial risk: did the value of my portfolio increase or decrease? Seems simple but remember that you can only assess changes in value (profits and losses) if the positions have a clear, undisputed price associated with them (known as a *mark*). This is usually true for equities, for example, but not always. Stocks can be halted for trading because of any number of reasons (corporate news, political instability, exchange technical issues, etc.), and when they do the market value of a stock is more guess than fact. In some less-liquid markets, such as mortgage-backed securities, there is no unambiguously agreed-upon mark for the securities. In those situations, the evaluation of market risk, and of profit and loss (P&L), is a matter of opinion.[5] I've traded some illiquid products in the past, and the mark was always a source of concern. This was because the amount of margin you had to put up depended on these questionable marks.

2. *Counterparty risk:* When you lend something (whether money or securities), counterparty risk relates to the possibility of the borrower defaulting on the loan. Counterparty risk is sometimes considered a subclass of credit risk, but here I'm going to treat credit risk as a subclass of a much broader notion of counterparty risk. Credit risk is specifically the risk of a borrower either failing to make an interest payment on a loan, or not repaying the principal itself. However, counterparty risk—that is, the risk of the borrower not repaying—is not limited to loans of money. If you lend shares

to someone for the purposes of short-selling, you now have a counterparty risk exposure to that borrower. When you trade exchange-traded securities, your counterparty is the clearinghouse. It's easy to forget about counterparty issues when that's the case, but clearinghouses have a long history of going under too!

3. *Liquidity risk:* Anytime you own an asset, you can consider the sale of that asset. If the market on which that asset trades is illiquid (i.e. it trades infrequently or in an unusual, slow or costly manner), then the ownership of that asset is subject to liquidity risk. You can't just sell it when you'd like to. I sometimes traded some very illiquid options, and that trading is all about liquidity risk. Since a given option is so infrequently traded, you have to mostly assume that you won't be able to trade out of a position before the option expires. That's known as "wearing" the position until expiry.

4. *Model risk:* Models are a useful simplification of the complex world we live in. Whenever models inaccurately represent the world and that inaccuracy materially affects trades or positions, you're faced with an instance of model risk. Chapter 6 will cover these issues. A common way in which models fail is when you implicitly assume certain states of affairs are impossible, although in fact they are quite possible. This particular sort of model failure will be covered in Chapter 8.

5. *Operational risk:* The mechanics of trading on financial markets can be quite complicated. Operational risk encompasses the possibility that you make mistakes in managing your positions or trades. There are innumerable ways to screw up in managing one's positions and trades, which is why good trading firms set up rigorous procedures to mitigate operational risk. A recurring nightmare I had when I first started trading options was that I had forgotten to send in my exercise decisions for expiring options, and as a result I had lost all the value of my positions. This doesn't happen in real life (the exchange usually does reasonable things), but it shows how terrifying operational risk can be.

6. *Technological risk:* Closely related to operational risk is technological risk. Trading in modern markets is a very technology-intensive operation: lots of procedures, lots of systems, lots of computers, lots of code, and lots of data. While having

computers to electronically trade in modern markets has made possible significant cost savings, there are few quicker ways to incinerate millions of dollars than to have a trading system go haywire because of a software bug. Even less dramatic technological risks can be extremely costly. Consider a trade whose models require an extensive statistical back-test. If the necessary historical data gets wiped out in a data-center flood, or because a technologist made a mistake in applying a software patch, that trade is no longer doable. Chapter 10 will have more to say about the role of technology.

7. *Reputational and legal risk:* Trading in financial markets inescapably involves establishing and maintaining good relationships with other entities. Traders need brokers, exchanges, and (for better or worse) regulators. The extent to which your relations have confidence in your ethical standards and your trustworthiness defines your range of free action. Untrustworthy people and firms will be kept on a short leash by others, with a resulting restriction on the kinds of profitable trades they can access. And there's no shortage of trade ideas with sketchy or downright illegal mechanics, as you'll learn in chapter 5.

You can plan for risk as much as you like, but there will always remain risks you can't account for. Random, weird things happen periodically in financial markets, and some of those will catch you unaware. The Flash Crash of 2010 provided me with a front-row seat for that lesson. The afternoon of May 6, 2010, was a busy but otherwise unremarkable day in US equity markets. Starting around 2:30pm, many stocks began to move down sharply on what appeared to be no news. Debate rages to this day about the cause of these moves, but the result was that US stocks moved down an average of 9%. Some stocks saw more extreme moves, with Procter & Gamble famously down 37% at one point based on no apparent news.

As saner heads began to prevail, discretionary traders began buying these stocks quickly and in large volume. This was a clear problem with market function, with stocks stuck in a weird feedback mechanism that would revert back to normal in the next few days. As markets rebounded over the next half-hour, these buyers—traders who had used quick thinking and an appetite for risk to arrest and reverse a market crash—began to show a profit from their trades. The reasonable thing to do was to sell back the shares they had bought. For example, a trader I know bought P&G when it was down 25% and began selling it back when it was down only 10%, representing a 15% profit over the course of 15 minutes or so. Great trading, right?

Not so fast. The entities (mostly algorithmic traders) who had sold when P&G was down 25% requested and received from the exchange busts on those trades. The trades were null and void, as if they had never happened. The trades when P&G was only down 10% stood, however, and as P&G rebounded to an unchanged level over the subsequent days, those sales represented a net *loss* of 10% for the traders who sold at that level. No good deed goes unpunished.

Evaluating and Measuring Risk

The ability to evaluate your exposure (and potential future exposure) to a variety of risks is an essential skill in being a good trader. After all, it is impossible to make good trades if you don't know, in a qualitative sense, which risks you believe you have edge to take, and which risks are ones you should either avoid or attempt to minimize. The act of trading is the act of taking risk. The job of a trader is to judiciously select the risks that will yield profit.

I've already touched on a few foundational principles in thinking about risk, and it's worth restating them here.

1. *Don't rely on one risk measure.* Risk measures all have strong and weak suits, and overreliance on one particular approach blinds you to the risks that exploit the weaknesses.
2. *Actively seek to understand the risks you could be subject to.* The easiest way to lose to a risk is not even to know that you were exposed to it.

Top-down Risk

Let's evaluate the general risk profile of a credit-default swap (CDS) trader. A CDS is a contract that represents the probability of default for a specific set of bonds, and its value is therefore subject to the prices of those bonds. It's clear that market risk is an important risk that a firm needs to be good at. But there are many kinds of market risk, as you'll see later in this chapter, and mistaking edge in one sort of market risk for another is an easy and dangerous mistake to make.

Perhaps less obvious is that a CDS trader probably needs to be skilled at taking operational risk too. CDSes are complex instruments, and the contracts that specify their payouts are long, complex, and full of arcane language and clauses. The Bloomberg columnist Matt Levine has, over the years, written many columns detailing the sometimes-odd specifications of these contracts, and the occasionally counterintuitive incentives that result from them. A good CDS trader needs to have a very good handle on the mechanics of how these contracts pay out in order to avoid getting exploited by other market participants with sharper-eyed readers of the contracts.

CDSes are also relatively illiquid instruments. Leaving aside the CDSes on big banks and other large well-established firms, a company's CDSes are often held by only one entity on either side of the contract. The secondary markets for these instruments are often non-existent, meaning that once you enter into a contract you're likely stuck with it for a long time. This illiquidity is a significant risk factor in the profitability of CDS trading.

Finally, given the close relationship between a company's prospects and the CDSes written on their bonds, it's useful to have a good productive relationship between the CDS trader and the company. There are many ways that companies can restructure their operations, each with different effects on the derivatives contracts written on those operations. Reputational risk (either in the positive or negative direction) is often an important consideration when trading distressed CDSes.

At the outset, as you can see, you have to have a good understanding of the nature of the trades you're attempting, and just as good an understanding of what it is about those trades that makes them profitable to do. This conceptual understanding of risk is crucial for what follows, and it must be revisited continually as markets evolve over time. It's easy to get complacent about an established trade that is making money and thereby to neglect new risks that appear over time.

Bottom-up Risk (A Worked Example)

Having examined the kinds of risks being taken, and the reasons why those risks are the right ones to take, it's time to get to the detailed risk analysis. Each trade is a very specific action, so let's consider one in detail. As an example, let's say you short[6] sell 10,000 shares of PTT Limited in Thailand. PTT is Thailand's largest company, and trades on the Stock Exchange of Thailand (SET). To what sorts of risks might you be subject with this trade?

1. *Market risk:* As always, the most obvious risk is market risk. PTT stock could go up or down in value. If it goes down you profit, and if it goes up you lose. However, as I will examine in more detail hereafter, it's not only the PTT-specific risk that you care about. If Thailand's stock market moves a lot, it's probably going to move PTT along with it. This isn't a risk in PTT specifically so much as a risk in Thailand in general. Similarly, since PTT is denominated in Thai baht, you care about the risk of the currency moving too. Also notice that PTT is an oil exploration company and is thus highly exposed to the risks of the oil markets in general. These are only the most obvious market risks to our PTT position, and it should be clear that there are many other sources of market risk that affect the value of PTT.

2. *Liquidity risk:* You have sold 10,000 shares of PTT, and you will eventually want to buy them back. Will there be a market for these shares when you decide to buy back? Since PTT is a very liquid and highly traded stock in Thailand, you probably believe this is a fairly small risk. But it is a risk nonetheless. Also note that you sold the shares short, meaning you borrowed shares in order to execute the sale. What if liquidity in the PTT borrow dries up? This can happen for any number of reasons, and if your lender recalls its borrow, you may be forced to buy back your shares before you'd like to. Even more dangerously, it's likely that the times you're forced to buy back will be times when the stock is trading artificially high (because of the difficulty in borrowing to sell). On those occasions, you'll probably buy the shares back for more than would otherwise be fair. Again, given that PTT is a liquidly traded company,

this is probably a small risk, but it's worth mentioning and at least considering.

3. *Capital risk:* In order to sell shares short, you are required by the exchange to post margin as collateral for adverse moves in our position. These margin requirements are set by fiat (i.e. mandated), by either the exchange, the exchange regulator, or directly by the government. If these rules change, you may be forced to post additional collateral against your short position, meaning the trade becomes more capital-intensive than it was before, and the opportunity cost of holding the position goes up.

4. *Execution risk:* When undertaking a trade in an unfamiliar market, especially in an emerging market, it can be difficult to ensure a good execution. The broker with whom you have a relationship may be relaying the order to another local broker, the mechanics of the market may be unfamiliar or may privilege local actors such as specialists, or there may be unforeseen costs or unanticipated procedures. Short selling may be banned entirely, for example, or may be subject to particular rules or exclusions. For these reasons, the risk associated with the mere act of doing a new trade can be considerable. It is therefore prudent to do test trades in any new market or security: a small trade that serves to flush out any of these issues before you start making larger or more frequent trades.

5. *Political risk:* When dealing with a foreign country, especially one with a history of political upheaval, it's quite important to consider the local political situation. Living in the developed world, it's easy to fall into the seductive assumption that the rule of law applies strongly everywhere. This is far from the case. A foreigner trading in an emerging market is frequently among the first "victims" of any political turmoil. Companies can get nationalized (especially oil companies), and the current shareholders can have their shares confiscated with reduced or sometimes no compensation.[7] In addition to confiscation, foreigners can be subject to retroactive ownership restrictions that limit the ability to buy (or sometimes perversely, to sell) stakes in local companies. The list of ways in which foreigners can be disadvantaged when trading in emerging and frontier countries is certainly not short.

6. *Communication risk:* All companies undertake actions at one point or another: declaring a dividend, a tender offer, a rights issue, a stock split, spinoff, merger—the list is quite long. Furthermore, depending on local laws, companies do not have the obligation to announce these in a fair and neutral manner. Insiders can sometimes get the information before the general market, or the information only gets translated out of the local language some time later, or sometimes the information is even mistranslated. All of these are risks that you bear when trading in countries of which you have no intimate knowledge, and where you do not have trustworthy and appropriately incentivized local expertise.

As you can see, even a comparatively simple trade carries with it an almost comically long list of risks and things that could go wrong. In the face of such a variety of risks, it can be tempting to tell yourself that thinking about and accounting for more esoteric risks is a mark of paranoia, not rationality. But as former Intel CEO Andy Grove famously said, "Only the paranoid survive" (Grove, 1999). Although Grove's book deals with more specific business risks regarding crises and how to deal with them, the quote in the title is nonetheless a perfect way to describe the mindset necessary in order to have long-term success in trading. The balance lies in avoiding taking undue risks without being paralyzed by them either. In the words of Winston Churchill, "There is a precipice on either side of you: a precipice of caution and a precipice of over-daring."

Thinking about and planning for extremely rare events is not considered reasonable behavior in everyday contexts. You rarely think about a meteorite strike when you go to the supermarket. Or having a bee fly into your throat and sting you when you're out for a jog. Certainly, the modern compendium of mental illnesses (DSM-5) takes a dim view of people who think everyone is out to get them. Yet financial markets are different: people really are out to get you, after all.

It is this near-obsession with thinking about all the esoteric ways in which things could go wrong that is the mark of an appropriately cautious and prepared trader. This is because the calculus is different. As you will see in Chapter 11, long-term success in trading requires an ability to discover new trades and to push into new and unfamiliar territory. The profitable trades are the ones that others

aren't doing, and typically there are very good reasons why. Institu-
tionalizing a prudent, near-paranoid mindset about risk really is the
only way in which pushing into new areas and finding new trades is
justifiable. Without it, the process of continually reinventing one's
trading would indeed be a pathologically risky endeavor.

It's worth noting that the other extreme, one of being paralyzed
by the variety of risks we're subject to, isn't helpful either. After all,
the people who keep all their capital in cash are unlikely to suffer
catastrophic losses, but they are also unlikely to profit very much from
that capital. Putting capital at risk is the way you profit, and being able
to accurately judge those risks is what makes taking them profitable.

Risk Systems

Having done the qualitative analyses, both from the top down and
from the bottom up, you need to architect systems to monitor the
risks we've identified, and to discover new risks. These systems fall
into three broad categories.

1. *Everyday monitoring:* Systems of this type are automated
   processes that produce periodic (real-time, daily, weekly,
   etc.) reports on the risk exposures of the firm. For example,
   market risk reports will show aggregated exposures to various
   risks and will raise alerts when preset warnings and limits are
   reached. Operational risk reports highlight possible trouble
   with the back-end mechanics of trading. Technological risk
   reports show the status of machines and connections, and
   there's certainly a lot of machinery to monitor.

2. *Scenarios:* The response of markets to news events and to itself
   is extremely nonlinear. Thus, everyday risk monitoring is hard
   pressed to provide valuable insights about risk exposures in
   the event of large moves and unusual events such as crashes.
   To assess risk for those events, some form of scenario or stress
   test must be used. By defining a specific set of realistic rare
   events that would particularly stress our positions and trading, you can assess exposures to those events. An example of
   such a scenario, for the purpose of evaluating market risk, is:
   "What would happen if all world indices fell 15% overnight?"
   To answer that question properly, you must also consider
   the state of the world in the event such a thing happens.

What other markets are affected? How are our relationships affected? Will you still be able to trade, to borrow money or shares? Thinking in concrete scenarios such as these helps sharpen our thinking about rare events. Of course, history is only a rough guide about these occurrences. Perhaps the most important scenarios to consider are ones that have never happened but that could plausibly happen.

3. *Novel risks:* The last category of systems is specifically unsystematic by design. This category is an extension of the top-down and bottom-up qualitative assessments you made at the beginning. You must continue to make those assessments and, as I've said, continually be on the lookout for new risks to which you might be subject. By its nature, this sort of effort is impossible to systematize, and involves a great deal of human creativity and experience. Once a new risk is identified, how do you define a specific scenario that tests for that risk? What new monitoring tools are needed for newly identified risks?

The Varieties of Market Risk

Having put market risk in the context of other risks, now is the time to return to the example of Ethel and Persephone at the beginning of the chapter. You will recall that Ethel made a bet on XYZ outperforming the market. In order to more specifically take the risk in which she believes she has edge, she also sold a broader market future as a hedge against her XYZ position. But was this the best hedge she could have made? What other hedges might she have considered?

Identifying Risks

Even in her simplified scenario, it is not as straightforward as it may seem for Ethel to figure out exactly which risk she has edge to take. Ethel may well believe that XYZ will outperform, but there are many reasons why that could be true. Identifying them is essential to creating a good hedge, and here are some very straightforward possibilities:

- Will XYZ outperform because its whole sector will outperform? Perhaps the cheapness Ethel identified is true not only for XYZ but also for every other company in its sector. If so,

then buying XYZ is a very stock-specific way of buying the
sector-outperformance risk. Better then to buy a broad sector
ETF and hedge with the market future. The same argument
applies, though possibly not as strongly, about XYZ's country
of incorporation.

- Is XYZ's outperformance due to its exposure to a specific
  sector or country? Maybe it's that XYZ has a lot of exposure
  to Vietnam, and perhaps Vietnam outperforming is the *real*
  source of edge. Again, perhaps the better trade is to buy a
  broad Vietnam index.
- Is XYZ's outperformance conditional on some event? For
  example, does Ethel believe XYZ will outperform more in a
  rising market than in a falling one? If so, perhaps Ethel should
  buy call options in XYZ and sell call options in SPY.

In practice, edge identification is exceedingly difficult. Many
trades that look different on the surface can in fact be the same
trade in disguise, and trades whose edge appears to derive from one
risk are actually bets on another risk.

Consider a market maker who, unbeknownst to him, actually has
no edge in making markets. However, during times when the market isn't moving up or down very much, the strategy of simply buying
on the bid and selling on the offer is likely to at least break even,
and probably make a bit of money. It turns out that this strategy is
synthetically the same thing as selling options.[8] The strategy of making markets in a stock, a strategy the market maker believes has edge
because of his skill at modeling the stock or because of his technological abilities, is actually merely the strategy of selling options on the
stock. When the stock fails to move very much, selling options generally makes money. But when the stock moves a lot, selling options
generally loses money. Does the market maker believe he has edge
in the stock's volatility risk? If he did, perhaps he should have been
trading the stock's listed options directly. Depending on the details
of the market making strategy and on the perceptiveness of the market maker, it can take a long time to discover that his edge (or lack
thereof) derives from a completely different risk than the one he
thought he was taking.

Optimizing the Hedge

Returning again to Ethel, let's say that after analyzing the trade properly, she decides that it's XYZ's sector (consumer staples) that she's

actually bullish on. So, she buys the $1 million of the ETF XLP and wants to hedge by selling SPY. How much SPY should she sell? As can be expected, the answer to this question is not plain and simple either.

Her first instinct should be to sell $1 million of SPY. When XLP and SPY go up or down the same amount together, the portfolio neither wins nor loses. But is this reasonable? It's impossible to say without looking at some historical data. Over the past year, XLF and SPY have been open and trading on 252 days. On each of those days, XLF and SPY have either gone up or down some amount. Let's plot the daily percentage returns of XLF and SPY against each other, to get an idea of how they co-vary.

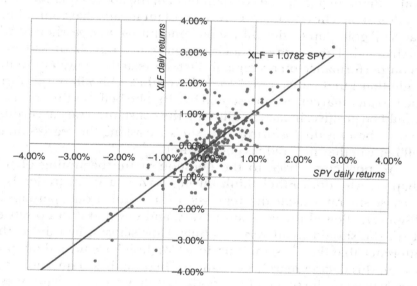

You can see that the points on our scatter plot seem to lie in a diagonal cloud centered at the origin. You can also identify some other interesting characteristics:

- The points should be roughly centered around the origin. Over a small timeframe like one day, the average return of any security is going to be quite small (i.e. nearly 0).
- The diagonal cloud means that generally, when SPY moves up then XLF does too, and when SPY moves down, XLF also moves down. This confirms our intuitions about SPY being a good hedge for XLF.

- The slope of the diagonal appears to be slightly larger than 1. This means that when SPY moves up 1%, XLF on average moves more than that, perhaps 1.1%.

You can make this visual intuition more systematic by running a linear regression on this data. You are looking for a relationship of this form:

$$XLF = \beta * SPY$$

This equation tells you that when you buy 1 unit of XLF, you sell β units of SPY to hedge and thereby minimize your market exposure. For readers with some experience doing linear regression, you may notice that I neglected the constant term in the above equation. This is a debatable choice. Any non-zero constant means that your model has XLF going up or down by some amount *on average* when SPY is unchanged. This represents a claim you're making about XLF and its outperformance on average. In fact, it's exactly equivalent to the trade that Ethel wants to do! *She* believes that XLF will outperform the broader market, as represented by SPY. She believes the constant should be positive, in fact. By allowing the constant to vary according to what best fits the historical data, she's are asking the regression to tell her whether her trade is good or not.

We now come back to the question at the beginning of this chapter: why does Ethel think buying XYZ is a good trade? Is it because she ran exactly this regression (or a similar one, perhaps in disguise), allowed the constant to vary, and saw that it was positive? If so, she should tread very carefully. How statistically valid is the inference that the constant is positive? Might it have turned out positive in this dataset merely by chance? These statistical questions are mostly beyond the scope of this book, but they are important ones.

Let's suppose that Ethel has reasons to believe in her XLF trade that have nothing to do with the historical performance of the ETF. Perhaps she is a fundamental analyst and so she has deep knowledge in the consumer staples sector. Suppose it is this analysis that informs her that XLF should outperform by 5bps per day, on average.

In that case, she now has a prior belief on a plausible value of the constant. If she entirely believes her analysis and believes that it was valid for the historical period in question, the she should set the constant to the 5bps number. This makes the regression accurately reflect her beliefs about the world. But it is more likely that either she doesn't fully believe her analysis, or maybe even more likely still, that her fundamental analysis doesn't apply to the historical data, or if it does, it's only partially. Ethel could choose to reflect this belief by setting the constant to some number between 0 and 5bps.

There are many other factors that come into play when evaluating how to hedge, when to hedge and how much to hedge. But at the core of the process is knowing how the trade you're doing makes money, and which risks you're taking in putting on the trade.

Risk, Utility, and Catastrophic Risk

One of the hedging considerations in the last section merits a closer look. Ethel asked what happens to her trade conditional on up moves versus down moves. Is she equally happy about a 1% profit as she is sad about a 1% loss? Probably. What about a 20% profit as compared to a 20% loss? At first blush, you might be tempted to assume that the same equivalence holds. However, consider the extreme: is Ethel as happy about a 100% profit as she is sad about a 100% loss?

It's clear these two situations are dramatically different. If Ethel wins 100%, then she's surely happy, but she's significantly sadder about losing 100% (that is, everything). In an important sense, losing everything is infinitely bad. Losing all your capital means that you're out of business. It precludes, for the rest of time, the possibility of making profitable trades. You have to start over, literally from zero. So, there is indeed asymmetry in the *value* of equal profits and losses if those numbers are large relative to your capital base.

This insight is far from novel. Economists have, since at least Jeremy Bentham, developed a robust notion of the idea of *utility*. Utility is the value that a person ascribes to some set of goods (and services), a value that may be quite different from their value in the market. In our context, we will mostly examine the utility of wealth. That is: what *personal* value is there to having a certain amount of capital?

We can imagine this utility as a function that converts a certain dollar value of wealth into another unit of measure (frequently called "utilons"). Using this concept, you can quantify your vague intuitions about happiness and sadness about outcomes.

A trader or trading firm having zero wealth, I've already said, should be considered infinitely bad. So therefore assign -∞ utilons to zero wealth. Conversely, infinite wealth should probably have infinity utilons, though large numbers might behave oddly. How much better is it for a person to have $20 billion compared to $10 billion? Having never had either sum, I find it difficult to say. But you can look at the behavior of multibillionaires to give us a clue. The Giving Pledge, a charitable organization established in 2010 by Bill Gates and Warren Buffet, is a campaign to encourage the very wealthy to donate a majority of their wealth to charity. Gates and Buffett themselves have pledged to donate the vast majority of their wealth, amounting to nearly $100 billion, over their lifetimes. Many other multibillionaires have subsequently made similar pledges.

Clearly, these billionaires find greater utility in giving away their billions than in keeping them. At a bare minimum, it seems like the value of having, say, $20 billion is not very much higher than having $10 billion. In fact, bizarrely, it may be lower! But let's be conservative and merely say that the utility of wealth, past some large number, is quite low.

The graph that relates wealth w to utility is:

- Very steeply sloping up at w = 0 from −∞.
- Very slowly increasing, or perhaps flat, at large numbers.

But what about the bits in the middle? You can get a sense of this by running through another thought experiment. Would you be willing to flip a fair coin for $100? If not, you can say that the utility of (1/2 (W−100) + 1/2 (W+100)) is lower than the utility of W. This indicates that the utility function is convex downward. In lab studies, economists have found that most people would indeed reject bets such as this, indicating that "normal" utility functions are convex downward around current wealth. Another way of stating this is that most people are *risk-averse*.

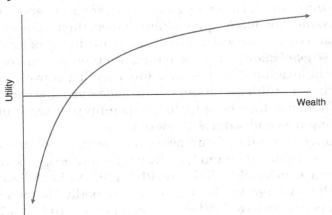

In practice it's quite difficult to (a) come up with a consistent personal utility function, and then (b) to act in uncertain situations according to this function. However, the exercise of thinking about this function can teach you a lot about whether risky decisions are consistent with one another.

Risk in Everyday Life

As the extended example with Ethel teaches, the story of risk and hedging in financial markets is fraught with complication. It is the same in everyday situations, not least because this complication can sometimes be hard to perceive. Considering how important the questions of risk and hedging can be, it's surprising that the manner in which they appear is frequently rather subtle.

Insurance

The most common situation in which you think about and evaluate risk is when you're shopping for insurance. The array of insurance products available to the average consumer is vast. Health insurance, home insurance, car insurance, and life insurance are the big ones, but insurance products are marketed and sold on just about any purchase. The electronics insurance sold at big box retailers probably comes to mind first, but consider the following less obvious insurance products you may already have bought:

- *Social Security:* Retirement savings are an important form of insurance. Life insurance mitigates the financial risk of your death (for your survivors), but retirement savings are an insurance against *living*. They protect against the possibility of living to an age where we cannot work anymore, but still need food and shelter. You are foregoing spending now in order to make sure that, if you end up living long enough, you won't be destitute past your working years.
- *Credit card payment protection:* Nearly all modern credit cards come with payment protection features. Fraudulent charges, a bad online retailer, even no-questions-asked returns are the automatic sort of insurance that you have simply by using a card when making a purchase. Many cards also carry automatic travel and rental car insurance.

- *Overdraft protection:* Many banks will automatically enroll new checking accounts in overdraft protection schemes. If you write a check that can't be funded by the money in the account (a bounced check), banks will charge an overdraft fee. Overdraft protection eliminates the fee by allowing you to pay for insurance against it. Consider it overdraft layaway.

The point of such a list isn't to label these insurance products as bad, or to be avoided. The real question to ask is: did I make a conscious decision to buy the insurance product? Did I make an honest effort at calculating the probabilities and utilities of the various possible futures? Frequently the answer is no, because such a task is typically difficult and sometimes uncomfortable (as with life and health insurance decisions). But the profit margins on some insurance products are so enormous that it's clear you shouldn't be buying them. Paying $120 per year for mobile phone insurance with a $50 deductible would require a phenomenally klutzy or accident-prone buyer for it to be a worthwhile purchase.

In fact, most small insurance products aren't insurance as much as they are taxes on an inability or unwillingness to set aside savings. If the klutzy mobile phone owner above simply set aside $10 a month to cover buying a new phone, the resulting self-insurance would end up being significantly cheaper than buying a policy from an external insurer. Seeing insurance through the eyes of a trader forces us to ask tough questions: *What is the risk that I'm hedging against, exactly?* and *What is the most cost-effective hedge?* Aside from large life-altering events, the answer is rarely to buy a commercial insurance product.

Job Offer Decisions

Consider Simon, a graduate computer scientist torn between two job offers: one with an established large company (Google, Microsoft, etc.) and another from a small software startup still trying to find Series A funding. The former is a significantly less risky job offer, in the sense that it's overwhelmingly likely the company (and the job) will continue to exist in 5 years. But the latter offers significantly greater upside potential, in the small chance that the startup is successful. How to decide?

In order to do so, Simon should try to sketch his utility function. How bad would it be to lose his job in 12 months? How great would it be to be employee #5 at the next Google? How probable are those outcomes? These are not easy questions to answer or numbers to estimate, but rational decision-making demands that he try. And in so doing, he may discover things about himself that he may not have known previously.

Can Simon find useful hedges? There typically isn't any startup-failure insurance available, but maybe if he takes the startup job he can stay in touch with the hiring manager at the large company. Similarly, he can take the large company job and stay in touch with the startup's founders. In fact, a large and diverse personal network of relationships is among the best career hedges available. This isn't a particularly novel insight, obviously. But thinking of these things in the context of risk and hedging helps you clarify and focus your behavior in a way that more general "good advice" typically doesn't. Thinking like a trader lets you understand the *why* behind common suggestions and advice.

Useful Paranoia and Natural Hedges

You've already seen how a good trader's mindset about risk can seem paranoid in more habitual social settings. However, it's not obvious that this is incorrect behavior. I talked in Chapter 1 about how humans are a mishmash of cognitive biases. Among the worst of these is *selective perception*, which is a form of *confirmation bias*. You tend to seek out and pay attention to information that confirms out preexisting beliefs, desires and preferences.

In the context of risk, the most salient example is the frequent inability to properly think of worst-case scenarios. In a meta-study on software development cost estimation (Jorgensen, 2007), the authors found that frequently, estimations of average-case and worst-case development time differed by a statistically insignificant amount. Even experts in estimation have a hard time thinking of really bad outcomes, even when it's their job to do so.

Consider now the case of a real family I know: two parents and one daughter. The father bought a car (a Dodge Challenger). Months later, the family bought a second car: another Dodge

Challenger, this time for the mother. Finally, a year later, a third car gets purchased for the teenaged daughter. Unsurprisingly at this point, it was a Dodge Challenger. Evidently the family really likes the car. But did the family consider the following risks:

- If they have any need to transport things that don't fit in a Challenger-shaped conveyance, they will incur additional expenses in renting something suitable.
- Any manufacturer's defect in the car affects them all. They have put all their transportation eggs in one muscle-car-shaped basket.
- If insurance rates change for the car, all are affected.

In general, they've made the risks in their transportation choices highly correlated. Should an adverse event occur, they have no natural hedge against it. While this may be a somewhat trivial example, the idea of natural hedges to adverse events is an important one, as the following example illustrates.

Remember the implosion of Enron in 2001? Among the most heartbreaking stories to emerge from the affair were the thousands of workers who had used their 401(k) retirement accounts to buy shares in Enron. When Enron subsequently went bankrupt, these workers were simultaneously unemployed and had also lost their retirement savings. By tying their current employment to their future retirement, these workers turned a bad-case scenario (losing one's job) into a near-worst-case scenario (losing one's job *and* losing one's retirement fund).

It seems likely that if they had taken the time to carefully consider all the possible futures, including ones where Enron goes bankrupt, these workers would have made different 401(k) choices. It's quite disturbing to consider possibilities like getting fired, laid off, or having one's employer go bankrupt, which is why you generally avoid doing so. But being clear-eyed about these and other "ugly" possibilities can be a useful exercise if it lowers the chance of truly bad outcomes. Considering risks clearly and dispassionately, like a good trader, lets you put in place preparations and hedges to mitigate their effect when they happen.

Summary and Looking Ahead

- Relying on one particular risk measure is a disaster waiting to happen. Remember Goodhart's law.

- Identifying the risks you're paid to take isn't easy: many apparent risks are actually other risks in disguise.
- Thinking about all the various ways that things could go against you may be paranoia, but it's the good kind of paranoia that makes the difference between survival and extinction.

In the next chapter, I'm going to continue looking at the core elements of trading by diving into another oft-misunderstood idea: liquidity. As you will see, the notion of liquidity isn't some esoteric fact about financial markets. Liquidity considerations turn out to be crucial in just about every important decision you make.

References

Grove, A. (1999). *Only the Paranoid Survive: How to Identify and Exploit the Crisis Points that Challenge Every Business*. Crown Publishing.

Jorgensen, M. M. (2007). "A Systematic Review of Software Development Cost Estimation Studies." *IEEE Transactions on Software Engineering* 33, No. 1, pp. 33–35.

CHAPTER 4

Liquidity

A couple of years ago, I received a call from someone at my bank. He called himself my "relationship manager," even though I'd never had any banking relationship that needed managing. He was the third relationship manager who had been assigned to me over three years.

He introduces himself, and says he wants to talk about some exciting new products the bank has put together. Now, having passed certain FINRA exams myself, I already know he's walking dangerous ground trying to sell financial products without going through important know-your-customer due diligence. But I humor him, asking, "What sorts of products?"

He begins reading from a script, describing some wonderful "notes" that the bank sells to select customers. He makes the notes sound a lot like buying some broad index, but somehow (magically) without the risk of losing much if the market drops. I've priced out these notes in the past, out of curiosity, and it was clear how incredibly high-margin these products are for the bank. I ask a few pertinent questions, trying to understand roughly how much the bank is making on these notes. He sees I'm skeptical. Then I ask a seemingly innocuous question:

"If I don't like these notes after I buy them, can I sell them?"

That question somehow wasn't in his script.

"We find our customers really like them, so that doesn't really come up much."

The obvious non-answer was clearly no, as I knew it would be. These notes (or structured products) are among the most illiquid products that

(*continued*)

> banks sell to retail clients. There is no secondary market for them, and banks never buy them back. Imagine buying a car that you couldn't ever sell back to anyone else, let alone the dealership that sold it to you.
>
> We had a conversation about his attempt at selling extremely illiquid, complicated, and high-margin products to someone whose name he barely knew. I had a similar conversation with his supervisor, at my request, a few days later. Every year, a captive audience of thousands of bank customers is sold products that, as far as I can tell, provide no economic benefit to the buyers but significant profit for the banks that sell them. And the buyers are just plain stuck with them, unable to sell them out because no real market exists for them.

Put on a risk using the most liquid instrument for that risk.

Liquidity Is in the Eye of the Beholder

The best way to define and understand the idea of liquidity is with examples. Let's first meet a few different kinds of market participants:

- Mr. Retail: a retail investor looking to buy 100 shares and hold them until retirement
- Ms. Fund: a fund manager with a $2 billion equity fund to manage
- Warren Buffett, looking to deploy some of Berkshire Hathaway's $40 billion cash pile
- Mr. Maker: a professional equity market maker in the US with excellent technology and connectivity
- Ms. Pension: a pension fund manager looking to hedge interest rate risk
- Mr. City: a municipal bond investor
- Ms. Arb: an equity-index arbitrageur

You will see how each of these participants views the concept of liquidity in the markets they trade quite differently. Let's examine a few different characteristics of these markets and their participants in order to understand how those characteristics affect the liquidity perceived by the participants.

Size

SPY is an ETF that contains the basket of S&P 500 stocks. It is the most liquidly traded ETF in the world, and its market is essentially always a penny wide. A retail investor buying 100 shares of SPY gets a great deal: markets are always at least 100 shares in size, and the spread that Mr. Retail is crossing is tiny (0.2bps from mid to offer). In fact, given Mr. Retail's small trade size, nearly every reasonable equity would seem highly liquid from his perspective.

If, however, Ms. Fund wanted to buy $2 billion worth of SPY (which is frequently all that mutual fund managers really do), the "headline" penny-wide market is of little interest to her. The act of buying $2 billion of SPY will significantly move the market up and away from her. For a $2 billion trade, the effective width is much larger. SPY is probably liquid enough that buying $2 billion of it isn't a ridiculous proposition if transacted carefully. But buying $2 billion of a medium-sized pharmaceutical company in the open market, or even $100 million for that matter, is not a reasonable idea. The market doesn't have enough liquidity to accept a trade that size without unduly moving the market.

Warren Buffett's trades can be even larger, and certainly larger as a fraction of the total shares outstanding. Buffett frequently buys companies outright, so the concept of market width is completely irrelevant. His main concern is explicitly how much of a premium he needs to pay to take over the whole company.

Frequency

Mr. Maker may not have very much size to trade. It's certainly less than our $2 billion fund manager, but probably only a bit more than Mr. Retail wants to trade. The important difference is that the market maker does these small trades in arbitrary directions hundreds of times a day. The previous three actors are all demanding (or *taking*) liquidity, whereas the market maker is, at least half the time, supplying (or *providing*) liquidity to whoever wants it. His job is to provide enough liquidity to induce people to want to trade the stock (and hence for him to make money), without providing too much liquidity.

What does "too much liquidity" mean? In this context, it means risking someone demanding more liquidity than the market maker can either afford to keep or to hedge. As an example, consider a market maker in Sanofi US ADRs,[1] ticker symbol SNY. In the US afternoon, when the European market is closed, making a market in SNY is a challenging task. In addition to modeling the fair price of a closed European security, the market maker needs to understand how large a market to make.

By providing liquidity to customers in the US, he exposes himself to a few risks. Primarily, the risk is that whatever position he accumulates will move against him overnight before he can hedge in the European market the next day. But also, if he makes his market too big, providing too much liquidity, the act of hedging will move the market against him. A trade that would have been good for a size of 1000 shares could be quite bad for a size of 5000 shares.

This idea of hedging with related instruments leads us to ...

Uniqueness

Ms. Pension needs liquidity in interest rate risk. But there is a wide variation in interest rate swap contracts: duration, currency, caps, counterparty, and other legal provisions. Each individual contract is unique and may well be infrequently traded. But looking at the aggregate market, "interest rate risk" broadly defined is quite large and mature. One can find contracts that are similar enough that by aggregating trading across the various contracts, there is more effective liquidity than is apparent by merely looking at one individual market.

Of course, there are differences among the various contracts. Most of the time these differences are not material, and one contract can be about as good as any other. But in times of market stress, the behaviors and hence values of these swap contracts can diverge dramatically.

Transparency

Bond markets typically behave quite differently from equity markets. With few exceptions (US treasuries, mostly), there is no listed market for bonds, and the only way to find out at which prices the market is trading is to call a dealer and ask. This opacity is an important factor in how the bonds trade. The lack of continuous pricing information constrains the liquidity of the bonds.

A similar result, through a different mechanism, operates in equity markets today, especially in the United States. US market structure is famously complex, and one of the results of this complexity is a phenomenon known as latency arbitrage. Every equities exchange keeps its own book in a given security. For example, one could find the national best offer (NBBO) of $19.45 is available on multiple exchanges: 1000 shares offered on NYSE, 800 shares on ARCA, 2000 shares on NASDAQ, and so on. But, if we attempt to buy 3800 shares for $19.45, we may find we only succeed in buying 800 shares on ARCA, your "local" exchange. What happened?

The answer is latency. When you sent the buy order, ARCA filled you on the 800 shares on its book, and due to a US regulation known as Reg NMS, it was required to route the rest of your order to the other exchanges. In the meantime, the extremely fast market makers saw your trade on ARCA and managed to cancel their offers on NYSE and NASDAQ before your order (routed via ARCA) arrived at those exchanges. You were latency arb'ed.

People debate how significant this problem is, and for whom, but it's clear that the apparent liquidity available in a US stock depends very much on your level of technological sophistication. Less sophisticated traders have access to less effective liquidity because of the latency issue.[2]

Heterogeneity

When municipalities issue bonds, they're the only ones who can sell the security on the primary market. Typically, those who buy these primary issues are not particularly heterogeneous either. Some are dealers whose job is to resell the securities on the secondary market, and others are funds whose mandate is to invest in municipal bond issues.

One day Mr. City calls his favorite dealer, and the dealer gives him a reasonable two-sided quote. Mr. City decides to trade. Days and months go by, trading in and out of these bonds, and he begins to feel comfortable with the size and width of the market in the bonds he's become familiar with.

Then, a fateful day comes when the Fed announces a surprise interest rate hike. This predictably makes the bond futures drop, and Mr. City's risk managers tell him that his bond portfolio is rapidly losing value. Sure enough, a call comes from his lenders to say they want some additional collateral posted with them. Mr. City decides to sell some of his bonds in order to meet this margin call. Understanding liquidity as he does, he decides to sell the most liquid bonds in his portfolio. He asks his favorite dealer for a quote and, to Mr. City's amazement, he refuses to make a two-sided market. He's got plenty of offers, but no bids! What happened?

It turns out that everyone else who owned these bonds (i.e. was long the bonds) is in the exact same situation, having to meet a margin call, and deciding to sell the most liquid stuff they have. For all intents and purposes, there is no one in the world who wants to buy these bonds. Everyone wants to sell. Evidently, the liquidity Mr. City thought existed was in fact there only under normal circumstances. The homogeneity of the participants in the market has created a liquidity crisis, with everyone rushing for the exits at the same time.

Risk and Liquidity

Fred is an excellent equities fundamental analyst. He believes that the earnings of financial firm Fifth Third Bancorp (FITB) will be better than the marginal analyst believes. Fred will want to trade into a position that wins $500,000 if FITB goes up 10% on earnings day. How many ways can he do this? Here is a nonexhaustive list:

- Buy FITB shares.
- Buy the FITB single-stock future.
- Buy FITB calls.
- Sell FITB puts.
- Buy XLF, the financial sector ETF, which contains 0.57% FITB.
- Buy SPY, the S&P 500 ETF, which contains 0.08% FITB.
- Buy the E-mini S&P 500 future.

Which subset of these trades should he do, and in which proportion? This is a difficult question, but fortunately this chapter's rule strongly guides the decision. What is the most liquid instrument for the risk to which Fred wants exposure? Let's look at these possible trades using a few different metrics:

1. *Spread to cross:* How wide is the market Fred is trading in? All things equal, the tighter the market, the lower the cost and the greater the liquidity.

2. *Size:* How big a trade can Fred make in the instrument? More liquid markets are typically larger markets.
3. *Margin:* How much capital does he have to put up as collateral to do the trade? Typically, more liquid markets have lower margin requirements.
4. *Specificity:* How close is the traded instrument to the specific risk factor to which Fred want exposure?

Buy FITB Shares

The most straightforward way to bet on good FITB earnings is to buy FITB stock. In order to win $500,000 on a 10% move up, Fred has to buy $5 million of stock. Evaluating this trade using the above metrics:

1. *Spread:* The market for FITB is 15.34–15.36. So, crossing a 2c spread is a cost of 1c. Buying $5 million of stock is buying 326k shares, so the trade would seem to incur a cost of $3.3k. However, as we've seen before, buying a large amount of stock will move the market against us. This is known as *market impact*. It's not easy to estimate market impact in general, but based on experience with a specific stock we can get a decent sense. In this case, let's estimate that if the stock trades $100 million per day, the impact of a $5 million trade is around $20k. You also have to double this number, because Fred will need to trade out of the position once earnings do occur. A good estimate is thus approximately $40k.
2. *Size:* As you've seen in the spread section, the spread Fred has to cross is a strong function of the size he wants to trade. FITB stock has enough liquidity to handle a trade of this size while still maintaining reasonable costs to do so.
3. *Margin:* You saw in Chapter 3 that Reg T requires Fred to put up 50% as margin on a stock position. As a professional he may have access to more advantageous terms, but he should probably assume a conservative regulatory treatment and thus take for granted that Reg T applies. Fred will have to put up $2.5 million in collateral.
4. *Specificity:* Buying FITB stock does reasonably isolate the risk factor Fred is going for. Of course, as you saw in Chapter 3, he's also exposed to the broad market, and so he may want to hedge his exposure to that. It's also the case that Fred has

FITB-specific risk that is unrelated to earnings. The earnings announcement could come out exactly as Fred anticipates, but if news comes out about a government investigation of FITB's mortgage security trading, Fred could still lose even if he's right about earnings. Large financial firms are complicated animals.

Buy FITB Single-Stock Future

A single-stock future (SSF) is a derivative whose value is based on the value of some stock (FITB in this case) at a specific future date. For example, much like an index future, the December future expires on the third Friday of the month. Unlike an index future, which settles to a cash equivalent to the value of the index, most SSFs settle to physical stock. The buyer of the future receives stock, and the seller provides it.

Why do such derivatives exist? For a long time they didn't, and even today they only exist in the most liquid stocks in the most liquid countries. This is an indication that their usefulness isn't universal. But SSFs do facilitate the management of long and short positions, especially across events like dividends, corporate actions, and other special situations. Let's examine Fred's trade as implemented through SSFs.

1. *Spread:* Since SSFs are a derivative of the common stock, generally assume that the market in it will be wider than in the common stock. This isn't always the case, especially in countries where regulations make trading common stock more costly or difficult, but in most developed countries SSFs typically have wider markets than their underlying stock. How much wider depends on the specific situation, but a good general rule is that it should be 30%–40% wider. Thus, in order to obtain the $5 million exposure he's looking for, Fred should expect to pay around $60k in effective spreads.

2. *Size:* Fred will find it harder to obtain the size he needs in the SSF. Though the SSF is hedgeable in the stock, and therefore its liquidity should track the stock, a good SSF market maker will fade his market faster in the SSF than in the stock. The arbitrage between the SSF and the stock isn't perfect, and there are many ways in which the SSF market maker would be worried he could be getting picked off (adversely

selected-against) by Fred (through an unannounced cash dividend or corporate action, for example).

3. *Margin:* So far, the SSF looks quite unattractive compared to trading the common stock. However, when it comes to margining, SSFs are frequently more capital efficient. While margin varies by country and by exchange, SSF margins are typically around 20% instead of the Reg T-mandated 50% for common stock. Thus, Fred would only need to put up $1 million in margin if he were to transact in the SSF. If Fred is capital-constrained, he may consider the SSF more attractive in spite of the greater cost.

4. *Specificity:* The SSF exposes Fred to almost exactly the same risk factors as does the stock. The only exceptions are if the company were to announce a dividend or other corporate action that would affect the SSF differently than it would the stock. These occurrences are rare, though they can be consequential when they do happen.

Buy FITB Calls

If Fred is interested in the upside potential of FITB through earnings, maybe he should buy call options, which gain in value only when FITB goes up. Many retail traders who want to bet on earnings find options attractive, and you'll soon see why that's the case. However, the fact that retail finds them attractive should immediately make you suspect they're really not *that* attractive, especially for a professional.

1. *Spread:* Trying to understand why a given option market's spreads are as wide or tight as they are frequently turns into an exercise in frustration. Many inscrutable factors affect option market width: stock volatility, costs, number and heterogeneity of market makers, exchange rules on tick sizes, whether the stock has a history of either large sudden moves or strange corporate actions or suspicious trading behavior, and so on. Which country the option is listed in has a huge effect too. Nonetheless, it's safe to say that option markets are typically wider than the common stock market on which they're based. As a derivative of the common stock, you should expect that they fade faster than the stock, much like in the example of the SSF. However, the big upside for Fred is that, depending on which call option he buys, the

leverage embedded in options means he can get the same exposure with a much smaller trade. Consider a call that is 5% out of the money and expires in 14 calendar days. If stock is trading around 15.36, this is about a 16.10 strike call. Assuming a fairly normal annual volatility of 25%, this call is worth around 7 or 8 cents. If stock moves up 10% on earnings tomorrow, as Fred expects, this option would probably move to around 0.83, for a profit of 0.75 per option. Thus, to obtain his $500k profit, he would need to buy around 6700 contracts (each with a 100 multiplier). An option valued at 8 cents probably has a market that's 0.05 - 0.10. For the size in which Fred wants to trade, he probably would need to pay closer to 0.15, meaning a cost of 0.07 per option, that is $7 per contract, or $47k for the whole trade. This cost is quite competitive with trading the common stock.

2. *Size:* A 6700 contract trade in a smallish financial firm is quite sizeable, but not outrageous. If Fred has a good broker, with good contacts within the options market making world, he should be able to get Fred the size he wants. However, a trade of this size is noticeable, and many people will pay attention to whether Fred ended up winning on the trade or not. Regulators in particular are very fond of looking at trading activity in upside calls leading up to an earnings announcement. A trader who consistently wins on those sorts of trades is at risk of being investigated for insider trading. However, even ignoring regulators, if Fred wins on this bet then the market maker will know that he lost $500k selling upside calls in FITB before earnings. He and his competitors will make note of it and be significantly more reluctant to do so in the future. Option liquidity is strongly affected by market maker memory, and losses are sticky in the brain.

3. *Margin:* The margining of options can be quite complicated, but fortunately since Fred is buying options the story is quite simple: Fred simply pays the options premium in its entirety at trade time, so Fred parts with $100k in premium paid. This small number is exactly why retail traders find options so attractive: the amount of capital required to make a highly leveraged bet is comparatively small. Of course, the probability of losing the entire premium is obviously much higher; options aren't a free lunch after all.

4. *Specificity:* Buying call options arguably provides even greater specificity than buying stock. If Fred's earnings call is wrong, and stock drops, buying stock exposes Fred to those losses. Buying calls, however, will never lose Fred any more than the premium he paid for the options. However, in the event of a small earnings surprise (say 2% instead of 10%), Fred will likely come out significantly worse off than if he had bought stock instead of calls. In a sense, depending on the calls Fred buys, the risk Fred is taking might be *too* specific.

Sell FITB Puts

Selling puts has a fine historical tradition in the United States. Many traders and fund managers have independently discovered the "genius" idea of selling insurance against crashes of all sorts. Most of the time, the world and its markets are normal, and selling this insurance feels and behaves exactly like picking up free money. And indeed, compared to historical probabilities, equity index options are priced at a good premium to those probabilities, meaning that from a mathematical perspective this should be a positive EV trade.

Nevertheless, these puts are priced rich for a reason. Selling puts makes a little bit of money 9 years out of every 10, approximately, and runs the serious risk of bankrupting you in that tenth year. You need only ask Victor Niederhoffer, a trader and fund manager famous for blowing up his fund in 1997, and again in 2007. As you'll see in chapter 9, selling puts is a great business until the day it really isn't.

In Fred's case, selling puts in FITB is not a particularly attractive idea. The puts won't pay off significantly more if Fred is right than if he's wrong, but if he's really wrong then Fred stands to lose a lot more than if he simply bought stock.

Buy XLF

At first blush, buying XLF in order to bet on FITB earnings looks like a bad idea. Though the spread in XLF is tighter than in FITB (1c wide on a $25 ETF), consider the effective spread Fred is paying in FITB. If all he wants is exposure to FITB, he needs to buy $1000 of XLF for every $7.50 in FITB exposure that he gets. To get $5 million of exposure to FITB, Fred would need to buy $667 million of XLF. Even if he managed to buy that much XLF paying only half a penny in spread (which isn't even remotely plausible), he'd still pay $133k in spread each way, or $266k in total. On top of it, he'd have an exposure of $662 million in other financial stocks that aren't FITB, which is certainly a large risk and would require a correspondingly large margin requirement.

So why are we considering XLF at all? It depends on what FITB's earnings mean. Or more importantly, what Fred thinks they represent. If the good earnings Fred expects are due to very FITB-specific reasons, then buying XLF is an obvious mistake. However, what if FITB is merely the first financial firm to announce earnings during this earnings season? Might the outperformance that Fred is betting on be a sector-wide thing? If FITB is considered a bellwether for the rest of the sector, the good FITB earnings will presumably reflect positively on the other financials that make up XLF. By buying XLF, he gets to bet on FITB earnings, but more importantly on the health of the whole financial sector. And to put on that trade, XLF is definitely a more efficient proposition than buying a lot of individual financial stocks. The specificity of the instrument must match the specificity of the desired risk exposure. The source of the edge (as you'll see in Chapter 5) crucially affects how he decides to implement his trade.

Buy SPY

The logical next trade to consider, if Fred is considering XLF as a possible trade, is to ask whether he should consider an even more broad-based instrument. If he's considering trading XLF, that means Fred's thesis amounts to believing that the whole financial sector (or at least a large enough part of it) is going to outperform. We know, however, how central the financial sector is to the whole economy. Is this bet really so financial-sector specific? Is it just some sophisticated version of "I think the economy is better than people think"? If so, then it's better to put the trade on by buying SPY, given the much greater liquidity available there.

Fred has now moved very far from the original bet on FITB's earnings. But if the underlying reasoning pushes him in this direction, then the rule about liquidity tells him he should use the most liquid instrument (SPY in this case) to express that view.

Conclusion

What should Fred do? It depends entirely on why Fred believes FITB will have good earnings. Let's assume, reasonably, that Fred believes it's mostly FITB-specific, and also that good FITB earnings will also positively affect other financials somewhat. Which trade should Fred choose?

Fortunately, he doesn't need to choose one instrument only. Fred can tailor his trade to obtain exactly the risk exposure he wants by trading a variety of instruments. His final set of trades could reasonably look like this:

- Buy 2000 contracts of FITB calls. This gets him a very specific and low-margin-requirement bet on earnings. It's also a reasonable enough size that he may not attract the attention and future recollections of options market makers in the event he does win big on his trade.
- Buy $2 million of FITB stock. Again, the bet is specific, and distributing his position between options and stock helps him hide it a bit better and likely reduces his market impact.
- Buy $1 million of XLF. Gaining broader exposure to the whole sector through a liquid sector ETF is a relatively cheap way to express the belief that good FITB earnings will affect the rest of the sector. Fred could also have considered buying XLF calls.
- Either sell some SPY or buy some SPY puts. Why? Because in addition to getting long FITB and the financial sector, he's gotten long the broader market. Fred probably doesn't want as much exposure to this risk factor as he gets with the above trades, so he probably wants to hedge some of it by shorting the cheapest-to-trade broader market instrument. Also, depending on how Fred's margin treatment works, this sort of hedging could actually reduce Fred's margin requirement (this is known as *portfolio margin*).

By thinking deeply about why Fred believes what he does, he can structure his trading in the most cost-effective and efficient way possible.

Liquidity in a Broader Context

Thinking about and assessing liquidity isn't just a job left to professional traders. Many financial products sold to the average person are less liquid than they might seem, and certainly less liquid than they should be.

- *Mutual funds:* There are somewhere between 8,000 and 10,000 mutual funds operating in the US, and close to 100,000 worldwide. Approximately half of the US funds are domestic equity funds of some description. Some of these, especially the larger ones from established companies like Vanguard, are very low-cost vehicles for retirements savings. The others are identical in all important respects except that their costs (management fees, and fees to open or close positions) can be an order of magnitude larger. These smaller high-cost funds act as illiquid investments in what should be very liquid stocks.
- *Annuities:* Many retirees are offered aggressively marketed annuities that are presented as a good and safe retirement income stream. Unfortunately, the problems with annuities are many. First, they are again significantly higher cost than they deserve to be, with broker commissions on annuities reaching 10% in some cases. Also, considering how the annuity seller hedges the risk, annuities provide shockingly poor investment returns. But just as importantly, once money is placed into an annuity it is usually exceedingly difficult to extract without incurring additional fees and penalties.
- *Structured products:* High-net-worth individuals are frequently marketed structured products (SPs) or structured notes by their brokerage firms. These products are almost universally a disaster. The brokers (or "investment advisers" with no fiduciary responsibility to the customer) receive large commissions for selling them. In addition, the secondary or resale markets on these notes is virtually nonexistent and therefore extremely illiquid. And finally, customers are subject to the credit risk of the issuing entity. While brokerage accounts are protected by SIPC guarantees in the event of a broker failure, SPs are not.
- *Loans:* Illiquidity in loans appears in a few places, but the most important ones surround the conditions for prepayment of a

loan. In many cases, loan contracts are written in such a way that paying off the loan early incurs a penalty for doing so. This penalty makes the loan an illiquid instrument: one that is difficult to get out of once entered into.

It might seem from the above that the concept of liquidity is specific to financial markets, and its considerations don't really affect everyday life outside of that realm. This view is very much mistaken. In fact, one of the most pervasive financial mistakes people make is to underestimate the importance and effect of liquidity constraints on their activities. Let's start with small examples and work our way to the larger ones.

Memberships and Contracts

Janine wants to start working out at the local health club, and she must choose between the following two options:

- *Membership:* A one-year contract for $40 per month, which entitles her to unlimited use of the facilities.
- *Pay-per-use:* A per-visit fee of $10.

The calculation seems fairly straightforward. If Janine expects to go to the gym more than 48 times in the next year, she should opt for the membership. Since that's less than once a week, and she figures she can muster the will to go once per week (on Saturday mornings, since weekdays are too hectic), she opts for the membership. Was this a wise decision?

If Janine is a typical Westerner, she has likely:

- Overestimated Janine-in-4-months's willpower to work out.
- Forgotten that she goes to the Caribbean for 2 weeks every winter, and she also frequently takes weekend trips to see her sister.
- Assumed that starting a new exercise program will result in no injuries that will put her out of action.
- Assumed that she will like the gym after having used it for a few months.
- Ignored the possibility that she will move, find a new hobby, a new boyfriend, a new job, get laid off, or any number of unforeseeable possibilities.

The fundamental problem isn't Janine's unrealistic calculation. No one is foresighted enough to anticipate every possible reason for missing gym visits, assigning appropriate probabilities to those events, and thereby making a truly accurate calculation. The issue is that she is locked into a gym contract that is a completely illiquid financial instrument. She can't resell it or otherwise escape, short of defaulting, the requirement to have $40 withdrawn from her bank account every month.

Janine should have, in her calculation, demanded a *liquidity premium* as compensation for the restrictions the membership placed on her. Many retail financial products have extremely poor liquidity, and an insufficient appreciation of this fact can lead to much hidden expense.

- *Phone contracts:* The traditional multiyear mobile phone contract is a classic example of an illiquid contract. If you find a better deal a few months later, the penalties for breaking the existing contract will likely make the new deal unattractive. Tying the physical phone to the contract is also a "feature" that decreases liquidity: when a phone breaks or one wants to upgrade, the lowest-apparent-cost option for getting a new one frequently involves renewing the contract, locking the customer in for even longer.
- *Car leases:* The story for car leases is very similar: a set contractual period, penalties for exiting the contract prematurely, not to mention the premium paid as compared to taking out a loan and buying the car outright.

Housing

Liquidity issues pervade housing markets. The usual path to home-ownership exposes people to a financial decision that would, it seems clear, be ridiculed if it were taken by any self-respecting public company. In particular:

- The process of purchasing the asset (a house, a condominium, an apartment) involves costs that typically approach 10% of the value of the asset. Among these are the broker fee, mortgage fees, title fees, escrow fees, various home and pest inspections, transfer taxes and fees, moving costs, and many others (such as the opportunity cost of the time spent searching).

- The home is typically financed through a mortgage whose debt servicing costs (the monthly payment) average 12–18% of household income (BLS, 2013).
- The home is bought and sold through an opaque cartel of brokers whose interests are demonstrably not aligned with those of their customers (Levitt, 2009).
- The ability to service the debt (the mortgage) is highly correlated with local economic conditions. This means that if you lose your job and need to sell your house, you will typically find it an exceedingly bad time to try to sell your house.
- Residential real estate has historically returned significantly below equity markets over long time horizons (Shiller, 2009).
- Aligning the move-out and move-in dates when changing homes typically entails frictional costs like paying an extra few weeks or month's rent, lengthening escrow, paying for storage, or paying for a hotel during the transition.

The facts on residential real estate investments for the average middle-class family are indisputable: financially it's a poor decision. This is not a cast-iron argument for not buying a house, however. There's no disputing that people do find a value in owning their home that doesn't derive from its actual financial value. But there are many people and organizations (the whole residential real estate industry, in fact) who have much to gain by hiding or minimizing the very real liquidity costs of buying a home.

Accordingly, if you argue that buying a home is a financially questionable idea, then renting must surely be better. Usually it is, though even here liquidity constraints bite more strongly than we generally imagine:

- Rental contracts are frequently written with a yearly term. If circumstances change and renters have to move (a new job, a birth, a death, etc.) they find themselves subject to restrictive constraints affecting their move-out date. These binding written agreements typically contain clauses that stipulate penalties that renters will incur for breaking the contract. The most common penalty mentioned is full payment of the rent for the remaining months on the contract.
- Setting up utilities when moving will inevitably cost both money (service setup fees, liquidity costs of entering into new service contracts) and time (having to wait for the cable guy to arrive sometime between 9am and 5pm).

The Job Market

Liquidity considerations appear in the job market in a variety of ways. Certainly, the most obvious is that finding, interviewing for, receiving an offer for, accepting, and starting a new job is usually a relatively long process. The illiquidity of the job market means participants incur costs as a result. Workers tend to want to stay in jobs even if they're not particularly happy there, and employers tend to want to keep the employees they already have, even if there could be better ones looking for jobs.

But even aside from this market-friction-induced illiquidity, other constraints and restrictions frequently appear in job offers and contracts that affect workers. Some of the more common ones include:

- *Deferred pay:* This is a broad category that includes things like employee incentive stock options and restricted stock, with their long vesting schedules. The idea is simple: by deferring payment to the worker to some future date, workers feel more inclined to remain than they otherwise would be. These are known as "golden handcuffs" in tech circles.
- *Noncompete clauses:* The commonality and legality of these clauses vary by industry and by jurisdiction, but wherever they appear these clauses restrict the ability of the worker to find future employment. By accepting a job offer with these conditions, workers are also accepting possibly significant restrictions on their future jobs.
- *Nondisclosure agreements:* By limiting the information and knowledge that the worker can communicate with others, these agreements constrain workers in subtle ways. Dealing with the question of "Can I legally say this?" does make the process of looking for jobs and interviewing for them more difficult.
- *Nondisparagement clauses:* These clauses constrain workers' right to free speech when the subject is their employers. Depending on how the clauses are written, even a throwaway "my job sucks" post on a social media site can be an actionable violation of the clause.
- *Rights to inventions:* Many engineering and design jobs have contracts that automatically assign ownership of worker inventions to the employer. Many of these clauses explicitly include

work and inventions that occurred outside of the employer's premises and hours. Thus, taking a job that has these restrictions constrains the sort of nonwork hobbies and interests that the worker can pursue.

Individually, each of these items may not significantly affect your behavior on a day-to-day basis. But when considering leaving a job and finding a new one, the aggregation of these restrictions can make the process more cumbersome and fraught with risk. It therefore pays to closely examine employment contracts before signing them, and in particular to consider one's preferences years ahead in the future when such restrictions could become more relevant and binding.

Finding Liquidity

So far, I've discussed liquidity in the broader world as something that restricts and constrains you. But how can you use the ideas of liquidity to help you?

Buying a Car

The efficiency of the used and new car markets depends on a variety of factors, not least of which is the specific car in question. It's clear that the market for an entry-level Honda Civic is more efficient than the one for a 1950s Ferrari 250 GT California Spyder. How to think about this variation?

The principle I propose, when searching for your next car, is to cast a net wide enough such that the marginal addition of a target or region doesn't affect the price appreciably. What does this mean? It depends on how specific you are about the type of car you're after. Highly specific requirements mean you will operate in an illiquid market, and broader acceptability will increase the effective liquidity of the market.

If you're after a very popular car, or a couple of them, and you're not too fussed about specific options on the car, there won't be much value in searching outside your metropolitan area. The liquidity of cars that meet your requirements is large enough that adding more regions to search won't decrease the already very low liquidity premium on that purchase.

Conversely, if you're after a very specific car, or one with very specific options, even if your local area happens to have the car in question, you're better off searching broadly anyway, across many metropolitan areas. This lets you accurately assess the market for the car. You're going to need to search a large area in order to increase the effective liquidity of the market, and hence decrease the liquidity premium you will pay.

A question you may be asking is: why is the liquidity premium paid by the buyer and not the seller? In fact, both are paying some liquidity premium to the extent that the desired transaction takes time to set up and execute. Sellers of cars in small markets take longer to sell their inventory, and buyers in small markets take longer to find and buy the car they're after. The cost of non-instantaneous transactions is a big part of the premium.

But how does this search actually decrease the premium? For new cars, at least, dealers are very attuned to the size of the market and are good at understanding exactly how specific your requirements and desires are. If you're after a specific car, merely telling the dealer (over email, of course) that you've been searching in areas far away will have them understanding that the effective market (i.e. the range of dealerships against which they're competing) is large. Of course, you do actually have to do the search: dealers know more about the market than you do and competent ones quickly sniff out any deception on the subject.

The Rise of Amazon

Increasing effective liquidity by increasing the effective market size is exactly the core principle behind the rise in popularity of online retailers. This is the concept of the "long tail" popularized in Chris Anderson's book of the same name (Anderson, 2008). By aggregating the retail experience across the whole country, and indeed the world, Amazon and similar retailers increase the market size of marginal products to a level high enough where there is sufficient liquidity to justify selling the product. Not only this, but by also handling the logistics (online store, warehousing, shipping, etc.) for Amazon partners, the latter can make ever more niche products profitable to produce and sell. Much like a financial exchange, Amazon, eBay, and the like standardize the mechanics of trading and the result is lower costs for consumers and higher volumes for vendors.

The Amazon effect has caused other retailers to tighten margins in order to compete with them. This benefits customers who have never used Amazon themselves. In liquid markets, the pressure to remain profitable is intense and unyielding. Looking at the difficulties of various booksellers over the last decade, it's clear that there have been some casualties along the way.

Of course, if Amazon were to become a dominant force in retail, to the point where they could begin to behave as a quasi-monopoly, then the liquidity story flips again. As you have seen, real liquidity only emerges when markets have a heterogeneous set of buyers *and* sellers. If the only seller is Amazon, then no matter how large the array of products on offer, the market is effectively being controlled by one entity and hence is no longer responsive in the way we would expect.

Finally, even though Amazon is famous for competitive prices and excellent customer service, it is by no means a guarantee that they will indeed have the lowest price. For example, many who sign up for the Amazon Prime membership find themselves consulting only Amazon when making online purchases. These people have artificially constrained themselves (after all, checking other online retailers really doesn't require much effort) and in so doing they have artificially decreased the liquidity of the market in which they're operating.

Summary and Looking Ahead

- The liquidity of a market is both subtle to define and well worth doing so. In fact, a lot of what traders in the market think about day-to-day has to do with the liquidity available for the trades they want to do.
- Thinking about the characteristics of a market and using the idea of liquidity to guide this thinking lets us see unifying concepts that apply to many disparate fields.
- Perhaps surprisingly, liquidity is a concept that transcends the financial markets where it's most thought about. Lots of everyday situations put us in liquidity traps, and paying attention to this fact lets us avoid them.
- Deep knowledge of the markets in which we operate is rewarded by being able to transact more cheaply, safely, and efficiently.

In the next chapter, we're finally going to get down to the meat: the edges that define our trades. As you will see, edge isn't some ephemeral or hard-to-define concept. The source of profitability in trading is very straightforward, though it is difficult to implement in practice. Most importantly, if your job as a trader is to go out and find edges, it's critical to understand what edge is and what it isn't.

Bibliography

Anderson, C. (2008). *The Long Tail: Why the Future of Business is Selling Less of More*. Hachette Books.

BLS. (2013). Consumer Expenditures in 2013. Retrieved from Bureau of Labor Statistics: https://www.bls.gov/cex/csxann13.pdf.

Levitt, S. S. (2009). *Freakonomics: A Rogue Economist Explores the Hidden Side of Everything*. William Morrow Paperbacks.

Shiller, R. (2009). *Irrational Exuberance*. Crown Business.

CHAPTER 5

Edge

In the early 1970s, Japan Airlines (JAL) had a problem (Parkinson, 2007). Japan's export-based economy was shipping a variety of manufactured goods around the world, which was good for JAL's cargo business. However, Japanese demand for foreign products was minimal: There was around a 7:1 ratio in the tonnage of cargo exported to cargo imported from North America. JAL was making money on the outbound flights but losing money on the resulting inbound flights. An enterprising young JAL employee, Akira Okazaki, was tasked with finding something in North America that Japanese consumers wanted to buy.

The item in question would have to be expensive *and* perishable, in order to justify the expense and speed of international air freight. Okazaki did his research, then sent a telex to another young JAL employee, this one in Toronto, Canada. The recipient, Wayne MacAlpine, was surprised but intrigued by the assignment: find out how much North Atlantic bluefin tuna was worth.

It turned out that the locals in Prince Edward Island, Canada, where the tuna was fished for sport, thought of the fish as more of a nuisance. Sometimes over 700 pounds, the tuna ruined cod-fishing nets and was considered too fatty to eat anyway. Sport fishermen who caught the bluefin ended up paying someone to dispose of it, such was its worthlessness as an edible fish.

MacAlpine sensed an opportunity and enlisted a sharp local fish processor named Albert Griffin to help. Soon JAL officials were making the trek from Tokyo to a small town in PEI to set up the logistics: Griffin would cool the bluefin, pack them in boxes made by a local funeral director (i.e. coffins), then ship them by truck to the nearest international airport, John F. Kennedy in New York City. From there they'd make the 14-hour flight to Tokyo to be sold at auction.

Finally, on August 14, 1972, the first Atlantic bluefin tuna was auctioned at the famous Tsukiji fish auction in Tokyo, birthing a new international era in sushi. The new trade in Atlantic bluefin, created by JAL out of necessity, broadened the appeal of sushi and in the process made JAL a lot of money. For many years, very few organizations could compete with JAL and the organization they had built to sell fish halfway around the world from where they were caught.

What Is Edge?

Why do some trades make money? Why do others lose money? How can you tell which one you're doing? You could look at some historical data, but there's rarely enough to be sure. For most trades worth doing you need something more than data, something very human indeed. This chapter is devoted to one of the most human characteristics of all: the telling of stories.

To this point, I've deferred discussing the concept of edge because I needed to establish some important concepts first (motivation, adverse selection, risk, and liquidity). But now is the time to give edge its full treatment. When we talk about edge, we are talking about *why* a given trade makes money. There are many ways of losing money in trading and precious few ways of making it, at least in expectation. Such rare beasts demand reasons for believing they exist. Of course, the efficient market hypothesis (EMH) denies the existence of trading strategies with edge. Efficient markets don't admit strategies that reliably make money, after all. However, the sumptuous marble foyers of investment banks and trading houses in New York, London, and other financial centers should be strong evidence that at least *someone* is making money in financial markets. But how?

In this telling, the term "edge" is simply the set of reasons, the explanation, why you think a given trade has a positive expected value. In other words, why does that trade make money on average?

> If you can't explain your edge in five minutes, you don't
> have a very good one.
> OR
> The long-term profitability of an edge is inversely proportional to how
> long it takes to explain it.

Understanding and Acting

The fundamental axiom of edge is this: all trades that have edge are profitable because there is some fact about the world that you *understand* and *can act on* that the marginal participant in the market doesn't understand or can't act on. Thus, describing your edge is explaining what you *know* and *can do*, which others do not and cannot.

In the sushi story, JAL had the unique opportunity to create a profitable business in shipping frozen tuna halfway around the world for two reasons. First, they understood both the Japanese market and also the economics of international air freight better than anyone else. But second, and perhaps most important, they had the unique ability to act on that knowledge: they already had the planes flying back empty to Japan. All they had to do was put the two together and the rest was history. Because of this powerful combination, only JAL was capable of doing that trade at the time.

Marginal Traders, and Why They're the Only Ones that Matter

You'll notice in the above definition of edge that you're comparing your knowledge and abilities to that of the *marginal trader* in the market. But who is this marginal trader? Consider any market with diverse buyers and sellers (say the market in Intel shares). If you decide to buy 1 share immediately, from whom are you buying it? You're not buying it from a very aggressive seller since that seller has already hit a resting bid and sold shares. Nor are you buying it from a very passive seller whose offer is far behind the best offer in the market. Your seller is exactly the most aggressive seller who isn't aggressive enough to hit a bid himself. This seller is known as the marginal seller.

Once you trade with the marginal seller, you need to determine who had the good side of the trade (in expectation). Ignoring costs for now, what matters in making this determination is who understands the state of the world better. Referring back to the axiom, it is clear that both you and the seller are capable of trading in this market, so there is no effective difference in ability (the "can" part of the definition). Over the long term, the side that better understands the nature of the world, and of Intel shares specifically, will end up making more money than the other side.

At first glance, you should be encouraged upon realizing that the relevant point of comparison is the marginal seller, as described above. In order to do profitable trading (again, ignoring costs for now), you don't need to be the very best. The best, most skillful participant doesn't matter. All that matters is how good you are relative to the marginal participant in the market. Speaking loosely, all you have to be is "better than average." This is obviously much easier than being the best.

In fact, "average" isn't quite right. It's more accurate to say that you have to be better than the trader of the median share. And therein lies the difficulty. Poor or uninformed traders have two important characteristics: (a) they typically don't trade a lot (because they lose money on average for every share they trade), and (b) they don't last long in the market (because even rich bad traders eventually run out of money). Skilled traders with edge both trade larger and also keep trading and expanding their trading over time. In any mature market, the really bad traders have either left or trade very small, and good traders (ones with edge) are everywhere, because they're the ones that survived. Evolutionary thinking applies quite directly when thinking about the evolution of markets. Having an edge in a mature market means understanding the world better than other traders, even ones who are already highly skilled. In fact, the marginal trader in modern financial markets is quite sophisticated and skilled indeed.

Telling Stories

In essence, edge is the story we tell ourselves that explains why a trade makes money. Describing edge in terms of "a story" makes it sound capricious and arbitrary, and I'm going to argue that that's actually a good thing. In describing an edge, the worst thing you can do is to put on the illusory mantle of mathematical or physical fact. Reasons and stories are inherently slippery notions for humans, and no amount of mathematization makes that fact go away. Math and logic help describe an edge clearly and accurately but they aren't, in themselves, the edge.

> When I first started trading, I thought the math was the thing. Stories were for retail traders who didn't have any edge, who were flipping random coins. I, on the other hand, was well trained in probability and mathematical reasoning: all I had to do was look at the data and the trades would emerge. So I did. I scoured some old price data for the stocks we were trading, looking for patterns in how they moved over time. And eventually I did find something, a small but seemingly real edge that I quickly showed the senior trader I sat next to. He seemed interested, but not in the graphs and data analysis I had done. Then he asked me a question that I wasn't prepared for: "Why do you think this makes money?" I had no answer since I never thought to ask that question. "You should probably figure that out, huh." In trying to answer that question, I learned much more than I expected I would.

Biases Big and Small

If the idea of edge is centered around the stories you tell yourself, then surely you should try to come up with some good stories! However, anyone who has been paying attention to behavioral psychology research in the last 40 years will be aware that humans are known to be far from ideal, rational decision makers. We are all subject to systematic flaws of reasoning. Many of these have been identified and catalogued, as we saw in Chapter 1. In the context of explaining edge (that is, "making up stories") some of these flaws are especially relevant and worth examining closely.

Overconfidence Bias

Overconfidence takes many forms. Among the most relevant, there is *illusory superiority*, where people consistently overestimate their own ordinal rank on some task. For example:

- **IQ:** (Furnham, March 2005) shows that men tend to overestimate their IQ by about 5 points (or half a standard deviation).

- **Other mental tasks**: The Dunning-Kruger effect (Kruger, 1999) shows that below-average performers on cognitive tasks overestimate their relative performance by more than high performers do.
- **Driving:** Many independent studies have shown that the vast majority of people (sometimes over 90%) consider themselves above-average drivers, in spite of the fact that only exactly half could be.

There is also *belief overconfidence*, where people consistently overestimate the accuracy or validity of their beliefs or answers. You can test yourself using various online tests at LessWrong.com (Vance, 2009). Most people find they have uncalibrated confidence levels, and in most cases their probability estimates indicate they are overconfident about their own actual knowledge.

This overconfidence bias bears a direct relation to the idea of edge as "the story you tell yourself." Stating that your edge in XYZ derives from the fact that "no one else has figured out that XYZ's sales in Chile will grow at 15% per year" may well be reasonable. But in order for this to be a plausible story, you should have good reasons as to: (a) why you believe this to be true, (b) why the marginal trader isn't aware of this.

The story had better explain what specific skills, knowledge, or abilities you have that sustain the plausibility that you do indeed know something about XYZ's sales in Chile which others don't. Absent this evidence, you should act like good Bayesian reasoners and assign a high probability to the hypothesis of overconfidence (or some other bias), and low probability to the proposition that this is a true edge.

Confirmation Bias

Confirmation bias concerns the tendency to avoid finding out you're wrong about something. This effect generally takes three forms, in sequence:

- **Biased search:** In the same way that you tend to read political news from sources that agree with your political beliefs, you also more generally seek out information that confirms your existing beliefs. How often have you argued with a friend about some general fact (for example, "playing violent video games makes you more violent"), and when you were asked to present proof you simply searched for articles and studies that confirm your position? Google will present you with many search results, so it's easy to pick out the ones that support your position.

- **Biased interpretation:** Most reasonably debated issues (which aren't simple questions of fact) are complex subjects. Results are often tenuous, hard to interpret, and difficult to summarize cleanly. The natural tendency is to pick out the aspects that confirm your beliefs and ignore the rest.
- **Biased recall:** Human memory is a fallible and finite resource. It is natural for you to try to summarize your understanding of the world by placing new facts into a schema that you've already developed. Although critical to being a functioning person, this schema is nonetheless a bias through which your memory gets filtered. You remember facts and events that confirm your beliefs and forget the ones that don't quite fit, in particular as they relate to your own performance. Many gamblers believe they're lifetime winners in the casinos or at sports betting, whereas they're actually significant losers (Gilovich, June 1983).

In financial markets, confirmation bias is a particularly dangerous one. With the wealth of data available in modern markets, and with the subtlety and noisiness of relationships, it's exceedingly easy to "find" a correlation or relationship where in fact none exists. Once "found," much like a gambler who's discovered a "system," confirmation bias makes it extremely difficult to eradicate the mistaken belief.

> I tested ideas and theories for why my Taiwanese trade made money. Dumb money, changes in regulations, poor competition, I thought of it all. But I couldn't come up with anything that sounded plausible enough to justify the results I was getting. Finally, my boss asked me, "How many ideas did you simulate before you found this trade?" Half a dozen, I responded. He looked skeptical. "Really? Including all the iterations, cleaning the data, selecting stocks in and out of your study, time periods, and so on?" I tried to count all the little variations that I had tested,
>
> *(continued)*

> but quickly realized I hadn't been remotely diligent enough to do that. I gave up. "Ugh, probably hundreds, I guess." I had my answer for why the trade I had found worked: because I had tried enough things that eventually something worked by mere chance. It was a statistical artifact, with no more edge than a grandmother playing the lottery. My biases had bitten me again.

The Competitiveness of Financial Markets

It is difficult to describe to the novice trader, or even to an experienced retail trader, exactly how competitive modern financial markets are. Investment banks, hedge funds, and proprietary traders all mobilize massive resources to develop tiny edges. It begins with hiring. The best of these firms spend many tens of thousands of dollars per hire in an attempt to woo the very best minds our universities produce.

These new hires are taught by some of the best traders and researchers in the business through a challenging and continuous training program. I've seen these programs first-hand. The material is taught and absorbed at a significantly higher speed than the classes at even the best universities. And it takes these excellent new hires somewhere between 6 and 18 months to become a net positive to the trading desk to which they're attached.

Traders stare at markets all day every day, and are extremely well incentivized to find edges, to find trades. Firms also employ the best programmers and technologists, and have some of the highest per-employee IT spending of any business. Not surprisingly, the research infrastructure available to study ideas integrates petabyte-scale databases with advanced analytics and custom tools.

The reason for this breathtaking deployment of resources is the extreme competitiveness of the market. In point of fact, there are no natural barriers to entry. Anyone can compete, if they have a good idea, and by modern venture capital standards they can do so with modest capital requirements. As a result, the edges of real-life trades are small.

It's easy to convince yourself, unless you've seen it firsthand, that your opposition isn't really that skilled, that motivated, that well-funded. Call it a specific form of overconfidence bias. But in my career I've met some incredibly sharp and motivated traders, and I'm sure there are hundreds more I haven't met. These *are* the people with whom you're competing. In modern markets, the vast majority of the orders and trades that happen are between professionals. So the marginal trader in modern markets is incredibly skilled, motivated and well-funded. Does the edge you've discovered, the story you're telling yourself, make sense in this context? Is it really possible that your competition, this competition, may have just flat out missed it?

Are Stories Really Necessary?

Given the problematic nature of edges, reasons, and stories, why bother? Why not eliminate these annoying human biases entirely? A style of trading known as *black box trading* attempts to do just this in financial markets.

Black box trading strategies concern themselves with finding signals. These signals are often small predictions about the future that appear with systematic regularity. By combining many (sometimes hundreds) of these signals, trading strategies can emerge that make money in expectation. They're known as black box strategies because crucially, the innards of the strategies are modeled as a black box. People running black box strategies don't know, and more importantly, don't care to know, *why* the regularity exists, merely that it does to a sufficient level of statistical significance.

In effect, these strategies attempt to eliminate the need for an edge in the sense of "a story that explains why this makes money." By relying on (presumably) solid statistical reasoning, you can eliminate all the biases and foibles of humans and their easily dismissed quaint stories.

This approach has its fans, but even the most systematic black-box strategy isn't fully systematic. For one, a human still needs to turn it on. And to turn it off, of course. What happens during a crazy time in the market, a time that any knowledgeable person can say has never happened before? The great recession of 2008–2009 is certainly one of these, as was the Flash Crash of May 6, 2010. Is it reasonable to keep a machine turned on that you know has never seen the kind of data that's being presented? The fact that the question is even a reasonable one to ask indicates that there is human decision-making involved. You can bar the front door with data, but humans and their stories end up sneaking in the back door.

Given all I've learned about (a) the pernicious nature of human reasoning and (b) the value of systematizing, practicing, and thinking about decisions rationally, I'm convinced it's not too smart to make those crazy days the very first ones where you're having to make consequential decisions about trading. It takes a very strong process to resist this tendency, and I know of many supposedly systematic black-box trading firms that, when the chips are down, become extremely human-centered. For this reason, the more reasonable course of action seems to be to build systems (in the sociological sense) in order to mitigate human biases. If you can succeed at this, it's likely to prove a more robust mechanism in the long run.

Constructing Reasons

So how do you construct robust stories? Or perhaps more importantly, construct robust and dependable processes that create believable stories? You've finally come to the essence of what it means to create a profitable trading organization. To find good edges, you need to build a culture of telling good stories. There's no recipe for this, but if there were no one would publish it in a book. Nevertheless, it's possible to identify some characteristics that such a process should possess. You'll see that all of these characteristics have something of the nature of a double-edged sword: some is good, too much is madness.

Creativity

You've seen that financial markets are extremely competitive arenas. Good ideas won't be obvious ones, but rather subtle and hard to find. This requires a process that rewards creative thinking. Paradoxically, ideas that at first glance seem clearly to be good ones probably aren't. The best, most creative ideas have the strange peculiarity of being half-great and half-terrible.

In the venture capital world, there is a truism that you should never fund obviously good ideas. This makes sense: if something is clearly a good idea for a business, then (a) why do they need *your* investment, and (b) why isn't someone already doing it? Looking back to the beginning of this chapter and our definition of edge, you can see the connection. Good venture capital investments are either ones that only you can see, or ones that only you can access.

We are left in the uncomfortable position of trying to create a process and a culture that rewards crazy ideas, at least to some extent, but not so crazy that you waste time and effort tilting at windmills. But then again, no one said this was going to be easy.

Persistence

The difficulty of being profitable in very competitive markets demands an odd sort of creativity, as you've seen, but also and most definitely it requires persistence. Coming up with ideas is great, but you have to be prepared for nearly all of them to come to nothing. The success rate on novel trading ideas is astronomically small, as well it should be given the competitiveness of the world in which we operate.

Competitive markets reward tenacity. Hitting your head against a wall of failure repeatedly and yet remaining undaunted by failure is a necessary condition for finding great new trading strategies. A good trade frequently emerges, slowly and haltingly, after people take three or four cracks at the same basic idea.

Of course, it should be clear that too much persistence can easily turn into pigheaded refusal to concede that something doesn't work. All too often, the mental biases you've already seen will lead you to hold onto something a little longer than you should, look for confirmatory evidence, believe the good parts of your results, and ignore or forget the bad parts. A good process rewards persistence, but only up to a point.

Quantitative Review

After some blood, sweat, and tears, you come up with an idea that makes sense and shows some promise on some preliminary data. It is now important to show the work to someone else who's knowledgeable in the area. The idea at this stage is to ask and answer tough questions about how you've gotten to this point. How did you arrive at this idea? How did you test it? What makes these questions crucially important is the phenomenon of data dredging, as you saw with my Taiwan "trade."

Put in a straightforward manner, data dredging is the practice of looking at some data and trying as many hypotheses as you can until you find one that works (i.e. a trading idea that makes money). The problem is that, since markets are such excellent random number generators, if you try enough ideas you're bound to find one that appears to work merely by random chance. Of course, no ethical trader would explicitly do this, but again, human biases complicate matters. When I was trying to find a trade in Taiwan, I wasn't trying to find worthless ghosts. It just happened as a result of the process I was using.

With modern computers and powerful software, it's easy to come up with an idea, look at some data, and then figure out whether the idea works or not. Since it usually doesn't, you go back and check to see if you've made a mistake. Maybe you change some parameters in a simulation or make some other adjustment that results in your basically testing a slightly different idea. You didn't set out to explicitly try different things, it just happened as a result of your trying reasonable things with the original idea.

This phenomenon isn't limited to trading, of course. Consider the recent so-called "crisis of replication" in the social sciences (Rogers, 2018). Can it really be true that the results of only 6 of 53 high-profile cancer biology papers can be replicated? But this isn't the result, as some news stories would have it, of nefarious academic researchers doctoring results in order to gain funding. That might be true for a few dishonest researchers, but for the most part it's clear that the people involved had the right intentions. It's just that the process of "finding" results was itself broken. Too many hypotheses were implicitly tested, and so enough of them got through by random chance.

Examining issues like this is the bulk of the quantitative review. The idea is to study the process by which ideas are scrutinized. In this instance, did you constrain yourself to a very specific dataset? Did you declare a priori which tests you were going to run and then stick to those tests? If you did some iterative testing, did you make sure to record all of the small changes made along the way? By asking these questions you can get a sense of whether the results are "real" or whether they're a random and nonrepeatable happenstance.

Of course, you can always go too far the other way, demanding an unreasonable standard of proof for a new idea. Again, markets are very competitive. Few good new ideas have an unassailable quantitative justification behind them. Furthermore, there's usually just not enough data and the signal to noise ratio is just too low. Having too high a bar doesn't let enough good ideas through. It's a balance.

Qualitative Review

Let's say you've come up with a good idea, and it seems to pass a quantitative test of its validity. It's probably time to show the idea and the work even more broadly. Given your biases, having someone else review the work so far is an essential part of creating a story that reasonable people can believe.

Of course, stories don't exist in isolation. If you're experienced in the markets you trade, you already have lots of stories about how things work, why they work, and how they relate to one another. How does this new idea fit into this framework? Is it consistent with what you know already? In particular, if this new idea is true, does it disprove beliefs you already hold? If a trade you already do, which you know to be profitable, relies on fact A being true, does this new idea implicitly require A to be false in order to work? Good ideas have to work well in a complex web of meaning. Does this idea prove too much? If this idea is good, where else should you see evidence of it?

As always, you can go too far in this direction. I've said that good new ideas are at least a little bit crazy. They really *should* upend or at least change some of our existing beliefs. If the new idea is perfectly consistent with everything you already know, how new can it really be? Again, there is a balance to the idea-generating process you're trying to create.

> In my experience, good trading ideas don't begin with Eureka-esque lightbulb moments. In every instance I can remember, great new trading ideas started with "hmm, that's interesting" or "that's odd". The human mind is a phenomenal pattern-recognition engine, and the well-trained trader mind is minutely attuned to the patterns of the market behavior.
>
> I don't mean "pattern" in the technical analysis sense, of course. In fact most traditional technical analysis fails to pass a rigorous statistical test precisely because TA begins *and ends* with patterns. Successful trading is about much more than pattern-recognition, but turning our natural facility for it into a useful oddness-detector is an important step in becoming a successful trader.

Practicality

A good idea is only good if it's workable. Good trading strategies frequently die at the last step with the "and can do" part of the definition of edge. There are innumerable ways that a good trade can end up being too impractical to actually execute:

- It requires too much capital.
- Costs are actually higher than predicted.
- Positions are more illiquid than they initially appeared.
- It requires relationships with other parties (brokers, exchanges, countries, counterparties) that are hard to establish or maintain.
- The technical requirements (speed of receiving data, speed of sending orders, computational power, latency, etc.) are too large or insurmountable given current technology.

A good process will take these and other considerations into account, but it will also be good at pushing on these restrictions. Frequently a good trade appears, has a seemingly insurmountable difficulty, and it is mere persistence that knocks down the final barrier. There may have been many others who looked at the idea, wanted to do it, but couldn't get past that last hurdle.

Go Try It

In the end, a lot of the answers are found simply by trying out things. Provided the sizes are small and the risk is controlled properly, frequently the best thing to do is to try a trade. It's important to create a process and a culture that encourages experimentation as well as simply going ahead and "trying it." The upside of doing so frequently outweighs the downside. As with everything else, of course, you can go too far in this direction and try everything under the sun, yet lack focus and diligence.

The Nature of Real-World Edges

The preceding discussion may make it seem that the nature of real-world edges is complicated and that to explain them requires a deep understanding of markets, huge datasets, a knowledge of advanced mathematics, and subtle reasoning. Proving that a given edge is indeed present, and being able to run a trade based on it, may well require all of those things. But explaining an edge does not. In fact, the competitiveness of markets makes the very opposite true. Bearing these considerations in mind, recall this chapter's rule:

If you can't explain your edge in five minutes, you don't have a very good one.

How can this be true? By way of explanation, let's describe some real honest-to-goodness edges that consistently make millions of dollars a year for the people who trade based on them:

- People who want to trade stocks need a middleman to make the process efficient and convenient. These middlemen, whom we met in Chapter 2, are known as market makers. Customers demand liquidity from market makers, the latter provide it, and in aggregate they make a profit for having done so.
- ETFs and other funds need to rebalance their portfolios periodically based on changes in the composition of the index they track. When these funds trade, people who provide liquidity should profit from doing so.
- Relationships between related securities should, over the long term, follow certain reasonable statistical properties. Identifying when these relationships are far from their historical averages can lead to trades that bet on the deviations disappearing over time. For example, the relationship between the on-the-run[1] and off-the-run treasury bonds.

Each of these trades is an easily explained profitable trade. I just explained them. The story of their edge is straightforward and understandable to anyone with a reasonable knowledge of financial markets. Of course, transforming this straightforward story of edge into a trading strategy that actually *is* profitable is no mean feat. Each of these trades is well known, well understood, and attracts plenty of competition. You have to be very good to win at this level.

You might object that these particular trades are easily explained, but perhaps some other more complex ones aren't. This could be true, but those edges are likely to be less profitable. The discussions in the preceding chapters about the competitiveness of financial markets give a clue about why this is the case.

The more complex the story of edge becomes and the more pieces there are to the trade, the higher the number of things that have to be true, to go right, and to remain true, in order for a trade based on this edge to be profitable. Moreover, as you know, markets adapt over time. A very complex edge with lots of moving parts is unlikely to be one that (a) is broadly applicable to many situations, and (b) remains profitable over the long term. Simple stories are robust and, even if they are competitive, they are reliable. Complicated stories are contingent and may disappear from one day to the next, as the following example shows.

The German Tax Dividend Trade

One of the more interesting and complex trades, one that was profitable albeit morally questionable, appeared in Germany in the mid-2000s. This German tax dividend trade was actually two separate but related trades known in the industry as the cum-cum and cum-ex trades (Reuters, 2016). The description of this trade relies on somewhat arcane knowledge, so don't worry if you don't fully follow it. Rest assured this was a real (and as you'll see, illegal) trade for many years, and the idea here isn't to understand its details exactly but rather to get a feel for what a somewhat more complicated trade looks like.

Many large German companies pay dividends to shareholders, and as in most developed nations, the holders of the stock must pay taxes on those dividend payments. In order to facilitate the efficient collection of those taxes, German exchanges and clearinghouses collect the tax at pay-date, and holders receive the after-tax dividend. This is known as the net dividend (i.e. the dividend net of taxes). Of course, if someone is short the stock (i.e. has borrowed in order to sell), then they owe the full dividend, known as the gross dividend. Stock holders who own shares up to a certain date (known as the record date) are entitled to receive the dividend, and those who buy shares such that the shares settle in a clearinghouse after that date do not receive the dividend.

To be sure, different entities have different tax rates: foreigners, German nationals, German brokers, and certain privileged German entities like charities. So, it can be hard for the clearinghouses to know what tax rate to apply when paying out the dividend. Standard practice is to withhold the maximum possible rate, and if it turns out a given holder has preferential treatment then they need to apply for a rebate from the German tax authorities.

The simplest version of the trade is the cum-cum trade. Someone who otherwise has bad tax treatment under German law temporarily sells their shares to someone (conveniently, their German broker or bank) who has better tax treatment. The German bank is the official shareholder on the record date, and thus can reclaim tax from the German government. Subsequently, the shares are then sold back to the foreign entity, and the extra tax rebate is split between the foreigner and the German bank. It is a straightforward tax arbitrage trade.

A more complex and significantly more questionable version of the trade is the cum-ex trade. Let's say that person A owns stock that will pay 10 million EUR in gross dividends. Due to withholding, A will only receive 7.5 million EUR. However, since they are entitled to (let's say) a tax rate of 0%, they can ask the German government for a refund of 2.5 million EUR. Now, let's say A sells shares to B after the ex-dividend date but *before* the record date of the stock (typically a span of 1 or 2 days). B will receive stock *without* the dividend. If during this period B then resells the stock with a tighter settlement schedule, C is technically the shareholder of record and is entitled to the dividend. If C has good tax treatment like A, then they can also obtain a refund of 2.5 million EUR from the German government. Thus, the state has paid out a refund twice *on the same shares of stock*.

This merry-go-round of ownership did happen up to 10 times on the same shares during the same dividend period, meaning the German government paid out ten times what it should have in refunds. Now ask yourself: does this sound like the sort of edge upon which one could build a business? For one, it relies on some very specific facts about German tax law and is only available for 2 days of the year for a given stock, since dividends in Germany are paid annually. But more importantly: it wouldn't take much of a change in laws or regulations for this trade to disappear, once the German government saw traders exploiting the multi-billion-euro loophole (Die Zeit, 2017).

In fact, this is exactly what happened, and both of these trades were outlawed in 2012. Not only that, but the German government (predictably) investigated the brokers and banks which facilitated the trade and ended up retroactively declaring the trade to be tax evasion! As a result of its relatively high level of complexity, this edge was also highly brittle and ultimately very risky indeed.

When Edges Break

The story of edge should be a relatively simple one, in order for it to be robust and reliable. Nevertheless, even simple edges do disappear over time. As you will see later in Chapter 11, markets are adaptive in the sense that they're a feedback system, which tends to decrease the profitability of trading strategies over time. As a result, it is naive to think that a profitable strategy will continue to be profitable forever. But what are the mechanisms by which edges disappear?

Usually, a good trade slowly gets slightly worse over time. As market participants improve their understanding of markets, and as those who don't improve get slowly outcompeted, eventually your trade will gain competitors. The edge in the trade will slowly decrease, the noisiness of your profit-and-loss (P&L) will increase, and it will become less easy to conclusively state "this trade makes money." Eventually, the edge in the trade will cross under the costs of putting on the trade, or perhaps more accurately, the opportunity cost of the trade you could otherwise be doing. At this point, you'll decide to pull the plug on the trade. While you're personally sad at this having happened, overall the world is a better place. The profit you were making was an inefficiency in the market that, over time, was squeezed away. This is the normal lifecycle of a trading strategy.

Rarely, however, a trade goes from being good to being bad nearly instantaneously. There can be a few reasons for this, but by far the most common one is regulatory. Regulations and laws change all the time, and compliance with those laws can have many disparate effects. Sometimes regulations introduce a cost (either more stringent documentation or disclosure, or a rule requiring splitting out costs that were once bundled) that makes the trade unprofitable. Another common regulatory change is to deregulate or open up a certain market to trading by new entities. For example, a country can open itself up to foreign investment or trading. Frequently this causes pain to local participants who were sheltered from the full competitiveness of global financial markets. Once the country's markets open up and sharp-elbowed foreign participants enter, a difficult adjustment period often ensues.

Another kind of regulatory change is when a rule changes the incentives of market participants, who in turn will change their behavior (such as in the German tax dividend trade). Sometimes these changes in behavior won't be obvious since trading on exchanges is anonymous. What will happen is that a trade that relies on some behavior will simply stop making money from one day to the next. You don't know exactly what happened, you just realize that the trade stopped making money.

Edges in a Broader Context

The notion of edge as a set of reasons why a trade makes money can be productively applied far from the world of trading. Recall that edges derive from something that you understand and can act on which the marginal participant doesn't or can't. In fact, the source of most profitable activity has this property.

Edges in the Workplace

Why is Apple such a profitable company? The obvious answer is that the cost of manufacturing their products is much less than the price customers are willing to pay for them. But why can't others do the same? Being Apple is a profitable business, and surely other firms would like to be as profitable. Why can't they become Apple?

The edge-based explanation is that Apple knows things and they can do things that others can't. What might those be? Here is a nonexhaustive list.

- *Brand:* What Apple has created is something approaching a cultlike following through decades of selling successful, desirable products. Apple can introduce products that trade on the success of past products, a feat that competitors have a hard time replicating.
- *Manufacturing prowess:* Apple has the size and supplier relationships to be able to aggressively drive down costs and obtain new technical innovations before anyone else.
- *Vision:* Apple knows what consumers want, perhaps even before they know it themselves.

- *Synergy:* Apple products work well together. People buy into a self-reinforcing ecosystem of products that makes the total greater than the individual parts by themselves.

The same sort of analysis can be applied to any business. What is the knowledge and what are the capacities that give the business its edge? Being able to answer this question properly, mindful of all the ways you can answer it poorly, is a powerful mechanism for organizing and improving a business.

This sort of institutional self-knowledge is something that should be part of the culture of a firm. Knowing how and why your employer is profitable should help you guide your own actions in your day-to-day activities. Conversely, job applicants should spend at least some time asking questions that elicit this knowledge from their interviewers. Be wary of companies whose interviewers don't have a good sense of the firm's edge. If they're the ones hiring new employees, and they're not fully aware of the firm's strengths and needs, how can they hire the right people? Down that path lies workplace dysfunction.

Your Personal Edge

The notion of edge also applies at a personal level. Considering the job you have, or perhaps the job you want, what is your personal edge? What do you know or what can do that your competitors don't or can't? The answer to this question defines your suitability for the job.

This idea of personal edge applies even more powerfully as a guide to what you should *want* to do. In his 1943 paper "A Theory of Human Motivation," Abraham Maslow identifies a pyramid of human needs. At the top of the pyramid lies self-actualization. While there is legitimate criticism of the pyramid and the identified hierarchy, it remains plausible that self-actualization is a goal worth striving for. In his book *Motivation and Personality* (Maslow, 1987), Maslow coined the phrase "What a man can be, he must be." Pardoning the linguistic misogyny of the time, this is a very succinct expression of the idea that you should do the things that maximize your personal edge.

For most of us, identifying our personal edge is not a straightforward thing to do. If you happen to have obtained three straight gold medals at the International Mathematics Olympiad, it's probably obvious where your strengths lie. Similarly, if you are continually crushing your competition in high school golf tournaments, you should probably keep that up. But more likely, your personal edge is a combination of competences and strengths that, when harnessed together, identify the sort of work you're likely to be best at. Since this is not a straightforward thing to do, the best you can typically do is try lots of things while you're still relatively young and then specialize.

The rule about edge applies quite transparently when thinking about your job too. If your personal edge is some convoluted story that requires lots of conditions and moving parts, it's unlikely you'll (a) find that particular job, and (b) hold it for very long. Better to identify a story that, by virtue of its robustness, is impervious to variations and changes in the world and in your own makeup.

Of course, over time your personal edge is likely to change as you progress and grow. Nevertheless, the principle of edge provides you with a lens through which to evaluate yourself and the possibilities open to you.

Summary and Looking Ahead

The story of edge is a complex and interesting one:

- Edge derives from something you *know* or can *do* that others in the market either don't know or can't do.
- The problem with stories is that human brains are suckers for them. But by working hard we can turn them to our advantage and thereby avoid innumerable ways of falling under their spell.
- Cognitive biases are a fundamental feature of human thinking, so we need to create a process that inoculates us against their effects.
- Real-world edges aren't complicated. Reliable edges, ones that persist over time, derive from fundamental features of the markets in which they operate.
- The idea of edge applies everywhere you need to operate in a competitive environment.

We've now developed a notion of how edge works—specifically, where the money comes from in a profitable trade. But I've yet to turn this story into an actual trade: a concrete mechanism for acting in the markets we want. The next chapter discusses these mechanisms, which we call models. As can be expected, many devils lurk when considering the actual implementation of trades, and the next chapter addresses those practical realities.

References

Die Zeit. (2017). Retrieved from http://www.zeit.de/wirtschaft/2017-06/cum-ex-scandal-tax-evasion-dividend-stripping-germany.

Furnham, A. J.-P. (March 2005). "Personality and Intelligence: Gender, the Big Five, Self-Estimated and Psychometric Intelligence." *International Journal of Selection and Assessment* 13, No. 1, pp 11–24.

Gilovich, T. (June 1983). "Biased Evaluation and Persistence in Gambling." *Journal of Personality and Social Psychology* 44, No. 6, pp. 1110–26.

Kruger, J. D. (1999). "Unskilled and Unaware of It: How Difficulties in Recognizing One's Own Incompetence Lead to Inflated Self-Assessments." *Journal of Personality and Social Psychology* 77, No. 6, pp 1121–34.

Vance, Alyssa. (2009). http://lesswrong.com/lw/1f8/test_your_calibration/.

Maslow, A. (1987). *Motivation and Personality*, 3rd ed. Longman.

Parkinson, D. (2007, July 12). *When Fish Began to Fly.* Retrieved from https://www.theglobeandmail.com/report-on-business/when-fish-began-to-fly/article689368/.

Reuters. (2016). Retrieved from https://www.reuters.com/article/germany-dividends/dividend-tax-scandal-how-banks-short-changed-germany-idUSL8N1991BN.

CHAPTER 6

Models

"Dad, why does the sun rise every day?"

"Because the earth goes around the sun. Didn't they teach you that in school?"

"Yeah, they did, but that doesn't explain it. Why isn't it always right there, in the same place in the sky?"

"Well, the earth also spins."

"Why can't I feel that? When I go on the merry-go-round, I can feel the spin."

"Maybe it spins too slowly. I dunno."

"But the earth is *huge*. It has to be moving superfast to get around once a day. Faster than a plane, right?"

"I guess. Look, school was a long time ago for me."

"Also, why are the days getting shorter? I can't play much after school before it gets dark. And it gets colder too. And the sun isn't ever high in the sky anymore, like it was in the summer."

"Look, son, that's the way it is. Days are shorter in the winter, and colder. They always were and always will be. You don't have to know why it happens in order to just put on a jacket and go on with your life."

"I guess. But if we don't know why it happens, how do we know it's going to keep happening?"

"I suppose *someone* knows why. Astronomers, scientists."

"I think that's what I want to be when I grow up."

The model expresses the edge.

Some Light Philosophy

As we will see later, models should be thought of as useful simplifications of the real world. This immediately raises two interesting questions:

1. What is the world made of, conceptually? What sorts of things exist?
2. What can we know about the world?

These two questions, the ontological and epistemological respectively, have vexed the greatest philosophers and scientists for at least a couple of millennia. So, don't expect any great new philosophical insights in this book. But these questions are at least worth mentioning since they bear an interesting relationship to the psychology and sociology of building models. What follows in this chapter is drawn from my experiences in trading, but it fully applies in any other setting where you need to build predictive models of the world. Whether you're a professional seller on Amazon, a buyer or seller of online advertising, or indeed whether you're trying to catch an Uber or Lyft, building models is a key component of how you make better decisions.

What Should Models Be?

Over the years, I have found that many disagreements about what models to build (and how to build them) have their root in fundamental disagreements about either ontology (what sorts of things are there), or epistemology (what is knowable). One particular debate where philosophical issues frequently appear concerns whether a model should be descriptive of a true underlying structure of the world (a generative model), or whether describing some observed regularity (a phenomenological model) is "good enough."

An example of a generative model is the Black-Scholes-Merton (BSM) options pricing model (Hull, 2017). It posits a specific manner in which securities prices move (a log-normal distribution with a given volatility), and also additional properties about the market in which they trade (no arbitrage, no transaction costs, etc.). Anyone with some knowledge of options pricing will quickly object that the BSM model is not a true reflection of the world. This is of course a valid objection, but what's important for this discussion isn't whether the model is correct. What's important is the fact that it *tries* to represent the world as it truly is.

By contrast, some of the best-known examples of phenomeno-logical models in finance are known as implied-vol models. In characterizing the prices of options on a stock, it's convenient to do something a bit weird. Every options price has, when run backward through the BSM options model, an associated volatility that has a one-to-one relationship to the original options price. So, instead of talking about an option's price, you can also talk about the option's volatility. The reason this is a bit weird is that it's incoherent. BSM assumes that stocks move with a given volatility. If the BSM model of the world were accurate, every option price would, when run backward through the model, yield the same volatility: the volatility of the stock.

In real world options prices, however, this is not the case. Prices for options with strike prices far from the current stock price end up costing more than BSM would predict. This means that these prices, when converted back to volatilities, yield a higher volatility than that of options with strike prices nearer the current stock price. This gives a picture similar to the one seen in the illustration below.

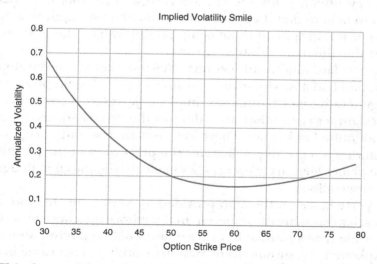

This shape of the volatility curve is known as the implied vol smile (it's more of a smirk, actually).

How is this relevant to the current discussion? It's simply that models that attempt to parameterize this implied volatility curve (or surface) of an options market are phenomenological models based on the observed volatilities. Fitting a curve through the points of the implied vol smile is simply an effort to match the observed options market prices. No claim is being made about the true nature of how stocks move. In fact, attempting to read any generative claims into such a phenomenological model of implied vol leads to logical inconsistencies. The model just wasn't made for that. And using any model, generative or phenomenological, outside its intended bounds is fraught with danger.

In practice, many models have both generative and phenomenological aspects to them, so there usually isn't a bright dividing line between them. So why is this distinction important? It's because when viewed from the right perspective, both kinds of models have "scary" implications when they're wrong.

Scary Generative Models

Imagine you have developed a generative model that posits an underlying mechanism consistent with observed behavior. As an example, consider Newton's law of universal gravitation. If that model eventually gains a long track record of reliability, it's easy to begin to believe that the model's fundamental assumptions actually *are* the truth, in spite of these being unobservable. This is known as "confusing the map with the territory."

By the late nineteenth century, Newton's law of universal gravitation had had a two-hundred-year history of rock-solid predictions. The generative mechanism was simple: objects have mass, and these masses attract each other according to the inverse-square relationship identified in the law. There was, nonetheless, one exception to this sterling record of predictions: the precession of the perihelion of the planet Mercury. Newton's law made predictions that disagreed with observations.

Overreliance on the map provided by Newton made more than a few scientists deny the experimental territory they were observing. And while it was justifiable to have an initial skepticism about the unexplained measurements of Mercury's orbit, as data came in over time it became a less reasonable position to take. It turns out what they were observing were relativistic effects for which they had yet to find a suitable model to explain. And indeed, one of the early successes of Einstein's general theory of relativity was the successful explanation (retrodiction, in this case) of Mercury's orbit. It took a free-thinking young scientist to ignore the map, see the territory more clearly than others, and provide the world with a new and better map, one that better fit the territory of reality.

Much more recently, the 2007–2008 financial crisis provided the backdrop for this now-legendary utterance by Goldman Sachs CFO David Viniar: *"We were seeing things that were 25-standard deviation moves, several days in a row."* If you take this statement about standard deviation at face value, Viniar was claiming that you were likelier to win the UK lottery 21 or 22 times in a row (Dowd, 2011) than to see the market behavior that was occurring. David Viniar had fallen in love with his models. Mistaking the map for the territory is a very common failure mode for users of until-then successful generative models.

Scary Phenomenological Models

Phenomenological models are scary in a more obvious manner, but scary nonetheless. Such a model makes no claim about why some (usually statistical) regularity is seen, and so it's exceedingly difficult to know if and when this regularity will stop existing. If the regularity is indeed statistical, it can potentially take a lot of data to convince the user that the world has changed. We will revisit this issue later in this chapter.

Disagreements about Scariness

Debate about which sort of failure mode is more worrisome frequently turns into an exercise in examining philosophical assumptions about the domain of the model. If you believe that the underlying true state of the world is definable and knowable, then you're going to be uncomfortable with a phenomenological model. You'd rather spend the necessary additional effort to develop a model that accesses that ground truth in a more reliable manner than a mere statistical regularity or curve-fitting.

Conversely, if you believe that the true state of the world is inaccessible in some fundamental way, the search for a good generative model will seem like a wild goose chase and a waste of time. Better to find a useful phenomenological model, and work on methods for improving it and understanding the extent of its applicability and its possible failure modes.

Philosophical assumptions are critically important for making good decisions about what's important and for deciding on which things it's worth spending effort. Yet in practice, this sort of conversation is often absent. As you've seen with human cognitive biases in previous chapters, it's easy to suppose that others view the world the way you do, and that your view of the world is universal and correct. Only by digging deeply and understanding why people disagree with your views can you start to uncover what, in this case, is a key disagreement about assumptions. Far from being a worthless exercise, it's the beginning of true understanding and collaboration.

> Options models are a fertile ground for arguments about models, and I see it all the time. As new hires learn about options and develop in their careers, they naturally gravitate to one side or the other of the generative/phenomenological divide. I think I straddle it as well as anyone, but I honestly do feel more attuned to the generative view. There *should* be a way of describing how stocks move, a model with a few understandable parameters that gives you a good account of market movements and hence prices for options. Correlated diffusions, jumps, copulas, rough vol, other jumps, the ways of describing stock movements can quickly get you lost in interesting but complex math.
>
> Unfortunately, having tried to come up with my share of unsuccessful "theories of everything," I've learned to appreciate how the messy real world exerts a power that can't be argued-with. The spots where my elegant model of the world broke down were exactly the places where there was money to be made by disagreeing with it. I'd try to fix it up in one place, but the messiness would leak in somewhere else. I'd like to say that I've given up on finding this grand unified theory of stock movements, but all it takes is a new paper or a new idea to draw me back into the rabbit hole. The heart wants what it wants.

Useful Simplifications

Assuming that you have sorted out your metaphysical and epistemological commitments, you can think about building a model. And yet the financial world is an exceedingly complex place. There are hundreds of thousands of securities, each of which can trade up to hundreds of thousands of times and have millions of market updates a day. Each of these securities is related to all of the others in complex, nonlinear, and state-dependent ways. The model needs to simplify this world in order to make sense of it, and that simplification must be useful. How do you evaluate usefulness? *The model expresses the edge,* not the other way around.

A model's usefulness is only meaningful in the context of the story you want to tell about the trade you want to do. In particular, even if a model makes good predictions about some future value or event, that knowledge is useless without also knowing how to take advantage of that prediction. More subtly, as I addressed in Chapter 5, if a model makes good predictions without that model's predictions being explainable in terms of the edge you claim to have found, it is difficult to have confidence in the model's reliability.

An Example from High-Frequency Trading

Let's imagine you've build a model to predict stock prices one minute in the future. Its empirical quality is unassailable: predictions it has made over the last few weeks, on fresh data it hadn't seen before, have been better than random with a high probability. So, you decide to create a simple trading strategy: when it predicts that the price in one minute will be above the offer (by some amount that exceeds costs), your system takes the offer, thereby buying. And similarly, when the predicted price is below the bid, it hits the bid, thereby selling.

After a couple of months of running this trading strategy you see two things which, taken together, seem inconsistent: (a) the model's predictions continue to be good, and (b) the strategy is losing money consistently. How can both be true? In fact, situations like this occur often in the world of high-frequency trading, and the solution takes subtle reasoning to identify. Also, as you'll see, the only way you know you need to reason in this way is because of your preexisting understanding about the source of edge in the model.

The solution to the apparent paradox is contained in the difference between the model's predictions and what actually happened. Specifically, the model predicts prices in a world where you didn't act (by definition, since it was trained on data we collected previously). But the strategy operates in a world where it *can* and *does* act. As an example of why this difference is important, imagine that when the model predicts a price above the offer, it is right 55% of the time, and it is wrong 45% of the time. On paper, this is a good model. Yet what if, in the 55% of the time it's right, you're competing with nine other skilled traders. In those cases, you only get 10% of the good trades (assuming you have similar technological abilities), and so the "good" portion is 10% of 55% = 5.5%. However, in the 45% of the cases you're wrong, no one is competing with you and you get all of those trades. Then $45/(45+5.5) = 89\%$ of the trades you do are bad trades. No wonder your strategy is losing money! Adverse selection rears its head again.

This is a case of a model that, although good in the sense that it makes valid predictions, doesn't express a useful tradeable edge. And a model without an edge to express is like a bicycle for a fish: perhaps a useful tool, just not for a fish.

Putting the Cart before the Horse

Abstractly, the view of model building as an exercise in expressing an edge appears to commit you to something like a two-step process: first identify the edge, then build a model that expresses that edge. In practice, this is rarely the case. More frequently, you begin with a notion of a trade (a theorized edge) and subsequently attempt to express this idea with a model. The process of developing the model, and validating it, provides useful feedback for the edge story you're developing. This is an iterative process, where the edge informs the model, which in turn modifies the edge. If the process is run properly, the edge and the model co-adapt in a way that satisfies the rule.

It is not uncommon to find, especially in academic literature, well-intentioned people inverting this process. They have found some new and mathematically interesting modeling technique and yearn to apply it to a real-world example. It is a model in search of a trade. While this is a valid approach for the purposes of publishing academic papers, it is dangerous to apply this sort of thinking to real-world trades, as the above example illustrates.

The reason for the danger should be evident. Having a model that makes interesting predictions does not, in itself, mean you have a trade. It's already difficult enough to find trades and to describe edges without fooling yourself. It's harder still if you have precommitted yourself to a specific model-based implementation of that trade.

Characteristics of Good Models

So, what do good models look like? According to the rule, good models are well-adapted to the edges they express. This adaptation guides the consideration and evaluation of models along a few different dimensions.

Robustness

The robustness of a model refers to its ability to maintain performance when you consider both aspects of the model and the world in which it lives and interacts:

- If historical data is used to train the model, does it perform similarly when different historical periods are used for training? If not, then the model probably isn't expressing a very reliable or robust edge.
- In particular, how does the model perform on a separate piece of historical data once trained? This is known as out-of-sample testing. Again, a model that performs well on data it's seen and poorly on data it hasn't seen is one whose edge is unlikely to be reliable.
- Once a model's parameters are determined, how does its performance change when these parameters are tweaked by small amounts? If a small tweak of a particular parameter significantly degrades the performance of the model, it's not robust.
- How sensitive is the model to the data sources it uses? If the data has outages, or starts to exhibit weird or stale information, will the model's performance degrade gracefully? Or will it start to incinerate money? This is a common failure mode for trading firms.
- How usable is the model in the real world? Does it require a lot of moving parts, is its architecture reliable or prone to breakage? An excellent predictive model isn't much good if the systems on which it runs are always going down with some fault or other.

When building a model, consideration of these factors frequently causes reconsideration of the edge the model was built to express. You may think an edge is reliable in principle, but if you can't manage to build a reliable model to express that edge, it's possible the edge itself wasn't so robust in the first place.

Addressing these and related issues is the way in which edges and models end up co-adapting during the development process, as I discussed earlier.

Hardware, Software, and Wetware

It is a seductive idea to think of models as abstract mathematical entities, always developed using powerful statistical methods, and implemented in rock-solid code running on bleeding-edge hardware. In fact, only the simplest models can be described this way.

As we've seen, a model is a useful simplification of the real world. If forcing the expression of an edge into a computer program destroys or even simply limits its usefulness, then this is a strong signal that putting the model entirely in software isn't the right thing to do.

In fact, the models for nearly all of the successful strategies I'm aware of live in some combination of a computer and a human brain (or possibly a set of them). This isn't a weakness of the traders or model builders, or of the computer tools available. It is a pragmatic acceptance of the fact that computers are good at some sorts of problems and calculations, and humans are good at other kinds.

Computers are good at problems that:

- Are well-circumscribed and well-described
- Are helped by speed of calculation (This is usually where there's a lot of reliable data that can easily be accessed.)
- Have inputs that don't vary very much from moment to moment or day to day
- Don't have important variables suddenly appear out of nowhere

Conversely, well-trained, sharp, and experienced humans are good at problems:

- That are poorly specified
- That have a large but sparse set of variables
- Where never-before-seen effects can appear at a moment's notice
- Where speed and reliability of calculation are not make-or-break aspects of the situation

It should be clear that these respective skill sets can be complementary. A well-designed model leverages the comparative advantages of both humans and computers to create a meta-model that is superior to one implemented using only one or the other. Thus, when I say a model is well adapted to express a certain edge, I'm saying that there is an edge-optimal division between the model parts living in a computer versus living in a human. I'll have more to say on this subject in Chapter 10.

Inspectability

Analogous to the discussion of black-box strategies in Chapter 5, it is useful to have the ability to peer into a model and understand how it's going about expressing the desired edge. Such a model is said to be inspectable. This is important for a variety of reasons:

- *Debugging:* Models break, and when they do it's useful to be able to inspect the model in order to debug it.
- *Confidence:* It's hard to place confidence in a model, from an operational risk perspective, if you can't (at least in principle) understand why it's making the predictions it's making.
- *Iterative improvement:* Having a black box model makes it significantly more difficult to update and improve it as your understanding grows and as the world changes over time.

The considerations of inspectability lead you naturally to ideas that are considered fundamental in the design of large systems. These ideas are particularly well-developed in the software engineering world, in particular surrounding the development of large codebases. Good model inspectability requires:

- A modular design. It's much easier to understand a large system (or model) if it's composed of a small number of less-large pieces that interact. Each of these pieces is in turn composed of a few smaller subpieces, hierarchically. The ability to abstract away consideration of lower-level aspects lets you understand the system at a high level, and conversely a well-architected system lets you examine and optimize small pieces of it without having to keep the whole structure in mind.

- A modular design requires good clean interfaces between modules. Defining properly the interaction of the pieces of the model usefully constrains the behavior of those modules in a way that lets you understand the result.
- Clean interfaces are generally small, and certainly no larger than required. The larger the set of interactions between modules, the more difficult it is to separate them conceptually. As Plato said in Phaedrus, we must *"carve nature at the joints."* That is, look hard for the logical places to put the divisions between modules.

It's worth noting that, although inspectability is desirable, recent trends in modern machine learning have pushed the world away from inspectability. Many of the most successful neural networks in a variety of fields are effectively large masses of neurons with millions of connections between them. It's virtually impossible to understand how a state-of-the-art image recognition network is managing to recognize a cat, for example.

Nonetheless, the idea of throwing up your hands and giving up on inspectability is probably giving up too much. Model inspectability and interpretability is an area of active academic and industrial research, and I'll have more to say about this in Chapter 10.

Data Management and Model Building

Nearly all modern models in trading require at least a little bit of historical data. Even if this data consists of a simple file or hand-written information about prior interesting events in the markets, data is the lifeblood of modeling. More commonly, historical data consists of large amounts of price, order, and news data stored in easily searched and accessed formats. The question becomes how to use this data properly when building and evaluating models.

Data Scarcity

The data exhaust of financial markets is truly huge. Conservatively, the activity of traders around the world produces tens of terabytes of data every day. Given this, it can seem odd to claim that data in financial markets is, in fact, somewhat scarce. But this is indeed what my experience has taught me. There are many reasons for this state of affairs:

- Even though terabytes of data per day get produced, any given edge only cares about a tiny fraction of that data. The headline number isn't as important as the amount of *relevant* data available to train models for a given strategy or edge.
- The data from today is not the same as data from five years ago. For nearly all types of models, the data from today is more important than the data from last week, let alone five years ago. This is known as *heteroskedasticity*. This is a long Greek word that simply means "the world changes, and so does your data." Mostly it changes gradually, but it can also change suddenly due to world events (elections, wars, etc.). So, even though you may have petabytes of data available to train your model, only the most recent data is relevant.
- Financial markets are extremely competitive, and a direct consequence of this is that they are noisy. What this means is that the edge you're seeking is typically quite small. In particular, it's small relative to the natural and fundamentally unpredictable amount of movement in market prices. Being able to predict even 1% of the daily variation of a stock is a big achievement. What this means is that the signal you're looking for is dwarfed by ineradicable noise 100 times larger than it. For this reason, comparing amounts of data to that available in other, less competitive arenas isn't really comparing like to like. The signal to noise ratio in, say, image recognition is significantly higher; it's not like we disagree on whether a picture is that of a cat very frequently, let alone 99 times out of a hundred.

You now begin to see that, even though data is ostensibly plentiful, it's actually in rather short supply and in fact it often turns out to be the limiting factor. For this reason, it's doubly important to take good care of your data and to use it properly.

How Much Data Is Necessary?

The first and most important way you can properly manage your data is to avoid using too much of it. This may sound counterintuitive: if data is scarce then surely you should use as much of it as you can get your hands on. But over the long term, the opposite is true: each use of a given datum makes it less useful for future models and strategies. As you train models on a given datum, the information it holds gets used by models. Then the more you revisit the datum in the future, the less new information it can give you. You are, in a very real sense, exhausting the information available in the datum. So, if you were to use "all the data" in a given modeling effort, you end up poisoning that well of information for future versions of yourself. Much like good management of oil wells or farmland, you must avoid overusing the resource in order to be able to use it in the future.

So, how much data is enough? The answer must of course vary by model and by strategy. But the key point is that you do need to go through the exercise of trying to determine how much data you need for a given modeling effort. The exercise amounts to answering the question: "How much data do I need in order to be sufficiently confident my conclusions are valid, and not just random noise?" Answering this question requires both experience and good knowledge of statistics. This is yet another area where experienced groups have a strong advantage over newcomers trying to break into the business.

Partitioning the Data

Once you've decided on the dataset you're going to use to build a model, you need to partition the data. You might assume that you should train your model on all the data you've set aside. However, this is not a good idea because of a phenomenon known as overfitting. I could, of course, talk about overfitting in very mathematical terms and there are many statistics and machine learning textbooks which provide such a treatment. In this book, however, I want to develop an intuitive understanding of the phenomenon, as a baseline that you can later refine with a more mathematical understanding.

Consider the following toy example. There is a set of datapoints, and you want to fit a curve to these points. This curve-fit is your (phenomenological) model.

The question is: how wiggly should the curve be? You could fit a simple straight line, or you could fit an extremely complex and wiggly curve that goes perfectly through all the datapoints.

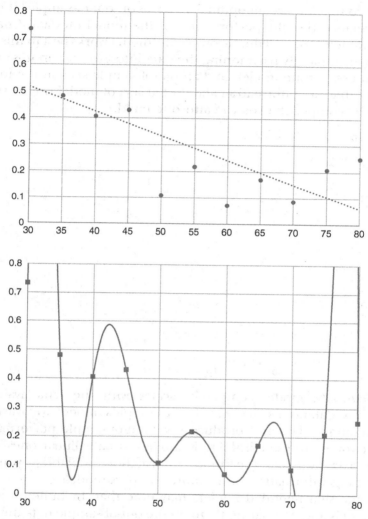

How do you decide which of these options (or the continuum of options between these two extremes) is correct for your application? You can, of course, use your well-honed judgment and make some decisions, but you can also do something a bit more principled.

Let's take a random half of the datapoints and fit the curve on those points. Then, look at the goodness of fit of the model produced on the other half. What you find, in this case, is that both extremes of model complexity are suboptimal. In terms of "out-of-sample" (OOS) performance (i.e. the performance of the model on data it hasn't been trained on), a medium-complexity model works best in this particular example. By partitioning the data into two sets: an in-sample set you use to train models and an out-of-sample set you use to test it, you can glean information about what sort of model (in the sense of model complexity) you can afford to build.

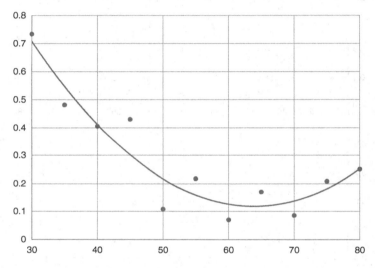

Generally, model complexity scales with the data available. With few datapoints, it's easy for a complex model to overfit to the in-sample data and produce poor out-of-sample performance. You're forced to use fairly simple models, usually linear ones. With more data available (i.e. more information available), you can extract this information with a more complex model.

Some sharp-minded readers may note that, by building multiple models and comparing them on the out-of-sample data multiple times, it's like you're building a big meta-model with the OOS data being somewhat in-sample. This is indeed a valid objection. For this reason, in practice you partition data into three sets: an in-sample set for building the actual models, a validation set used to find good model "hyperparameters" (such as model complexity), and finally a true OOS set that you touch as little as possible (ideally only once).

It should by now be clear that there is a tension between iteratively improving models and the desire to avoid overfitting the model to the available data. Remember, the more you go back to the well of data, the more you exhaust the true information contained therein, and the more you end up fitting models to an apparent signal that isn't actually there (in the sense of being reliable in the future).

The Process of Building Models

The tension described in the last section leads us to a natural question: when is a model good enough to put into production? If you stop the process too early, you leave some value on the table. If you work "too" hard and squeeze the data too hard, you end up overfitting and producing a model that won't have as much value as it could have going forward.

The answer is, as always, given by experience. However, you can find guidance from the chapter's rule: the model expresses the edge. You should, if you understand the world well enough, have good bounds on how good a given strategy can be. Or more concretely, how much edge is there to be had anyway? If you have good reason to believe you can extract, say, 1% of edge from a one-day return in a stock, then it seems pointless and dangerous (given the foregoing) to keep working to improve a model that is achieving (in OOS tests) 0.98% of edge. Conversely, if you've built a model that's achieving 0.1% of edge, then you need to either (a) work harder to improve it, or (b) revise your beliefs about how much edge is available. This is again part of the mechanism of models and edges co-adapting to one another.

Development versus Production

A more practical tension also exists when building models. When doing the research work to create a model, it's useful to have a development environment that favors fast iteration and convenient tools and libraries. In order to provide this convenience, these tools (such as Python/Numpy in the machine learning world) are not generally optimized for speed or robustness, characteristics that are critically important when running models in production. Thus, you are frequently left with a situation where you develop a model in one computer/technical environment but need to run it in production in a completely different environment.

This is a well-known problem, and there have been many efforts through the years to reduce the pain of this transition. But the important thing is to recognize that this tension exists, and to avoid the strong desire to paper it over by assuming that it's a minor issue. In fact, one of the many ways that trading firms get into trouble is in transitioning trading strategies from a development or test environment to a production environment.

One famous example of this is what happened to Knight Capital on August 1, 2012. On that day, Knight released into production a system designed to take advantage of a relatively new NYSE program called Retail Liquidity Program (RLP). The code that implemented Knight's RLP functionality reused an internal signaling flag that was originally used only in testing environments. Internally known as Power Peg, this old functionality (unused by the time the new code was released into production) was used to move stock prices in the test environment in order to verify the functioning of other parts of the system. When the new code's reused flag triggered the old functionality, Knight's systems started to aggressively trade stocks in the real market. For 45 minutes, Knight's "test" system was actively moving stocks in the real world, and hence actively incinerating money. Knight ended up losing $440 million in those 45 minutes and the event resulted in the eventual purchase of the firm by Getco a year later.

When Models Break

You know from the discussion in Chapter 5 that edges don't last forever. The same is true for models. In fact, the question I examined in Chapter 5 is much subtler and, having now discussed models in detail, we can revisit the question in this context.

Suppose a strategy that was consistently making money no longer does. You need to examine the situation to assess the root cause of this new behavior. The most important question you need to answer is whether the edge disappeared, or whether the edge persists but the model needs to be changed or updated.

How Much Variation Is Expected?

Before assessing why a model or strategy has changed its behavior, it's important to establish whether it did indeed change at all. After all, very few trades are such consistent earners that daily, weekly, or monthly variation is negligible. Randomness in strategy performance (P&L, amount traded, etc.) is an inevitable part of running trading strategies in modern competitive markets. Of course, the general subject of change-point and outlier detection has a rich history and remains an active area of research in statistics. I cannot give the subject the treatment it deserves in this small section, but I can nonetheless highlight issues and ideas that are worthy of consideration when thinking about strategy behavior changes.

To begin with, you need to understand the true value of historical data. Jordan has been running a strategy for a couple of years. He has around 500 datapoints that represent the daily performance of his strategy. He decides to calculate statistics on these parameters—for example, the mean or average P&L—and also the standard deviation of the P&L. He does so and sees that the strategy makes an average of $2,000 per day, with a standard deviation of $10,000 per day. Today was an unusual day, and Jordan sees the strategy lost $58,000. This represents a Six Sigma negative excursion. If you assume that P&Ls are normally (or Gaussian) distributed, you'd say that such an excursion is phenomenally unlikely (0.00034% to be exact) and he'd have to conclude that something about the strategy has changed.

In fact, such a conclusion is likely to be premature. For one, P&Ls are almost never drawn from such a well-behaved distribution as a Gaussian. Most distributions in finance, and P&Ls are no exception, have much fatter tails. That is, the probability of large deviations from "typical" behavior is much larger (by orders of magnitude, quite plausibly) than implied by a Gaussian distribution. You can likely confirm this is true by looking at the historical data and seeing which fraction of days have exceeded a Six Sigma event. And sure enough, Jordan looks at this data and sees that the strategy has made or lost more than $60,000 on a few occasions. Of course, similar analyses and arguments can be made when looking at multiday streaks of behavior.

As you can see, historical data is valuable in evaluating this sort of question, but it's easy to misread the data by making unwarranted assumptions about how well behaved the distributions are. Let's now suppose Jordan's strategy lost $200,000 instead of $58,000 and that there is no historical precedent for such a large excursion. Can he now safely conclude that the strategy has experienced an important change?

Maybe. In these situations, it's rare that data alone can conclusively determine the answer one way or another. For example: was this day special in some way? On US election day November 8, 2016, the markets behaved in ways that were quite atypical for a normal trading day. It's quite likely that strategies trained on data that does not contain days where yellow billionaires implausibly become president will exhibit very unusual performance. It would again be premature to conclude that the strategy exhibited a change merely because of its performance on this day.

It would also, frustratingly, be premature to conclude that just because November 8, 2016, was a special day in US history that you should disregard it and continue on assuming it was a forgettable outlier. In this case, the surprise election result upended the consensus on how the US federal government would function for the subsequent four years, and stocks in industries as varied as healthcare, oil, and defense did indeed exhibit a permanent step-change in their behavior from one day to the next.

Again, there is little substitute for experience. These questions are hard—among the most difficult, in fact—and this book can only gesture in the direction of the issues that must be confronted.

Assessing Strategy Changes - A General Approach

The process of trying to figure out why a strategy doesn't work anymore generalizes to just about any model of the world. Say you're a buyer of digital ad space, as on Google or Facebook. You make money by reselling that ad space to your clients, and your edge comes from being able to identify mispriced ad space. One fine day, you realize that your clients aren't willing to pay enough for the ad spaces to justify the price at which you bought them. But what was the nature of this change? In particular, was it sudden or gradual? If sudden, then it could be an edge issue if:

- Something fundamental about the world has changed. Perhaps a new boycott of Facebook is depressing ad rates.
- A competitor of yours has changed their behavior.
- A new competitor has entered, or an existing market participant has left.

- A new regulatory regime has come into effect. Perhaps Google changed its auction algorithm and you didn't notice the change.

Sudden changes in performance could be model issues if:

- Something in the external technical environment has changed (the ad platform released a new programming interface with either new or restricted functionality).
- Something in your internal technical environment has changed (new machines, software upgrades, network topology changes, etc.).

It's worth noting that changes can be seemingly small ones and nonetheless have an important and in fact dominant effect. This phenomenon of small changes having large effects is a phenomenon of systems with feedback. A small change causes a small change in the behavior of a small number of participants, but each of those changes in turn causes other small changes, and the cascade effect (caused by the feedback effect of people reacting to each other's reactions) ends up causing a regime shift in the behavior of the whole business (in this case, online ads). In any competitive pursuit, it pays to pay attention to the details.

Gradual changes can also be caused by either edge or model changes. Edge changes could be a candidate if:

- You see evidence of new participants competing for the trades your strategy wants to do. If, for example, the profit margin on your ad reselling has steadily shrunk from 50% to 20%, a likely candidate explanation is more competition for the same trade.
- Strategies with related edges experience similar degradations over time. Is your problem just with Facebook ads, or are Google ads also affected?

Gradual changes can be model issues if:

- Other strategies with similar edges haven't seen degradation (or at least, as much degradation) in performance over the time period.
- If the story of edge encompasses the possibility that model parameters naturally get stale over time, even if the edge persists.

- A form of Goodhart's law applies to gradual model changes. Over time, the statistical regularities upon which your model relies to express the edge will become disconnected from the fundamental source of the edge.

Models in the Real World

So far, the discussion in this chapter has been trading-centric. And it's not necessarily easy to see how to apply elsewhere these ideas about models and how to think about them. In order to do so, you need to go back to the beginning of the chapter and remind yourself what a model is: a model is a useful simplification of a complex world. The excellent statistician George Box once famously said, "All models are wrong. Some are useful." And indeed this is the vein in which we proceed with the discussion of how to think about models more broadly.

Humans Are Model-Building Machines

Even if you've never built a model for trading in financial markets, I can assure you that you're already an expert model builder. Nearly all intentional action in the world requires at least a rudimentary model of the world in order to predict beforehand the results of your considered actions. Babies learn to walk by building a model of the walking problem: how leg and arm muscles react to signals from the brain, how surfaces react to being stepped (or fallen) upon, and so on. Of course, such model building isn't an explicit conscious process, but it's nonetheless model building. Some of the strongest and most useful models contained in your brain were developed (through painstaking trial-and-error) before the age of five.

It's probably not productive to closely examine these sorts of autonomous models with the framework developed in this chapter (unless you're a gait analyst). So, let's examine the sorts of models that you build semi-explicitly to see what insights you can glean about them.

Models of the World

The most obvious sort of mental model you learn to develop concerns the world in which you live. Which lane should I pick on the freeway? How much softer really are my clothes when I use fabric softener? Do I get indigestion after I eat spaghetti with meatballs? You build all sorts of models every day, just to get through your life. Yet rarely do you subject these ad hoc models to rigorous testing.

In many situations, the sort of testing rigorous enough to be valid can feel like a waste of time: the benefits of an improved model of traffic flow on the freeway probably aren't worth the effort of creating a statistically valid A/B testing plan and carrying it out. But for those who are so inclined, by nature if by nothing else, these little daily-life models serve as good practice for developing the right mindset about models. This mindset can, in turn, be put to a significantly more productive use in situations where the difference between a good and a bad model is important.

Models of Other People

The most important aspects of your life, as the social animal that you are, concern your relationships with the other social animals in the vicinity. And in this area, the quality of your mental models of the behavior of others largely define how successful you'll end up in life. Work, relationships, and family life are all arenas where your interactions with others make the difference between a happy, successful life and one that's less so.

Interestingly, the distinction I drew at the beginning of the chapter between generative (G) and phenomenological (P) models ends up being valuable when studying mental models of other people. Contrast a model of the form "my boss is just a grouch" (a P model) to one of the form "my boss has a stressful job, maybe one that's more stressful than he can handle" (a G model). In the world of trading it can be difficult to make a judgment about the value of a P versus G model in some specific situation. You'd like a G model if you can get it, but sometimes you have to settle for a P model. However, in developing models of the behavior of others, an accurate G model will almost always be better and more useful than even an excellent P model.

G models about other people get at their fundamental motivations. You're not just finding statistical regularities about the behavior of others, but rather you're trying to inhabit their world, understand how *they* see their own lives so that you can understand *why* people make the decisions they do and behave the way they do. Building a good G model about a person is more difficult, but it yields significantly more value in the long run if you're going to be interacting with that person over time. You can ask yourself hypothetical questions: "What would they do if I did X?" or "If Y happens, how are they going to react?" and, with a good G model, you can actually get useful counterfactual answers.

As I said, building such models is difficult and therein lies the value of the ideas developed in this chapter. You know it's easy to fool yourself about subjects containing little information and a lot of uncertainty. Well, there are few subjects as complex as the thoughts, desires, motivations, and preferences of another person. What better arena, then, to remember the characteristics of good models: robustness; inspectability; the way in which data is used to generate, validate, and test models; and so forth.

In fact, recent work in neuroscience has validated this approach to understanding how the brain works. The Predictive Processing Model (Clark, 2015) posits that the brain operates in exactly the way that it should if it were fundamentally a model-building engine. The brain works to minimize the surprise experienced before a state of events, and the most parsimonious way to minimize surprise is to build an internal representation (or model) of the outside world. And indeed, the approach has already provided interesting new ways of thinking about mental illnesses such as psychosis.

You can also see connections to traditional moral philosophy in thinking about modeling the behavior of others. To have a good G model about someone else is to have some measure of empathy and compassion for that person: what they're like, what they think and feel, putting yourself in their shoes. Pragmatically, developing the skill of empathy and compassion for others is, aside from a moral good in itself, an excellent way to understand better the people who surround you. More people working to develop good G models of others is surely a small step to a better world.

Models of Ourselves

Given all I have said about our phenomenal ability to fool ourselves, it should come as no surprise that some of the best ways to avoid this involve the development and deployment of good models. In this case, these good models are about ourselves. Tying in our discussion in Chapter 1 about motivation, we can restate our first rule ("Know why you're doing a trade before you do it") as a rule about mental models of ourselves ("Develop a good model of your own motivations"). The idea of knowing yourself at least as well as you know anyone else ends up becoming an exhortation to really spend the time to understand yourself, and to build the best models you possibly can about your own nature.

Summary and Looking Ahead

- Thinking about models is thinking about how they fail. All models are wrong, but some are useful.
- When building a model, having a clear view of whether you're building a phenomenological model or a generative model gives you a better understanding of its possible failure modes.
- Managing the data used to build a model is an exercise in tradeoffs, which let us build good models now and also in subsequent efforts.
- We're all natural-born model builders. Building good models about the people around you lets you understand them better and provides an avenue for empathy and compassion.

In the next chapter, I'll be doing a deep dive into the subject of costs. It turns out that cost is a much richer subject than "that boring thing you try to minimize." Thinking clearly about *all* the costs to which you're subject opens new windows into the nature of long-term success in trading. It also has things to teach you about the nature of innovation in general.

References

Clark, A. (2015). *Surfing Uncertainty: Prediction, Action, and the Embodied Mind*. Oxford University Press.
Dowd, K. J. (2011). How Unlucky Is 25-Sigma? Retrieved from https://arxiv.org/pdf/1103.5672.pdf.
Hull, J. (2017). *Options, Futures, and Other Derivatives*, 10th ed. Pearson.

CHAPTER 7

Costs and Capacity

In the *Seinfeld* episode "The Bottle Deposit," Newman sits on his couch. He's using an old mechanical adding machine and a pad to work on permutations for the "Michigan deposit bottle scam."[1] Spools of used adding machine paper litter the table, and maps of the northeastern United States are pinned on the wall. He taps out a series of numbers, pulls the handle, and reads the result, then looks at what he's written on his pad.

NEWMAN: Damn!
               Frustrated, he sits back. He notices a framed photograph of his mother. A thought occurs.
NEWMAN: (voice-over): Oh, Mother's Day. Wait a second. Mother's Day?!
               He starts typing figures into the adding machine rapidly. He mouths numbers to himself, shrugging as he makes estimates. When he finishes, he tears the paper strip from the machine and compares it to figures on his pad.
NEWMAN: (triumphant) Yes!
               In celebration he swigs from a bottle of soda.
               [later]
               Newman hurries up to Kramer's door and hammers on it with his fist. He waits a few seconds, then impatiently hammers again.
NEWMAN: Come on Kramer!

The door opens to reveal Kramer midway through a shave, holding a razor, with foam on his face.

KRAMER: Wha ... ?

NEWMAN: It's the truck, Kramer. The truck!

KRAMER: Look, Newman, I told you to let this thing go.

NEWMAN: No, no, no, no, no. Listen to me. Most days, the post office sends one truckload of mail to the second domestic regional sorting facility in Saginaw, Michigan.

KRAMER: (interested) Uh-huh.

NEWMAN: But, on the week before holidays, we see a surge. On Valentine's Day, we send two trucks. On Christmas, four, packed to the brim. And tomorrow, if history is any guide, we'll see some spillover into a fifth truck.

KRAMER: (realization) Mother's Day.

NEWMAN: The mother of all mail days. And guess who signed up for the truck.

KRAMER: A free truck? Oh boy, that completely changes our cost structure. Our G and A goes down fifty percent.

NEWMAN: (excited) We carry a couple of bags of mail, and the rest is ours!

KRAMER: Newman, you magnificent bastard, you did it!

NEWMAN: (triumph) Let the collecting begin!

> If you think your costs are negligible relative to your edge, you're wrong about at least one of them.

Introduction

All trading activity entails cost. Some of these costs are obvious (like brokerage fees) and others are subtler (like market impact). Without accurately assessing the cost of a trade, it is impossible to understand the profitability of a trade. It's quite easy to think of costs as "a thing you're forced to think about", that is, a technical detail that's important but not particularly interesting. In fact, properly accounting for the costs of trading can teach you a wealth about the trade you're attempting to do, and about trading in general.

As you'll see, by taking an expansive view of costs you can actually think broadly about the nature of innovation itself, whether in trading, in technology, or otherwise.

Categorizing Costs

In this chapter I'll argue that the two most important characteristics of costs are their visibility and linearity. These two aspects almost entirely define how you should think about a cost and how it affects your thinking about a trade and its edge.

- *Visibility:* How clearly seen is a cost or fee? Some costs are very visible, like the salaries of your employees, or the brokerage fees on a trade. Others are much less visible.
- *Linearity:* How does a cost scale with the amount of trading you do? A linear scaling means the cost is proportional to the amount of trading: if you trade twice as much, a linear cost will double. Again, an example would be a brokerage fee. Costs can be sublinear, linear, or super-linear in the amount of trading.

	Visible costs	Invisible costs
Linear costs	Quadrant 1	Quadrant 3
Nonlinear costs	Quadrant 2	Quadrant 4

The diagram makes it seem as though there is a bright dividing line between the categories of cost. As with nearly everything else I've discussed so far, this isn't exactly true. The level of visibility, for example, constitutes a continuum from very visible through to extremely hidden. Similarly, the linearity of a cost can also vary greatly. Any function that maps an amount of trading to an amount of cost incurred can work, in principle. But, in practice, most of those functions are monotonically increasing in the amount of trading. In other words, if you trade more then you pay more in costs. How much more depends on the function. So, the quadrants above *are* at least a little bit artificial. Nonetheless, in what follows, partitioning the world of costs into these quadrants lets me speak more generally about their characteristics and the partition is a useful mental shorthand for thinking about costs.

Quadrant 1: Visible Linear Costs

We begin with the easiest category to think about. Here is a partial list of costs that fall into this category:

- Brokerage fees
- Ticket charges
- Exchange fees
- Clearing costs
- Financing
- Margin

Traders and trading firms are generally explicitly charged these costs (they're visible), and they scale almost exactly with the amount of trading done (they're linear). Because of this visibility, these costs are the easiest to account for prior to a trade occurring, and also the easiest to attempt to minimize over time. So how do you minimize these costs?

The best way to minimize quadrant 1 costs, much like what you'd do as a good consumer, is to shop around. Brokerage fees, for example, can be quite variable across different broker-dealers, depending on the relationships you've established and how they view the business in which you're engaged. Frank conversations about the deals you think you can get elsewhere can be a good mechanism for lowering your costs with existing relationships.

Nevertheless, it doesn't necessarily pay to squeeze your relationships as hard as possible. As an example, SAC Capital famously paid higher brokerage fees than nearly any other sophisticated Wall Street hedge fund (Eavis, 2013). Given their reputation as sharp operators, it's reasonable to assume they were getting something of value in exchange for these excessive fees paid. It's in this context that you shouldn't be surprised at SAC Capital later being investigated and eventually shut down as part of the New York attorney general's investigation into insider trading at SAC Capital and other sophisticated hedge funds.

The general point is not, of course, to condone illegal activity through the overpayment of brokerage fees. It's more to understand that any business relationship has to be mutually beneficial in order to be fruitful over the long term. Minimizing costs is good business, but not to the point where it poisons the relationship with counterparties and other firms that facilitate your trading. Finding the happy medium isn't easy, but it's certainly true that neither extreme is optimal.

In the finance world, there's an implicit understanding that traders pay broker fees, and brokers return those fees in the form of dinners and other "relationship building" activities at the broker's expense. Many people find it a bit distasteful to be honest: the firm pays the fees, but the trader gets the kickback. Other people like to milk the system for all it's worth, so the broker needs to figure out which category you fall into.

I like a nice meal as much as the next guy, but after a long day of trading the last thing I wanted to do was sit for idle chitchat with brokers to whom I didn't relate very well. This caused problems sometimes, since brokers didn't know what to do with me: the trading I did paid plenty of fees but I never personally got anything back in return. My friends tell me I'm very boring that way, but mostly I just wanted to get home to my family. The funny thing is that the brokers who figured this out developed, over time, better rapport. They were relieved they weren't forced to play the usual client-appreciation game, and as a result the client appreciation took the form of something much more valuable: a productive business relationship. I learned you're sometimes better off with a quick drink every few months than a never-ending stream of high-end steak dinners, no matter how tasty.

Quadrant 2: Visible Nonlinear Costs

Many of the costs that fall into this category are fixed or semifixed costs of doing business. There are very few truly fixed costs, of course, so the distinction is mostly to do with whether the costs stay fixed from day to day (irrespective of amount traded) over the course of a few months or so. Again, a partial list:

- Rent
- Salary
- Equipment
- Connectivity
- Market data
- Legal and regulatory costs

As organizations get larger, these costs also get larger, but as I've said, this relationship is a function of organization size and not a function of the amount traded. A large organization that doesn't trade one share will still pay these costs, after all.

Other costs that fall in this quadrant are subtler and relate specifically to the business of trading. Some of the more interesting ones are position limits. Defined narrowly, a position limit is a cap set by a futures exchange on the number of contracts an entity can be long or short in a given future, option, or option underlying. The historical origins of these limits on derivatives contracts are somewhat nebulous, but they generally derive from the desire of "fundamental" traders of commodities to limit the influence of "speculative" traders in these products.[2] In practice, the actual limits are typically quite high and are unlikely to be approached by anyone but very large trading organizations. However, thinking of position limits more broadly, you can see their influence even for smaller traders.

An example of a different kind of position limit is that of foreign-ownership restrictions that exist in many countries. These laws restrict the fraction of local businesses that can be held (i.e. owned) by foreigners. For example, in Canada, telecommunications carriers are prohibited from having more than 20% of the voting shares held by non-Canadians (Lexology, 2017). Other countries can have different restrictions. The effect of these restrictions operates as a position limit on the aggregate of foreign traders in that stock.

Every trade by an entity subject to the restriction that decreases the margin to the limit operates as a cost for that trade. Even if a given trade is profitable on its own, its profitability is decreased in proportion to the probability that a future desired trade will be prohibited because of the limit. Thus, the cost is reasonably visible in the sense that these limits are well publicized and accounted for, but very nonlinear since this probability is not a straightforward function of how much we trade.

Over my career I've worked in many different offices, from low-end tilt-up office parks to high-end prestige offices with expansive views of the great cities of the world. One memorable office had the unfortunate property that during strong rain, the window leaked and my right-most monitors got wet. I had to cover them with a towel whenever the skies opened up. Even worse, the air conditioning once broke during the two hottest weeks of the year. We rented some portable AC units that looked like something out of the movie *Brazil*, wore ice vests, and ate a steady supply of smoothies and frozen yogurts until the building AC coughed back to life.

Nicer offices mostly eliminate these sorts of events, but that comfort comes at the expense of a set of war stories that I still reminisce about today. There's a lot to be said for the cohesion and bonding that comes from feeling like you're besieged on all sides by competitors and even the building you're in. Posh offices cost more, and maybe they come with more intangible costs too.

Quadrant 3: Invisible Linear Costs

There are a few costs that fall into this category, but for a trading firm the most important of these by far is trade depreciation. This idea goes by many names in the literature, but they all refer to the same phenomenon: the very act of trading profitably destroys the profitability of the trade. I've already touched on this idea a few times in the preceding chapters and it's no wonder that it runs like a thread through this book, connecting together different concepts:

- The fundamental fact of adverse selection we discussed in Chapter 2
- The way in which risk and liquidity interact in Chapters 3 and 4
- The proper development of stories about edge in Chapter 5
- Determining whether models are still valid and valuable in Chapter 6

The idea of trade depreciation is so fundamental that it's worth looking at it from various angles. Right now, I'm interested in a more analytic understanding of the phenomenon. What are the mechanics? How is it that your current trading makes your future trading worse?

The key insight is one you saw in Chapter 2. Every trade you do sends a signal to the market about your beliefs. If that trade is a profitable one, the signal is like a beacon to would-be competitors: "Here lies money!" Perhaps competitors can't uniquely identify your profitable trades specifically. But, if they're given enough time, they can actually piece together sufficient information to understand enough of the trade such that they can duplicate it (perhaps poorly). And even poor imitators, given enough time and enough of them, will eat away at the profitable trades you've identified.

The more you trade, the more information you leak to the world.[3] Thus, the cost is a linear (or nearly linear) one. It is perhaps controversial to view the future reduced profitability of a trade as a cost to a present (not-yet-less-profitable) one. Yet this idea of the present value of a cost is in fact quite a mainstream approach in accounting. When companies buy capital goods, they begin depreciating their value immediately. The capital good is still perfectly usable, yet you account for it by reducing its value over time. Why is this a valid approach when thinking about a trading strategy? Simply because it helps guide your decision-making on where to deploy resources.

You run a trading firm with $5 million in working capital and you're considering deploying two strategies, A and B. You believe each of these can trade $10 million per day and make $1,000 while using the $5 million of capital allocated to it. However, you have good reason to believe that the edge upon which strategy A relies is likely to disappear rather quickly, whereas the edge of strategy B is a more durable one with a slower rate of decay. Without accounting for the cost of trade depreciation, you would be indifferent to deploying strategy A or B, or perhaps you'd allocate half the capital to each. When you look at the depreciation rates, however, it's optimal to make a different decision. But which decision? Should A or B get more capital? The answer is less obvious than it might appear.

- *Argument:* A relies on some short-lived information that is likely to disappear quickly. You should allocate your capital to A until it starts to disappear, then transfer to B.
- *Counterargument:* Why is profit from A any better than profit from B? Money is money, so if you agree that A and B are equally profitable on day 1, they should get the same amount of capital allocated to them. Once A decays, we transfer capital to B.
- *Argument:* B is the more useful long-term strategy, in the sense that its lifetime P&L will be higher than A. You should invest your resources in B early, so that you can get on the learning curve of improving B. If you're successful, you may even create a sort of first-mover advantage where your continued innovation makes it even more difficult for competitors to get a toehold in the trade.

You can likely come up with more arguments for the relative allocation of resources to A and B. In the end, there is no knockdown argument because all the little details I haven't specified do matter. For example: what is the source of A's edge? Is it a one-time thing (like a new market opening up, or a trade based on short-lived news that recently came out), or is it something that, once you start trading, others will quickly see and copy? Or is it a bit of both? How improvable do you think B is? All of the questions critically affect your allocation decisions. Again, the important thing is that you now have a framework for thinking about these decisions. Without such a framework, you'd be making the decisions anyway, implicitly, but without full knowledge of the effects of those decisions.

Estimating Depreciation Rates

A natural question now arises: if you agree that you need to account for the depreciation of a trade in deciding how much capital to allocate to it, how do you come up with these depreciation rates? As you might expect by now, this is one of the most difficult questions to answer in trading. The story you're after is now a second-order story. One that tells you how your story of edge will cease to function over time, and so crucially dependent on the details of the edge and the models. Here are some useful directions:

- What is the source of the edge? How robust is that source, and how quickly do the people against whom you're trading react? If, for example, the source of your edge is your ability to connect and trade in some exotic market, you can probably figure out who else would be interested in doing a similar trade, what hoops they need to jump through to duplicate your efforts, and so on.
- What depreciation rates have you seen in similar trades in the past? This information is useful but, much like in the discussion on data in Chapter 6, care must be taken to interpret it correctly.
- What are your current or theorized hit-miss ratios? Trades that (a) you accurately believe are profitable and that (b) have extremely high hit rates (i.e. no one is competing with you for these trades) tend not to last very long. Conversely, if you believe you are entering an already competitive trading environment, any edge you accurately believe is there is likely to be more durable.

A Little-Appreciated Fact about Trade Depreciation

So far, the discussion of trade depreciation has either explicitly or implicitly assumed that you're undertaking profitable trades. But what if you're doing trades you expect to lose money? Recall the discussion on risk in Chapter 3, where you saw that it can be quite rational to lose money hedging in order to achieve a better risk profile for a trade. So how does trade depreciation work with "bad" trades? As it turns out, bad trades get better! Recall that every trade you do is a signal to the world. Your hedging behavior is, over time, reliably signaling "I don't know anything, I'm happy to lose money here." The world will react to this signal by competing to trade against you. This competition is good for your hedging trades: the competition will, in aggregate, provide you with a better price over time and your hedges will lose less money.

In fact, you can restate the insight about trade depreciation more simply: over time the edge of any trade goes to zero (ignoring trading fees, financing cost, etc.). Whether it started on the positive or negative side is not important; over time the world will adapt and markets will become more efficient. And efficient markets, by their very definition, do not admit profitable or unprofitable strategies. All strategies in a perfectly efficient market (again, ignoring other costs) have an expected value of 0.

Quadrant 4: Invisible Nonlinear Costs

All the costs that don't fall into the other categories falls into this one. As such, this category is a bit of a catchall, and at least for this reason, the costs in this category are the most difficult to perceive, think about, and account for. Let's look at a few examples in this category to get a sense of what we're dealing with, and to see how this analysis can generalize to other Quadrant 4 costs.

Herding

Most trading firms like to think their profitable trading strategies are unique flowers, developed in a hothouse of intellectual discovery and brilliance. However, the more self-aware subset of these traders realizes that, in most cases, there is very little that's new under the sun. As you saw in the introduction, people have been trading for millennia so it stands to reason that inventing a brand-new trading strategy whole-cloth is an unlikely proposition.

More likely, again in most cases, is that a given strategy has many other close cousins. Other firms have either (a) independently discovered something substantially similar to your strategy, (b) you've snatched some intellectual property from someone else, or (c) someone else has done the same to you. Success, famously, has many parents and this is certainly true in trading. For example, many of the world's greatest hedge funds and proprietary trading firms owe their genesis in one way or another to Ed Thorp's Princeton/Newport Partners. Similar things are true of the offspring of DE Shaw and Renaissance Technologies.

Given this fact, it's worth examining in detail the situation where your strategy operates where parallel versions of a substantially similar strategy are also operating. Just such a situation occurred in 1998 around a few trades that most memorably were operated by Long Term Capital Management (LTCM). The story of the collapse of LTCM (and the near-collapse of the financial system) is elegantly detailed in *When Genius Failed* (Lowenstein, 2001). In what follows I extract the important details so that you can draw the appropriate lessons regarding the dangers of herding behavior.

LTCM was a hedge fund that famously had two Nobel Prize–winning economists (Myron Scholes and Robert Merton) among its partners. During the spring of 1998, LCTM was considered the best, most skillful hedge fund in the world. Broker-dealers competed to improve their relationships with the firm, extending loans and lines of credit under very favorable terms. And so it was that in 1998, the trades that LTCM was involved in included:

- *Short equity volatility.* Essentially, LTCM was selling insurance against large moves in the equity market. Perhaps not surprisingly, the perceived edge on this trade was derived from some of the work that Merton and Scholes did to win their Nobel Prize.
- *Long illiquid high-yield bonds, short low-yield high-quality bonds.* Their bet was that the spread on the yields between the two would shrink.
- *Long Russian government debt, denominated in Russian rubles.* They were betting on the stability of the Russian economy and the associated value of the ruble.

There were, of course, many other trades that LTCM was involved in but these suffice to describe the general characteristics of the trades in which they engaged. Generally speaking, they had insurance-selling characteristics: these trades did reasonably well when markets behaved normally but had the potential to suffer large losses if markets began acting oddly or panicking.

As it happens, this is exactly what began to occur in earnest on August 17, 1998. The Russian government announced that it would no longer service (i.e. make interest payments for) debt held by foreigners and began measures to devalue the ruble. Along with other difficulties in Asian emerging markets, this caused the broader market to flee riskier investments in favor of safer harbors during the oncoming storm.

It's important to note that, although there was a general "flight to quality," the incredible variety of securities, instruments, and trades in modern markets means that even under stress, markets don't all move in the same direction. Nevertheless, LTCM's positions did indeed *all* begin to move against them in the summer of 1998. How could this be? LTCM's partnership was reputedly the most skillful on Wall Street. Could they really have gotten *everything* wrong?

Of course, the answer is no. And there is a different and more interesting explanation for the incredible correlation between LTCM's supposedly uncorrelated positions: the very fact that LTCM held them. Recall that LTCM was the world's best and most famous hedge fund. Everyone wanted to facilitate their trades, and everyone wanted to imitate their trades. So much so that the prop trading desks of the brokers who traded with LTCM also put on the same trades as them. Monkey see, monkey do.

In practical terms, what this meant is that, even if LTCM's positions in a given trade were reasonable (albeit somewhat large), the aggregate of the market doing LTCM-like trades was, by some estimates, factors larger. For example, say that LTCM was long 5% of the market in illiquid high-yield US corporate bonds. As a practical matter, the aggregate pseudo-LTCM representing both LTCM and its herd of imitators could have had as much as 15–20% of that market. In times of stress, when these leveraged bets begin to suffer losses, it's natural that some of the less well-funded imitators would receive margin calls (as I described in Chapter 3) that they could not meet. The result is a fire sale of those positions, which exacerbates the losses in these markets. These markets lost much of the heterogeneity of participants, since a lot of the money invested in them was invested for the same reason and was subject to the same constraints. Thus, LTCM's herd of imitators made its positions significantly more subject to quick movements, untethered from financial fundamentals, which not even LTCM could weather.[4]

Even if your own trades aren't as large or systemically important as those of LTCM's, the principle of herding nonetheless applies. Trades that make money attract imitators, and fashionable trades even more so. Examples are legion of trades whose participants individually had prudent risk management practices, especially in regard to trade sizing, but whose fashionable nature created a herd of participants all acting virtually identically. The effect is that, when markets move against a given trade with these characteristics, those markets can move with significantly more speed and ferocity than any historically based or reasoned judgment could predict. Herding risk is a cost worth accounting for.

The story of LTCM is usually told as a cautionary tale of hubris and ivory-tower academics meeting the messy real world and eventually losing. But it's hard to draw practical, useful conclusions from such a reading of the events of 1998. "Be less hubristic" sounds great but is really hard to turn into practical information. The view of LTCM as a story of concrete mistakes in trading (sizing, herding, etc.) is more useful from two perspectives: first actually avoiding the mistakes LTCM committed, and secondly as a way to draw more general lessons that can apply even if you're not "the greatest hedge fund on earth."

Accounting for Herding Risk

The key to thinking about herding risk is to evaluate as dispassionately as possible how well-known is the edge upon which the trade is based. Some small trades that emerged sui generis are quite plausibly one-offs, but most profitable trades are known and have been known for decades. If those trades have recently had a good run of profitability, it stands to reason that there is a larger herd of people trading that strategy than when the trade wasn't as profitable. Thus, recent (depending on the trade, weeks to months to years) performance is an important component of herding cost.

Another important component is the liquidity and heterogeneity of the markets involved. What you're trying to assess is what fraction of the total trading volume in the markets can be attributed to people doing the trade you're doing. If the fraction is large (anything over 10% should be considered large, given the typical leverage ratios in modern trading) then it's likely that herding is a significant risk and hence cost to the trade.

Finally, you should evaluate, much like the analysis in Chapter 3, what other markets relate to the traded one. How well matched are the risks, and what can cause that matchup to break down under stress? You're looking for pools of liquidity that you could take advantage of in a stress event. Such judgments are not easy to make and require both creativity and experience in the markets in question. It pays to have a long memory of all the ways markets can become crazy.

Reinventing the wheel happens often in financial markets. After the first few years of my trading career, I had a decent understanding of how markets worked and as a result I was always on the lookout for new patterns and trading ideas. I had more enthusiasm and ambition than experience, however, which meant that many of the things I "discovered" were either trades we were already doing on another desk, or well-known trades we *weren't* doing, for good reasons.

Later in my career I saw the same phenomenon with newer traders I was mentoring. It seems every equities trader goes through the stage of "discovering" the mean-reversion trade between Berkshire-Hathaway A versus B shares, or Royal Dutch Shell shares in London and Amsterdam. Bond traders reinvent the on-the-run versus off-the-run trade, and foreign exchange traders find carry trades between currencies. It's easy to ridicule, but first you have to find the well-known things before you find the subtle things. I always tried to encourage people to keep looking, in the same way I was encouraged when I first started out.

Opportunity Cost

Another interesting Quadrant 4 cost is opportunity cost. This is simply the cost incurred through not doing something that would be profitable if you did it. You may ask why you didn't do this profitable thing, and the answer is typically "because I was doing something else." You may also suppose that this is an easy cost to account for, but as you'll see, matters relating to opportunity cost are complex.

Let's again consider a situation with two strategies, A and B. You're currently doing strategy A, which earns $1,000 per day. You estimate that if you were to do strategy B it would earn $600 per day. The opportunity cost you're paying by not doing B is $600 per day. Clearly stopping A in order to do B is a losing proposition (to the tune of $400 per day) but things are rarely this clear-cut. For one, what if you can find a way to do both A *and* B? If you can find efficiencies in the way you execute A (manpower, compute resources, capital, etc.) while minimizing the impact on A, then you can use the freed-up resources to start doing a bit of strategy B.

In practice, these sorts of clear-cut situations rarely present themselves. In a well-functioning trading organization, there is a set of strategies you're currently executing, and a set of strategies you'd like to execute if you had the resources to do so. The real decision to be made, assuming you know what strategies you'd execute if you had the resources, is how many resources you should divert from executing your current strategies to the task of making your execution itself more efficient. There is a very real tradeoff between maximizing the value of the strategies today as compared to the benefits of improving efficiency so that you can grow your capacity to execute strategies.

This sort of resource-allocation problem isn't unique to trading, of course, and there is a rich literature on how to approach the question. For these purposes, the important part is the insight that such a tradeoff indeed exists. In trading, fortunately, the problem is made somewhat easier by the fact that, for well-functioning strategies, it's very difficult to devote all your resources to pure execution/maximization even if you did want to. As a simple example, financial markets have largely well-defined trading hours. Even if you'd like to maximize the profitability of your exchange-listed US options trading business, there is very little you can do to further that immediate goal before 9:30am and after 4:00pm. Markets simply aren't open. To the extent that you have resources available outside those hours, aside from maintenance and other housekeeping tasks, you can devote them to either improving your current strategy's efficiency or on working on new strategies.

Of course, this isn't the end of the story. Resources are famously nonfungible. That is, not all resources are made equal: people vary in their skill sets and inclinations, and there is also variation in any number of other human factors (relationships with counter-parties, brokers, and exchanges) or even tech resources to some extent (location of computers and servers, their interconnection, software, etc.). By understanding these details, you can make good decisions on creating and maintaining a plan for addressing the maximization-today versus find-efficiency-for-tomorrow tradeoff.

Unknown Unknowns

In the preceding discussion on opportunity cost, I've assumed that you have a good sense of what strategy B is, what it looks like, how to implement it, and so forth. In practice this is rarely the case. Ideally, you should have good ideas for the next marginal trade you'd implement if you had resources to spare, but these "adjacent" strategies are rarely the dominant concern when considering opportunity cost. In any competitive market, the lion's share of the cost of not doing something is contained in the ideas you'd pursue *if you knew of their existence.* This sort of exploratory opportunity cost ends up being (a) extremely difficult to account for and (b) a defining factor in the success and failure of companies long-term.

First brought to popular attention in *The Innovator's Dilemma* (Christensen, 1997), the idea of disruptive innovation has, in the last 20 years, gained an almost dominant perch in the strategic worldview of modern business. The core of the theory is that large companies with established large market share in mature markets lose during technological transitions because they overinvest in marginal improvements to current products and businesses and underinvest in ideas that could supplant those businesses. The canonical example of this process is Kodak, which went from a dominant position in film photography to bankruptcy in a quarter century by virtue of missing the digital imagery revolution. As if to punctuate the cautionary tale with an irresistible piece of schadenfreudian irony, Kodak was one of the original innovators of the digital camera.

On the heels of the book's positive reception, every management consultant worth their salt was coaching companies on how to immunize themselves against disruptive change, and how to restructure themselves to favor more agility and flexibility. For a time in the late 1990s and early 2000s, everything was disruption. And, as can be expected with a revolutionary pseudo-philosophical theory that takes the business world by storm, the inevitable backlash eventually came. The pushback reached its zenith with Jill Lepore's 2014 *New Yorker* article "The Disruption Machine" (Lepore, 2014). In it she lays out a case partially against Christensen's academic scholarship, but she mostly criticizes the manner in which the lessons of his work have been applied in the broader business world.

So, what do I make of this universe of ideas, with the benefit of some detachment and distance? Lepore is certainly right to point out inconsistencies and arbitrary (some might say handpicked) limits and breakpoints in Christensen's original studies. And it is true that, under some subsequent more expansive and philosophical formulations of the disruptive innovation idea, the theory becomes more of an unfalsifiable folk religion than a scientific or even predictive theory of business.

But in spite of these valid criticisms, it's hard to argue against the idea of disruptive innovation as a coherent explanation for the historical developments in competitive tech and tech-adjacent businesses. Kodak really did screw up a golden opportunity in the 1990s, and Uber/Lyft really did cause the value of a New York taxi medallion to drop from around $1.3 million in 2013 to around $160,000 in 2018.

The important aspects of disruptive innovation, of the unknown unknowns that represent threats to a profitable business, concern the question of how to account for these factors as explicit costs of a business. It's relatively easy to intone the words "disruptive innovation" as a sort of mantra, but those words don't help guide strategic decision-making: what to work on, what to spend money and time on, and how much to do so. At a more abstract level, the answers to those questions end up being inseparable from the organization of the business itself. And it's those questions I want to examine here.

In studying the history of organizations that have weathered technological disruptions and themselves created them, one stands alone: AT&T in the first half of the twentieth century. And, as described in meticulous detail in *The Idea Factory* (Gertner, 2013), the part of AT&T known as Bell Labs was the engine of innovation that permitted this nearly uninterrupted run of dominance for over 50 years. All this happened during arguably the greatest period of innovation in human history. So, what was so special about AT&T and Bell Labs? It turns out the answers lie partly in the economics of being a monopolist, as can be expected. But mostly, and from this perspective most instructively, the answer is sociological. It was the structural and sociological organization of Bell Labs that made it so special.

Bell Labs and the Sociology of Innovation

To begin with, you should understand exactly the role that Bell Labs played in the development of technology in the twentieth century. A highly abridged list of Bell Labs discoveries, developments, and firsts follows:

- Eight independent Nobel Prizes awarded to Bell Labs researchers
- The invention of synchronized images and sound in movies (1926)
- Radio astronomy (1931)
- Stereo audio recordings and transmission (1933)
- The solar cell and the first P-N semiconductor junction (1939)
- The transistor (1947)
- The foundations and most important results in information theory (1948)
- Modern cryptography (1949)
- Lasers (1958)
- The MOSFET transistor, the building block of all modern computer chips (1960)
- The first communications satellite, Telstar (1962)
- Nearly all of the technologies necessary to mass-produce computer chips (1960s)
- UNIX (1969)
- The C computer language (1972)
- Fiber optic communication (1976)

- The main cellular telephony architectures and technologies (1970s and 1980s)
- The C++ computer language (1979)

It's no exaggeration to say that without the inventions of Bell Labs in the twentieth century, the world would look substantially different. So, what was it about Bell Labs that allowed this incredible density and production rate of world-changing inventions? Many different people have tried to answer this question, not least the people who worked at Bell Labs during this time.

Among the most perceptive, at least in public remarks, was the long-time president of Bell Labs Mervin Kelly. In a 1950 address to the Royal Society in London, Kelly described the organization of Bell Labs as having three groups:

1. A group of scientists and engineers who did the really exploratory basic research
2. A group of engineers who kept abreast of the work of the first group with an eye to integrating their discoveries into existing problems faced by AT&T
3. A group of engineers and technologists whose job was to actually put into production the new ideas and products developed by the previous two groups

Such a division of labor is eminently reasonable, and not particularly unique to Bell Labs. The interaction among them, however, was certainly unique for the time. The boundaries between the groups were quite porous and not particularly well defined. Kelly remarked that Bell Labs operated as a sort of organism, with exchanges of ideas going across all three groups. In addition to formal meetings, a culture of informal get-togethers was encouraged as a matter of policy. Even the most senior and famous researchers at Bell Labs (some of the most eminent scientists in the world at the time) were expected to receive even the most junior employees when the latter had questions and requests.

The effect of this culture was to make the transmission, understanding, debate, and development of ideas the primary currency of the labs. Many modern workplaces have attempted to duplicate the outward trappings of such a culture, with well-stocked breakrooms, ping-pong tables, and such. But ping-pong tables do not, in and of themselves, create the open and collaborative culture evidenced by Bell Labs. Creating such a culture takes a concerted effort by senior employees, both as a formal matter of policy and as informal cultural behavior, to enforce those norms of openness and curiosity.

Another unique-at-the-time characteristic of Bell Labs was its emphasis on continuing education. Again, many modern companies pay lip service to this goal, usually by (partially) funding employee continuing education at local universities or colleges. Bell Labs did something more difficult and valuable: they developed their own syllabus of graduate-level courses and taught this syllabus to any and all interested employees on the Bell Labs campus. This was more than just after-work talks; this was a concerted effort to teach everyone who was interested as much as they could manage to learn, all taught by the very scientists who—in many cases—invented the fields they were teaching.

The third important characteristic evidenced by Bell Labs concerned the relationship between scientists and the real-world effects and consequences of their work. To put it simply, even the greatest scientists were expected to get their hands dirty. To help with this undertaking, Bell Labs employed technical staff who, even though they might not have had the advanced degrees of their scientist bosses, were more than a match for them in practical knowledge of how to build devices, instruments, and products. Culturally, Bell Labs held this technical staff in high respect, which again provided avenues for the transmission of ideas across groups of people.

Finally, we learn from John Pierce, a maverick in electronics and one of the directors of the Telstar project, about the value of failure. He claimed late in life that one of the important values of the Bell Labs approach to research is that a given line of investigation could be allowed to fail, and that such a failure wouldn't reflect badly on the people involved in the project. While in a more mainstream development environment such an idea would be considered heresy, in a research environment where "most ideas are bound to fail," such an approach is critically important. Without the protection of being able to *fail successfully*, very few would be motivated to take the risks necessary to do truly groundbreaking work.

Summarizing, we can identify three main sociological facts about Bell Labs that, if people like Mervin Kelly are to be believed, created the conditions for such a creative workplace:

- Hire the best people possible and create a culture where openness and transmission of ideas are the highest ideal.
- Invest heavily in educating your workforce. Don't outsource the task of designing the curriculum, nor the one of teaching it.
- Connect basic research to real-world problem as much as possible. Segmentation and stratification of concerns is a structure to be assiduously avoided.
- Failure is a necessary counterpart to exploratory research. Failed projects do not reflect badly on the project team.

Given all we've been told about disruptive innovation in the last two decades, it's easy to view the above list cynically as a set of platitudes about creating a good work environment. Yet arguably, the reason they seem like platitudes is because the ideas are easy to co-opt. It's straightforward to create the veneer of openness, of education, of practicality, but another thing altogether to actually put these ideas into true practice. And let's not forget, Bell Labs pioneered this sociology of innovation nearly a century before people like Clayton Christensen studied these ideas.

The Landscape of Trades

Each of the costs examined above lives in a competitive world of alternatives. For example, if one exchange begins to charge too much in fees, another exchange can begin to provide lookalike services at lower fees.

A similar competitive landscape applies to the total cost of doing any given trade. This leads us, finally, back to our rule about costs:

If you think your costs are negligible relative to your edge, you're wrong about at least one of them.

This rule is saying that magical super-profitable trades don't really exist in the real world. If a trade appears to have far more edge than other available trades, then that appearance is illusory. But why?

Overestimating Profitability

Consider the landscape of all possible trades. This is an extremely high-dimensional space, with an axis for every possible variable in a trade's implementation. A given specific trade (edge, model, etc.) represents a point in this very large landscape. Since nearly every parameter can be varied in a continuous manner, and since I've already defined a good edge as one that's robust to small parameter variations, the region around a given hyper-profitable trade must also be essentially profitable. This is akin to saying that the region around the very peak of a large mountain is also high in elevation. Continuing down the mountain, nearer the base, applying this continuity argument tells you that there must exist a large region of at least notably high profitability. In fact, the whole region surrounding the hypothetical hyper-profitable trade, a region defined by reasonable variations in the parameters of the trade, is somewhat profitable.

It should be evident why such a large and obvious region cannot exist in a competitive world. Perhaps you can posit that you're the first to have discovered one particular super-profitable spot in this extremely multidimensional space of trades. But the idea that there is a largish region of high profitability that has somehow eluded every single one of the world's traders? That seems unlikely. Much more likely is that you have misunderstood something about the trade, specifically how profitable it is.

Underestimating Cost

One of the very best ways to overestimate profitability is to underestimate costs of all descriptions. So how do you test your beliefs about costs? For Quadrant 1 costs, the visible near-linear ones, the best way to evaluate them is to simply do a small trade, known as a test trade, to examine all the steps in the process. It's not uncommon, especially in frontier countries and other new markets, to be completely unaware of very market-specific costs, taxes, or restrictions that materially affect a trade until you actually do a trade.

It's worth noting that cost, broadly considered, is the reason for the rise of index funds and ETFs over the last 20 years. After all, the reason that mutual funds underperform their indices (as a group) isn't that they do bad trades. It's simply that they do too many trades, and the cost of this excessive trading is the cause of the underperformance. As the late great Jack Bogle, founder of the Vanguard fund empire, successfully spread the story of cost-based underperformance, the broader investing world shifted to the modern model: one that takes cost into account as *the* primary consideration for retail investors.

Another common underestimation of costs appears when trying to scale a trade up in size. Suppose you do a test trade and see that everything checks out. Now it's time to trade in real size. Yet once you do, you see that your trade loses its profitability. Sometimes it's relatively easy to see why: machines and systems that can't handle the trading in some way, or perhaps the trade isn't nearly as automated as you expected and requires more human capital to run (decreasing its profitability). But frequently, sizing up a trade kills its profitability because of market impact, a Quadrant 3 cost. It's easy to underestimate how markets react to your new presence in it, and typically you find that you can trade far less than you expected before the market adjusts to compensate for your presence. This market impact is an important component of trade depreciation, and it's hard to get good estimates of it without actually doing the trading.

It's also easy to underestimate day-on-day depreciation of a trade. A profitable trade attracts attention, and even if you're the only person doing the trade on Day 1, by Day 4 there will be a crowd of people trying to figure out the trade and how to get in on it. Profitability is conspicuous and breeds imitators. Your brokers in particular will love to tell your competitors, perhaps in oblique and polite conversations over dinner, about the hot new trade you seem to be doing.

Finally, have you underestimated the cost you should be paying your people (traders, technologists, operations, and support) to facilitate this highly profitable trade? No matter what powers of moral suasion and airtight employment contracts you may possess, if your employees see that a trade makes a lot of money and they're only getting a small fraction of it, you may find people voting with their feet and setting up a competitive operation somewhere else. This phenomenon is indeed the genesis of many modern trading firms. I will have much more to say about this and related issues in Chapter 9.

The Ownership of Trades

This last point about trades getting copied or taken also opens the door to a broader question of what trades are, really. Are they intellectual property: something you own? Certainly, case law in the Western world upholds this view. I'm going to argue that it's much more productive to view trades in a different light, no matter their legal status. As I said in Chapter 5, a profitable trade is due to something you know or can do that the marginal participant doesn't or cannot. And there doesn't seem to be much in the way of ownership surrounding either of those concepts.

Imagine being an explorer who discovers a previously uncharted mountain valley. You consider this valley breathtakingly beautiful, and so you decide to build a small cabin and live there peacefully and in solitude for the rest of your days. Life is hard but this wonderful solitude is, as it was for Walt Whitman, what you've been seeking all these years. Nevertheless, your absence back home is noted, and since at least a few people know where you were exploring, one of your friends decides to go look for you. Eventually she too stumbles on this valley, shares your view about its transcendent beauty, and also decides to move there. You see your friend's cabin every so often, and although it does limit your blissful isolation in small ways, it doesn't affect your life all that much. It really is a beautiful valley and the fishing is superb.

Fast forward a few decades, and it's clear that the backpacker hostel, dive bars, and endless tour companies have definitely ruined the place. The mountain valley is still in the same physical spot, but it's no longer the beautiful mountain valley you had discovered.

While you might have been able, in the beginning, to buy up all the mountain valley land and erect large walls surrounding it, in the trading world such actions are difficult, costly, and don't work very well. In practice, you're never the owner of a trade, merely a caretaker. And the better care you take of it, the longer you'll enjoy the fruits of your labors.

Summary and Looking Ahead

- Far from being a boring technical matter, properly thinking about and accounting for costs opens windows into some quite fundamental ideas about innovation and progress.
- The most interesting and important costs to consider, over the long term, are the ones that are hard to see and hard to estimate.

- Building a culture that is robust to the inexorable cost pressure of trading is critical for long-term success.
- Hyper-profitable trades rarely exist, and if they do they don't live long.
- It's more productive to view trades as discoveries rather than property.

In the next chapter, I'll cover some of the more abstract and philosophical ideas in the book: what sorts of things are possible in the world, and how you can understand the distinction between "it can't happen" and "it's never happened." And more concretely, you'll see that many of financial history's greatest disasters came about through assuming some event was impossible, as opposed to it being an event that hadn't happened yet.

References

Christensen, C. (1997). *The Innovator's Dilemma.* New York: HBR Press.
Eavis, P. (2013). Retrieved from https://dealbook.nytimes.com/2013/07/25/sac-case-threatens-a-wall-st-cash-cow/.
Gertner, J. (2013). *The Idea Factory.* New York: Penguin.
Lepore, J. (2014, June 23). "The Disruption Machine." *New Yorker.*
Lexology. (2017, 02 16). Retrieved from https://www.lexology.com/library/detail.aspx?g=545805cd-814e-433c-b141-09bba35a1247.
Lowenstein, R. (2001). *When Genius Failed.* New York: Random House.

CHAPTER

Possibility

Six Impossible Things before Breakfast

In Chapter 5 of Lewis Carroll's *Alice in Wonderland,* Alice meets the White Queen, who says she's 101 years old. Alice says she can't believe her, to which the Queen responds by asking her to try. Alice responds, "One can't believe impossible things." Undeterred, the Queen responds, "I daresay you haven't had much practice. When I was your age, I always did it for half-an-hour a day. Why, sometimes I've believed as many as six impossible things before breakfast."

It's easy to dismiss this exchange as yet another nonsensical piece of dialogue, but like much of Alice in Wonderland, there is something about it that resists such a dismissal. Is it possible to believe in impossible things? What does it feel like to do so?

Western philosophy has a firmly-rooted tradition of splitting extremely fine hairs when talking about something as seemingly basic as what's "possible." Partly this is because philosophers do like to split hairs. But these distinctions—ones that we've learned to draw over the millennia—are real ones. The result of all this hair-splitting is that by now humans have a hefty account of what we mean when we say *possible* or *impossible.* Here, I will only touch on the parts of this work that are relevant for this chapter, but for those of you interested in this fascinating area, the Stanford Encyclopedia of Philosophy is an excellent starting point (Kment, 2017).

Logical Possibility

If something is said to be logically possible, that means that it cannot be proven false by logic alone. Conversely, something that is logically impossible can be shown to be false by mere application of the rules of logic. A married bachelor is a logical impossibility since the commonsense definition of "bachelor" expressly requires the person to be unmarried. Simple examples such as these illustrate the point, but for more complex matters it can become difficult to determine whether some conceivable state of affairs is *actually* ruled out by the judicious application of logical deduction.[1]

Getting back to the White Queen, it's clear that it's not really possible to believe in logically impossible things. They're internally incoherent, so it seems a stretch to be able to believe in them. There's no coherent "them" in which to believe!

Physical Possibility

This type of possibility considers things that are possible in our actual universe. For example, a moon made of blue cheese is certainly logically possible. But it isn't physically possible since the tidal forces experienced by the moon would soon rip apart any celestial body with such poor structural rigidity. This may be a silly example, but the reasons for the physical impossibility of a blue cheese moon contain, implicitly, a wealth of information and knowledge about the actual universe in which we live.

Under this definition of impossibility, it's actually quite easy to do as the White Queen says, and "believe in the impossible." In fact, much of science advances because researchers seriously entertain the possibility of "impossible" things (at least, as far as existing scientific theory goes). You then design experiments to test how impossible they actually are.

The requirement for actual knowledge is the key distinguishing factor when thinking about logical versus physical possibility. Evaluating the former does not require any knowledge other than understanding the rules of logic. You simply examine the definition of terms, and keep pushing down to more basic definitions, until eventually you (hopefully, if you're a good-enough logician) find either a proof of impossibility or an example that proves a claim isn't impossible. By contrast, in order to understand whether a claim or concept is physically possible, you do need to understand the world. For more subtle claims, your understanding may well have to be very good. You may have to run experiments to test ideas and claims. At any rate, you certainly can't sit back in an armchair to make determinations about physical possibility.

The Inductive Hypothesis

Bear with me as I pick up the second bit of philosophical scaffolding you'll need: an understanding of induction. As a motivating example, I ask: how did the ancients know at sundown that the sun was going to rise again the next day? (Munroe, n.d.). They didn't really *know* properly speaking. They certainly weren't clairvoyant about the future, nor is anyone today (to our knowledge). But very few people at the time would have bet against the proposition that the sun would rise tomorrow. After all, they had seen it rise for about as long as anyone could remember, without fail, and it would have seemed like a reasonable supposition. Perhaps without realizing it, they were making use of the inductive hypothesis.

What's Special about Today?

The inductive hypothesis merely states that, if one has seen some regularity in the past, it makes sense that it should continue in the future. This is an eminently reasonable hypothesis, and in fact without it we wouldn't be able to make almost any claims about the world. For instance, all of science is predicated on the notion of physical laws that don't arbitrarily change. A famous example in philosophy demonstrates these ideas.

Consider two hypotheses: (A) all things that are green will remain green, and (B) some of the things that are green are in fact grue: they'll be the color green until August 14, 2021, at which point they will transform into the color blue. Obviously, hypothesis B is laughable. But why exactly is it laughable? You may appeal to your knowledge of physics: we've never seen any such color transformations in the past. But hypothesis B cares not for your science: it posits that of course you haven't seen such a transformation before, since it's never happened before. This grue business is a one-time transformation. In fact, there is no scientific or narrowly rational argument that would make us believe A over B. And yet we do.

The reason we believe in A and discount B is because of a meta-rational reason: what's so special about us? The universe has been around for over 10 billion years. If we ask ourselves what's so magical about some specific point in the universe's development that would explain a one-time change in the laws of physics, we come up empty. The meta-rational argument is "what's so special about today"?

It's hard to overstate the importance of induction in how we learn about and view the world. Regularity, the idea that things will behave as they did before, without arbitrary changes, underpins our ability to learn about the world. It would be hard to learn to walk if floors randomly changed their hardness or moved about randomly. It would be hard to learn how to deal with people if their personalities changed from one day to the next. And it would be particularly difficult to learn about the probability of a normal coin coming up heads if this probability itself changed over time. As we'll see, this last example hits quite close to home when thinking about financial markets.

Induction in Financial Markets

So, what does all this philosophy have to do with trading? It's that we need induction and the inductive hypothesis (IH) to have any hope of making money trading. If the arbitrage between two securities disappears randomly from one day to the next, there's no arbitrage to be done. If people randomly decide to start or stop trading a given stock, you can't have a business making markets in it. We need regularity in order to make plans and predictions. But markets have an inherent and ineradicable randomness, and this makes the IH an unreliable tool. The key question we have to ask ourselves, in order to justifiably use the IH is "is the future going to be like the past?" In order to answer this question, we have to look at the relevant properties of markets:

- *Markets are stochastic.* As we saw in Chapter 2, the world is so complex that it's impossible for any one entity to fully understand why prices move as they do. We can't avoid modeling the world as containing some fundamental randomness that we'll never, in a practical sense, be able to remove.
- *Markets are self-organized feedback systems.* The information transmission that is enabled by markets means that all actions are reactions to either news about the world, or previous actions.

You need induction, but the combination of the above facts makes using it a dangerous proposition when dealing with financial markets. This leads to this chapter's rule.

> Just because something has never happened doesn't mean it can't. Corollary: Enough people relying on something being true makes it false.

I've already discussed at length the characteristics of financial markets that make them fundamentally random. What you need now is a detailed account of how feedback works in the context of trading.

Feedback Systems and Their Stability

Feedback is a property of systems whose outputs are coupled to their inputs. For example, it is this property that gives explosives their power. There is potential energy stored in the chemical (or nuclear, in the case of nuclear explosives) bonds of the material. The feedback mechanism works as follows: the act of releasing the potential energy in some molecules (or atoms) triggers the release of potential energy in adjacent molecules or atoms. The output (this release of energy in the form of heat or momentum) is used as an input to the same reaction.

The above is an example of positive feedback. Negative feedback is also possible and in fact it's a central property of living things. A simple mechanical example is that of a household thermostat. If the house gets too cold, a bimetallic strip changes shape, triggering a switch that turns on the furnace. Once the house is hot enough, the bimetallic strip changes back, turning off the switch and hence the furnace. Your body has similar mechanisms (known as homeostasis) for regulating heat, as well as hunger, thirst, heart rate, breathing, and just about every other chemical process that imbues you with life.

Financial markets are also feedback systems. The act of trading creates an information signal to you, your counterparty and other market participants. That information makes everyone adjust their beliefs about the world, and those adjusted beliefs create a reason for action, that is, more trading. The output (trading activity) is coupled to the input (changes in information about the world).

Markets demonstrate both positive and negative feedback behavior, usually concurrently.

A standard example of a negative feedback strategy is one that bets on *mean reversion*. The idea here is that some information came into the market, someone traded on that information (for example buying), but that markets adjusted their prices (up, in this case) too much as a result of that trading. The overadjustment can have many causes, the most common being that the people providing liquidity (usually market makers) faded or backed away quickly in the face of the buying pressure and thus the current price is temporarily higher than its long-term fair value. Mean reversion strategies attempt to identify these situations and provide additional liquidity, which pushes prices back to a fairer level.

There are many positive feedback strategies, and some of them do have a bit of a bad reputation, at least historically. This is reflected in the regulations that many markets now have in place. The reason for this is the intrinsic instability of positive feedback. Negative feedback is a stability-seeking phenomenon: movement in one direction induces a countervailing action to slow it down. Eventually things settle out to a stable level given enough negative feedback. Positive feedback, however, pushes prices in determined directions, and the very movement induces more movement in the same direction, with no natural endpoint. Reasonably, this scares regulators who are interested in well-functioning and orderly markets. Nonetheless, the fundamental idea of a *momentum strategy* is not particularly controversial. If you believe that a recent move in a direction has more movement to go yet, it makes sense to bet in the direction of the recent move.

The interplay of the two kinds of feedback is complex, but you can derive some useful intuitions from a common example.

Depending on the kind of feedback that traders are used to thinking about, it's possible to have some lighthearted fun with traders who run their strategies based on the other kind. Mean-reversion trades like market-making make money as long as moves are small and revert, but they can lose a lot on positions that get run over by news or a big trade. Momentum traders like to call market making "picking up pennies in front of a bulldozer." Most of the time you get the pennies, but if you're not careful you sometimes get the bulldozer.

The simplest retail trade that most people can think of is "It's gone up recently, I should buy because it will keep going up." The vast majority of the time that doesn't work because market prices are generally pretty fair. But momentum trades are based on exactly that simple idea, which is why mean-reversion traders think of momentum as somehow simplistic. After all, momentum traders look for sophisticated ways of putting on a trade that your grandmother would understand.

The best traders recognize that both effects are always at play, and I've found that the important thing is to understand how, when, and on what timescale different effects dominate. But every sub-culture has its harmless jokes, and trading is no different. It ain't *that* complicated, after all.

A Normal Market in a Stock

Consider the market in some medium-sized equity BAZ. Though the actual market microstructure may vary from what follows, these simplifications do not change the story in any meaningful way. Let's assume, as is typical, that there is a wide variety of market participants: market makers, indexers, long-term investors such as pension funds, hedge funds, and so on. During normal operation, market makers provide two-sided markets in BAZ. If someone wants to buy BAZ, almost definitely they will be buying it from market makers.

Market makers try to keep very little inventory in the stocks they trade, since inventory costs capital. You can therefore assume that market makers start off with a net zero position in BAZ. If someone wants to buy 1000 shares, some market maker Phil will sell to them. But how does Phil sell something he doesn't own? Quite simply, he borrows the shares.

In nearly all reasonably liquid stocks, there is a robust market in the borrowing and lending of shares. This is a completely separate market from the one in which shares are bought and sold, but the two interrelate, as you will see. So, in the example, Phil borrows 1000 shares from some lender, say a large pension fund. The pension fund is incentivized to lend their shares, since (a) they get paid a small fee (a few basis points, typically) for the loan, and (b) they're not going to be trading these shares anytime soon.

In this "normal" mode of trading, everyone is happy. The buyer of the shares (let's say it was a hedge fund) got the BAZ exposure they wanted; the market maker is happy because he collected half the bid-ask spread; the lender is happy because he's getting some extra yield out of his long-term holdings in BAZ. Certainly the brokers and exchanges are happy because people traded and trading generates fees.

Let's pause to consider the feedback mechanisms at work. The hedge fund demanded some liquidity, and the market maker provided it. The hedge fund is betting that the price will go up. Given the small size traded, that bet has to be because of some fundamental belief about the stock. Because the size is small, the market impact is small, and so it cannot be the very *fact* of their trade that would move the price up. In this example, there is no real feedback effect.

Conversely the market maker, having sold, is betting that he will be able to buy the shares back at a lower price. He is betting on mean-reversion, but again because the size is small, there is no significant market impact and so whatever feedback effects exist are minimal.

The lender only cares about the long-term performance of the stock. As such, she doesn't care, over a small timescale, which way the stock moves as long as they get paid their few basis points to lend the stock.

A Bigger Trade

Now consider a hedge fund that wants to buy 10 million shares. They start accumulating the position, with market makers getting short the whole time. The hedge fund is having market impact now, and given the sustained nature of the buying, the impact is positive (prices going up). You can see that the hedge fund is winning on their trade simply because they continue to buy. Their own trading is (partly, at least) what's causing the price to rise, which makes their previous trades look good. Again, the people who sold to them didn't originally have any position; they're merely market makers borrowing shares from pension funds and selling those shares short.

It turns out that this particular hedge fund manager, Carl, is a confident and brash sort of person. After he has accumulated some BAZ, he publicizes his position, announcing to the world how much he loves the stock. This phenomenon of "talking your book" is not uncommon among famous hedge fund managers. Publicizing their position encourages others to follow their lead and again improves the P&L of the trade. As usual, this announcement from Carl, plus the recent price increase, attracts attention from other hedge fund managers. Some agree with him and start buying too (which only helps Carl). Positive feedback is now at work.

Other fund managers, including Bill, disagree and in fact believe the stock is now overvalued because of the recent price rise. This is a negative feedback trade: the recent buying is now inducing people to bet against the price increase. And so, Bill starts borrowing and selling shares to bet against Carl. The market makers buy their short position back from Bill (probably at a higher price than they sold) and lick their wounds from getting run over by Carl's massive bet. But if they were sharp maybe ended up making some money from the frothy back-and-forth exchange of information.

Now the situation looks like this: Carl is massively long BAZ, but the shares he "owns" are in fact borrowed shares that Bill has sold to him. All of this activity is of course being conducted almost entirely with borrowed money, meaning they're putting up some amount of capital as margin on their position but the bulk of the buying and selling is occurring with money borrowed from someone else.

The Squeeze

Carl is betting on positive feedback. Bill is betting on negative feedback to Carl's original trade, but it would help Bill's position if some positive feedback could be activated in the selling direction. If Bill is right and the broader world ends up agreeing that BAZ is now overvalued, the fall in BAZ will have Carl facing margin calls on his position. If Carl's pockets aren't deep enough, he will have to sell some of his BAZ position to finance the margin call, leading to further price falls, until the price gets back to a "fair" level.

If Carl is right, he might get an even bigger payoff. Other people are now piling into this trade. It's been working for Carl, after all. The continued increase in price, now due almost entirely to market impact, draws even more people in. This is positive feedback in action. All of these people are buying from people who borrowed shares to sell: Bill and his fellow shorts.

At some point, however, Bill and his friends run out of shares to borrow. The pension funds they're borrowing from don't have an infinite supply, after all. This is a disastrous situation for them. Now, someone selling short can't borrow the shares they need to make delivery. A second and more powerful positive feedback now kicks in. The short sellers now need to buy back shares to make delivery. This causes upward market impact. The person they're buying from may not have shares to sell, meaning offers to sell the stock begin to disappear. Everyone wants to buy: the original buyers *and* the short sellers who need to buy back in order to make delivery. But there is no active market participant available to sell. This situation is famously known as a short squeeze.

The only way the short squeeze gets resolved, in this hypothetical example, is for the pension fund manager to realize that the price of BAZ has gotten to insane levels and hence she decides to sell her "long-term" holding. Everyone would want to sell BAZ if they could, but selling BAZ is a large-edge trade that only the true long-holders of BAZ *can* do. Once this happens, the new availability of sellers in the market causes a price drop. The friends of Carl who piled in late will now be the ones suffering margin calls, which will cause them to sell. The positive feedback now runs in the downward direction, and the price eventually regains sanity.

Some Comments

Stocks that have gone through a squeeze do take a long time to return to normalcy. Market makers are skittish about trading stocks that can have such enormous moves, and various other entities also restrict themselves from trading "crazy" stocks. These stocks can maintain their mark of Cain for many years after such an event.

The example above is idealized, with the participants clearly defined. In practice these situations have much more "fog of war" surrounding them, with speculation and rumor ruling the day. Many other market participants are affected too. Options traders see unusual trading in upside calls, and speculation starts up. Indexers are also subject to unusual behavior, depending on how the company that runs the index decides to adjust it based on the "patently crazy" prices of stocks in squeezes.

Nevertheless, the idealized story shows the salient features of markets. Normal markets demonstrate a balance between positive and negative feedback, with a large enough reservoir of capital to absorb the behavior of all sorts of market participants. But these normal situations are only an unusual occurrence or brash personality away from turning into pathological situations where the forces of feedback lead to some of the most interesting events in financial markets. I'll go through some of them towards the end of the chapter.

The Anti-Inductive Behavior of Markets

You've seen how both noisy signals (or more properly, low signal to noise ratio) and feedback (both positive and negative) make for a system where induction is hard to justify as a baseline rule of rational inquiry. More fundamentally, if some state of affairs isn't ruled out by either the laws of logic or the laws of physics, then it's possible for it to occur even if it never has. But what does this mean for financial markets specifically? It turns out that the action of the market itself causes not-impossible things that have never occurred to become likelier to occur. This constitutes the corollary of this chapter's rule.

The greatest modern example to illustrate this corollary is one about US housing prices in the period from approximately 1991 to early 2007 (FRED, 2018). Using the Case-Shiller index as a rough indication of house prices in the US, we see that during this period house prices increased by 6% per year for over 15 years. This means that house prices more than doubled over this period. This incredible increase occurred in spite of real GDP growth averaging a little over 3% over this period. It's natural to ask what caused this outperformance in housing costs over such a long period of time.

By now, researchers of all stripes have produced papers and books on the subject and yet the question is still far from settled. Nevertheless, I'm going to concentrate on one relatively uncontroversial cause: the amount of money lent to house buyers. In 1991 there was approximately $3.9 trillion of mortgage debt outstanding, and in 2006 there was $12.9 trillion outstanding. That's a growth rate of 8% per year. Every year for 15 years, American house buyers owed 8% more on their houses than they did the year before. With so much more money being borrowed to buy houses, it's little wonder that house prices increased significantly more than GDP. Now it's even more logical to ask: who was doing all this lending, and why?

To answer this question, you need to look at the market in mortgage lending, and in particular that of mortgage-backed securities (MBS). Traditionally, the business of mortgage lending worked as follows: retail regional banks used some combination of demand deposits (people with checking and savings accounts) and short-term borrowing to provide capital in the form of mortgages to long-term borrowers wanting to buy housing. This was a profitable business because the rates the banks paid to borrow money were lower than the rates they charged for the mortgages. That is, this was a profitable business for the banks provided that:

- The rates at which the banks borrowed remained below the rates at which they lent.
- People didn't prepay excessively on their mortgages.
- Most importantly, people didn't default (fail to pay) excessively on their mortgages.

All of these factors had good historical data on them, and so the business could be considered stable. However, starting in the late 1980s some enterprising financiers realized they could squeeze a bit more profitability out of this business with some smart financial engineering and a few innovations:

- Instead of restricting the mortgages to one particular kind of buyer or one particular region, they could cover mortgages across the whole country. This allowed them to:
  - Market bond-like securities whose coupon-like payment came from mortgage payments across the country. This was more profitable because:
    - Financiers didn't need to have much in the way of real deposits to fund the lending. The money came from the buyers of these bond-like MBSs. This lowered costs.
  - This lower cost structure was further enabled by the geographic diversity of the mortgages underlying the MBSs. One of the most important risks, default risk, was not very correlated between mortgage holders under normal conditions, but even under poor economic conditions the correlation across *regions* remained low.[2]

This last point deserves more discussion, since it forms the core of the argument I'm going to develop below.

Correlations and Low-Probability Events

What is a correlation? There is, of course, the standard mathematical definition with which many readers are surely familiar. But more intuitively, you can say that correlation is the phenomenon where two different random occurrences aren't independent. That is, seeing the result of one random occurrence tells you something about the other random occurrence even though you haven't seen it. Some examples:

- Whether it rained last night and whether my driveway is wet are correlated. Typically, if my driveway is wet then it's likelier it rained last night, and vice versa. Of course, my driveway could be wet because my neighbor watered her plants. Conversely, it might have rained last night but my driveway dried by the time I woke up. But in general, wet driveway means rain. This correlation is positive.
- Whether a famous actor is a good actor and whether they're attractive are correlated, but this time negatively correlated. A great actor will likely become famous no matter their attractiveness, and an attractive person could become famous even if they're a bad actor. Thus, supposing that a person is famous and attractive, it's less likely they're a good actor. This is known as the explain-away effect (Pearl, 2018).

Now ask yourself: what is the correlation structure of mortgage defaults? Most of the time, defaults are fairly independent. A given person defaults on a mortgage because of a job loss, or a health emergency, or some other life event that is specific to them. Knowing that one person has defaulted on a mortgage doesn't give you information about whether their neighbor has or not. This is a useful and important fact for banks: if it writes a number of mortgages to a variety of customers, the likelihood of enough of them defaulting to cause the bank problems (i.e. not being able to pay back depositors or creditors) is small and manageable.

Of course, there are times when mortgage defaults are indeed correlated. Consider the mortgages held by the residents of a town where the majority employer is a steel mill that just closed down.

In that situation, many people are likely to be out of a job, and therefore it's likely that when one person defaults on her mortgage, their neighbor is much likelier to do so as well. This is a historically well-known phenomenon, and as a result the US government has, over the years, instituted rules and entities to help regional banks mitigate the risk of these sorts of locally correlated defaults.

Correlations and the Financial Crisis of 2007–2008

This was the state of affairs in the 1990s, when financial mortgage issuance began to take off (Gorton, 2010). As I said, a good understanding of default correlation was a crucial component of the securitization of mortgages through MBSs and related instruments. The issuers had pored through the historical data and realized that, even if certain regions of the US saw periodic ups and downs in economic fortunes (and hence downs and ups respectively in default rates), nationwide there was little to no correlation across regions. It made perfect sense to construct securities that contained a variety of mortgages from a variety of regions. This way, the mortgage-to-mortgage default correlation could be decreased as much as possible.

As this market grew from a relatively small one to a large portion of the market that lent to house buyers, the assumptions upon which these products were built became central to the whole market itself. In essence, the world began to put on a large and very specific bet: mortgage defaults, and house prices themselves, wouldn't all go down simultaneously across the United States. On the face of it, this seemed like a reasonable bet: it certainly hadn't ever happened before. But, as you're learning in this chapter, having a large portion of the market rely on a regularity that isn't strictly required by the laws of logic or physics creates the conditions for its violation.

How did this feedback process work in this case? Consider the state of affairs going into the summer of 2007:

- Mortgage issuance had more than tripled in 15 years.
- The institutions that lent this money did so using structures that had less capital to cushion losses than did traditional mortgage issuance.
- MBSs, which lent money to borrowers, relied fundamentally on the assumption that, even in bad economic scenarios,

default correlations inside portfolios would stay within the very low levels seen historically.

- Many house purchases were made under the assumption that house prices would continue to rise, using exotic mortgage structures like NINJA[3] loans and interest-only (IO) ARMs[4] (Lewis, 2011).

The conditions were thus set for a feedback system that relied on low correlations to directly create the very high correlations that could destroy the functioning of the mortgage market:

- Issuance of mortgages increased nationwide, relying on low nationwide default correlations.
- In order to compete in this large and growing market, underwriting and verification standards decreased nationwide.
- Once ARMs started resetting, defaults increased across the country.
- These correlated defaults caused early losses in some MBSs.
- Funding for new MBSs dried up.
- Mortgage issuance rates decreased, which decreased the growth rate of house prices, and in places decreased house prices themselves.
- These decreased house prices caused more defaults of subsequent IO ARMs.

Aftermath

The crisis in the mortgage markets beginning in 2006 caused large ripple effects in other lending markets across the world, leading to the financial crisis of 2008. It's easy but wrong to lay the blame entirely on this cause, however. The whole world had created and used more credit than at any other time in history, and the models and assumptions that underpinned that lending also had many of the same characteristics as those of the US mortgage markets. The same mechanism, with somewhat different players, repeated itself in corporate debt, emerging market government debt, and many other less well-lit markets. The story, in the context of this chapter, remains the same: relying on the impossibility of possible events is unwise, and furthermore frequently causes those previously "impossible" events to occur.

Probabilities and the Effect of Correlation

You've seen from an intuitive perspective how the correlation structure of a given market or set of products can dramatically affect its behavior. But for perhaps the only time in the book, it's worth taking a more mathematical approach to the question. The interaction between correlation and small probabilities is not only extremely important for good risk management, but it also has some deeply counterintuitive properties that a mere intuitive understanding cannot show.

Consider a complex high-reliability system, like a nuclear power plant or an airplane. Because of human safety considerations, we require that such systems have very low probabilities of failure. These are very complex systems, and the number of different possible failure modes is large. A rational response to such high reliability requirements is to engineer redundancy in the subsystems that make up the whole system. And it is this redundancy that I examine here.

Assume that the subsystem in question must operate correctly in order for the whole system to operate. In airplanes, for example, engines must work in order for the plane to stay aloft. Medium and large planes are built with at least two engines, with the plane designed so that it can still be flown safely even if one engine fails. Suppose you demand that the engine subsystem have a probability of failure no higher than one in one million per year. That is, if you had a million of these airplanes flying for a year, you'd expect, on average, no more than one of them to have a total engine failure. Of course, you might get lucky and have none of them fail, or unlucky and more than one might fail,[5] but you require that *on average* no more than one should fail per year.

A natural question is to ask how reliable each of the two engines must be in order to satisfy the one per million engine-subsystem failure rate. In order for there to be a total engine failure, both engines must fail. If you assume the probability of failure ($P(fail)$) of engine 1 and 2 are the same, and these engines are independent of each other, then you need that $P(fail)^2 < 0.000001$. Thus, each engine must fail with probability no higher than 0.001, or one in one thousand.

So far so good, but the sharp-eyed reader will likely see a key (and possibly questionable) assumption made in the above analysis. Specifically, I assumed that the engine failure probabilities were independent of each other. That is, their correlations are zero. Is this a reasonable assumption? Even without deep knowledge of the aircraft industry, you can imagine ways in which the failure rate could be positively correlated:

- Engines can fail because of flaws in their design. If those flaws are exposed in specific situations the airplane might experience, then the failure of one engine could be caused by conditions to which the other engine is simultaneously being subjected.
- Engines can fail because of poor maintenance. It's reasonable to assume that the maintenance practices that one engine sees are similar to those of the other engine. Again, this causes positive correlation in the probability of failure.

So far, I've made mostly heuristic arguments, but it's important to back up these arguments with some numbers. You can do this by looking at the total engine failure probability as a function of the correlation coefficient[6] of the two individual engine failure probabilities. You already know that P(total failure) = 0.000001 if the two engines are uncorrelated, and you can easily deduce that P(total failure) = 0.001 if they're perfectly correlated. But what about in between?

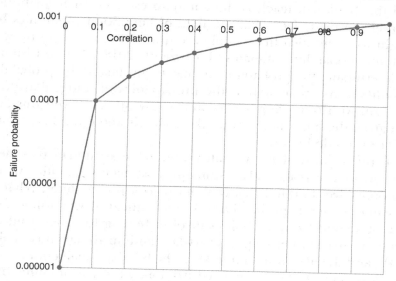

If you've never seen this sort of analysis before, these plots should shock you. Even a relatively small correlation of 0.1 increases the probability of total engine failure from one in a million to one in ten thousand. This hundredfold increase in the probability of failure comes from just a small correlation of 0.1! To give you an idea of how small a correlation of 0.1 is, it would take 400 independent measurements to be 95% confident that the correlation wasn't zero. In practice, such small correlations are extremely difficult to detect using only data-centric statistical techniques.

The behavior of rare events and how they're affected by even small correlations is a subject that, in my opinion, doesn't get enough attention. It's easy enough to understand the idea in a general and heuristic manner. But, until you look at the actual numbers in a small and easy-to-understand example such as this one, you can't fully appreciate the problem. Anyone involved in thinking about risk and unlikely events really does need to learn how small a correlation it takes to make rare events orders of magnitude more likely.

Practical Techniques for Evaluating Possibilities

Given the importance of thinking clearly about probabilities and correlations in evaluating any uncertain outcome, one important skill this book can teach is the ability to estimate such quantities. Among the many facts that the field of behavioral economics has taught us is the idea that people are quite bad at coming up with abstract probability estimates (Cartwright, 2018). We consistently underestimate: the probability we may be mistaken, the probability of unlikely events, as well as the probabilities of things that don't conform with our prior beliefs, and many others. Given this fact, and given the importance of thinking clearly about random events, how can you do better?

It turns out we have a small saving grace as human reasoners: while we may be really bad at estimating abstract probabilities, we *can* train ourselves to think clearly about *concrete* probabilities. What do I mean by concrete probabilities? In the context of what follows, the idea of a concrete probabilities involves betting for small (but not insignificant) amounts upon everyday random things: dice, coins, cards, and the like. You want to keep the bet sizes small enough that you don't engage other financial irrationalities and non-linearities like loss aversion and risk aversion. You do, however, want to keep the notional amounts large enough that they're meaningful: betting cents on a question isn't likely to engage much mental effort, whereas betting $10 likely will for most people.

What I'll develop is a calibration technique that lets you transfer your trained understanding of concrete probabilities in well-intuited situations to more abstract ones. Even if someone has never played dice games or coin flipping games, most people still have reasonably accurate ideas of how surprising some events can be. Suppose I ask you to roll a standard fair six-sided die, and before you do, I predict that you'll roll a 4 (for example). You roll the die, and sure enough a 4 comes up. Think of your intuitive level of surprise at my correct prediction. You wouldn't be shocked, by any means, but you'd be at least a little surprised.

Now consider some other abstract probability, say the chance that you'll be able to make your friend's party. She asks you how likely you are to make it, and you say 90%. Now compare the two probabilities. What would surprise you more: my correctly predicting a die roll, or something happening that would prevent you from getting to the party? If you're like most people, the latter would surprise you much less. You used your understanding about a concrete probability (for which you do have at least somewhat well-calibrated intuitions) to help you calibrate your beliefs about a more abstract situation. In my experience, people who say they're 90% certain to make some social function are, in fact, less than 50% likely to make it[7].

You can use this calibration exercise in any context where you need to accurately estimate abstract probabilities, not just in low-stakes social situations. Over time, you can develop some skill in using calibration exercises like this to elicit truer estimates of your own beliefs than you might otherwise be able to access. It's an interesting exercise in self-knowledge. You may believe something, but when the belief is presented to you in a more practical context, you realize your true beliefs are actually different.

I estimate I've interviewed somewhere between 1500 and 2000 people in my life. In the majority of those interviews, I've asked the candidate how confident they were in some answer they had given me. No matter what number they give me, I give them the calibration exercise. The results

(continued)

of the exercise span the spectrum. Many people have a small "aha!" moment when they realize their stated confidence doesn't match the surprise in the exercise. They learn that these estimates aren't arbitrary, and they learn a way to get better at making them over time.

Less frequently, people doggedly claim their surprise levels are the same, simply because the math says they should be. It's difficult to reason with them, so sure are they of the math. It's hard to make a good trader out of people with this inclination, though it is possible. The worst ones give a confidence of 100% and fail to update their beliefs no matter how ridiculous the hypothetical ("Really, you're surer of your answer than that you're not going to get struck by lightning in the next 5 seconds?"). Even after I patiently explain the point of the exercise, if they persist with their unshakeable confidence it's clear that they're not made out to be a trader.

Taking It up a Notch: Bet on It

The calibration technique I just showed you is a useful introductory exercise in becoming better reasoners about uncertain events. But you can sharpen your intuitions further by introducing some skin in the game, as Nassim Taleb likes to say (Taleb, 2012). Consider the trivial example of the party again. Let's say you've gone through the above exercise and conclude your true probability is in fact 75%. Your erstwhile host now proposes the following bet:

"If you're truly 75% sure to come, then let's bet on it. If you make the party, I pay you $10. If you miss the party, you pay me $30. If the 75% probability is accurate, on average you stand to make or lose nothing. In fact, to incentivize you to bet I'll only make you pay $25 if you fail to attend. You should want to take this bet, since on average you stand to make money."

If you're like most people, this proposal *feels* very different from the calibration exercise I introduced earlier. Betting on your beliefs gives you the visceral experience of uncertainty: possibly making or losing actual money. And if there is even a little of the natural trader in you, you'll find that this prospect will greatly sharpen your senses and desire to think clearly about the situation. Assuming the stakes are relatively small, if you're uncomfortable making this bet then that tells you your 75% estimate is too high. Even though on paper you should make money on this bet, your gut tells you that you won't.

This feeling is valuable information. Again, you are eliciting information about your own beliefs merely by framing them in consequential ways, ways that require you to be more honest and self-aware about these beliefs.

Some Historical Episodes

Financial markets provide a constant stream of unusual events and episodes. In this section, I'll look at some of the more interesting ones in the last few decades. Some of them are well known, others less so. The thread that weaves all of them together is the idea that even the most unlikely events can occur, and that frequently, reliance on their unlikelihood or impossibility in fact makes them more likely.

Portfolio Insurance and the 1987 Market Crash

In 1973, a paper was published that changed the course of the financial world irrevocably. In all likelihood, the ideas contained in "The Pricing of Options and Corporate Liabilities" (Black, 1973) by Fischer Black and Myron Scholes would eventually have been developed and published in other forms. The idea of risk-neutral pricing of derivatives was an idea whose time had come by the mid-1970s, much like the ideas surrounding special relativity in the first decade of the twentieth century. Nonetheless, the publication of this paper changed how the world of finance thought about derivatives, and this change was large and permanent.

The paper in question develops the theory of hedging (and hence pricing) equity options and other kinds of options. Before this development, options traders priced options using a variety of methods that, to varying degrees of success, functionally emulated the arguments contained in this paper. But the paper gave everyone a mechanism for pricing these derivatives by showing how to dynamically hedge them. This turned options trading into a pseudo-arbitrage business instead of a business wholly reliant on traditional market-making skill.

Relevant to this story, the paper gave the world a method of replicating the payoffs of options without needing to actually have options-like products to trade directly. By trading an underlying instrument (say a stock) in a specific way, you can simulate the portfolio of holding any vanilla option[8] on that stock. And so, in the late 1970s, Hayne Leland and Mark Rubinstein realized that they could use the ideas of dynamic hedging to create options-like products that (a) didn't actually exist as tradeable instruments and (b) for which there could be a market to buy. They focused on creating a product known as *portfolio insurance* and started Leland O'Brien Rubinstein Associates (LOR) in 1980 to market these products.

The idea of portfolio insurance was pitched to large institutional investors who were long the US stock market. The investor would purchase this portfolio insurance, which was a fancy name for buying a put on the US stock market. The buyer would pay a premium every month in exchange for the right to sell a broad US market index at some predetermined strike price. For example, let's say that the S&P500 index was trading at $300. An investor with a $1 million portfolio to protect could pay approximately $15,000 per year in order to obtain the right to sell $1 million of the index at a price of $270. Why would this be attractive? Consider a market crash where the index falls to $250. The investor has a right to sell the index at $270, which counteracts the losses on the portfolio. In fact, the "put" option the investor has bought has capped his losses in the event of a market crash at $30/$300 = 10% of his portfolio. By paying $15,000 per year, he has guaranteed he can't lose more than $100,000 on his investments.

This portfolio insurance (PI) product sold very well indeed, and by the fall of 1987, there were a number of investment banks selling insurance-like products. It's difficult to estimate the amount of portfolio insurance issued, but it was easily in the billions. At this point, it's worth examining the details of how this financial alchemy was cooked up.

An investment bank selling PI is selling a put on the index since the investor is buying one. Of course, such a put doesn't actually exist, and the bank certainly isn't in the insurance business. The way the bank sells such a thing is by synthetically replicating it by trading according to the Black Scholes formula. Recall, the put profits when the market goes down. So, if the investor is promised those profits, and the bank doesn't want to take those losses, the bank has to sell the index as it is falling. In fact, it needs to do this in the most continuous manner possible in order to match the payoffs the bank has promised its clients. If the index goes down 0.1%, the bank has to sell a small amount of the index. This is usually most efficiently done using futures, though it can sell baskets of stocks in the index as well. Even more efficient is to set up machines, at the time a recent innovation in stock markets known as *program trading*, to do this hedging automatically. Because the hedging had to be performed all day, every day, based on a well-understood formulaic strategy, it was a natural candidate for automation.

Though it may not be obvious from the above, creating portfolio insurance in the manner described above creates a feedback system. And by 1987, the world had set up an enormous market-wide feedback system, wherein the effort to protect against market crashes set up the conditions to make any such crashes more painful and severe. Let's examine the feedback in detail.

- The market, through normal random movement, moves up and down.
- On a particular day, the market moves down, perhaps more than is typical.
- PI providers' trading machines react, in order to maintain a good hedge for their PI products, by selling.
- This additional selling order flow causes market-makers to react in the usual way, by reducing their bids. Prices go down some more.
- This further decline prompts even more machine selling.

On October 19 1987, a day known as Black Monday, benchmark equity indices in the US fell in the vicinity of 22%. Throughout the day, exchanges like the NYSE were overwhelmed by thousands of orders from program trading systems attempting to sell as markets dropped and dropped (Carlson, 2006). Index values were meaningless, impossible to accurately calculate with so much chaos occurring. People were panicking, certainly, but the dominant effect was machines that were essentially programmed to panic. The whole crash episode, ironically, was exacerbated by an idea that tried to smooth out losses during those very crashes!

Incinerating Money in Japan: The Dentsu IPO

Is it possible to sell shares in a company in an amount greater than the value of the company? You would think not, but UBS attempted just such a thing on November 30, 2001. In Japan, the fourth-largest advertising company in the country was doing an IPO (initial public offering). Dentsu placed 135,000 shares at 420,000 JPY, making the total value of the issuance 57 billion JPY (~460 million USD).

At 9:00am that day, UBS Warburg intended to place an order to sell 16 shares at 610,000 JPY. By mistake, they actually entered an order to sell 610,000 shares (more than the number of shares being placed) at 16 JPY. Readers with experience in North American or European markets may laugh at such a mistake. Surely that's *such* an obvious transposition that no one would make such a mistake! But Japanese markets have a few interesting quirks. One is that stock prices vary enormously. While in the US, prices are usually somewhere between $5 and $100, in Japan prices could easily be 100 JPY or 1,000,000 JPY. Furthermore, Japanese stock tickers are numbers, not letters as in the US. Thus, the order "sell 100,000 shares of 100 at 1000" is just as reasonable (potentially) as "sell 100 shares of 1000 at 100,000."

Furthermore, Japanese "bust" rules are notoriously strict. Most developed markets have "obvious error" rules where if a trade was due to an obvious error in entering prices, quantities, or tickers, the trader in question can ask the exchange to bust the trade and the exchange usually does. Not so in Japan, where trades stand no matter what.

On that day, UBS noticed its error at 9:02am, by which point they had already sold 64,915 shares, almost half the full offering! By then, this enormous selling had brought the price of Dentsu to 405,000 JPY. Knowing that there was no chance of busting this trade, UBS immediately started buying back shares, and did so for the rest of the day. They managed to recover 18,339 shares, but the episode left UBS Warburg with a loss in the vicinity of $65 million. All from one erroneous order left in the market for two minutes.

This was far from the only Japanese "fat-finger" episode in recent memory. Four years later, Mizuho Financial lost over $300 million in a similar situation with a stock named J-Com. Interestingly, UBS was one of Mizuho's counterparties in this trade and, perhaps chastened by the events four years prior, they voluntarily agreed to return some of their profits. Karma being what it is, UBS was again involved in another fat-finger event in 2009, this time with Japanese bonds. Since that trade occurred outside of market hours, the exchange discovered the error before markets opened the next day and UBS avoided a multi-billion-dollar loss.

"Impossible" Events in 2008

The financial crisis of 2008 was very fertile ground for creating "impossible" events, that is, things that no sane trader would have said were even possible six months prior.

- **US short sale ban:** US markets are famously some of the freest in the world: regulation is consistent and it generally allows market participants to act as they will with few restrictions. And yet, in the wake of turmoil in financial markets throughout the late summer and early fall, the US SEC announced on September 19, 2008, that they were instituting, with immediate effect, a ban on the short selling of financial stocks (SEC, 2008). The list of stocks comprised 799 financial services firms of all types and sizes. Such an act would have been considered impossible even three months prior. The list eventually grew to include over 900 stocks, with stocks being added in an ad-hoc manner with no prior announcement. Such an abandonment of regular market operation struck many traders around me at the time as something more akin to a developing market in the throes of an existential crisis than the behavior of the most developed and well-functioning market on earth.

- **Volkswagen becomes the biggest company in the world:** There is no upper bound on the price that a squeezed stock can get to. Perhaps the most famous example of a short squeeze occurred in the shares of Volkswagen AG (Reuters, 2008). Due to a combination of interesting factors (an attempted takeover by Porsche, the government-centric ownership structure of Volkswagen, plus some acrimonious relationships between two rich aristocratic German families), Volkswagen briefly became the most valuable company in the world. If you had asked a trader how much a very large stock like Volkswagen could squeeze up to, even an estimate of doubling would have been met with some laughter. Small companies could have short squeezes like that, but surely not one of the largest automakers in the world. In late 2006 the stock was worth under 100 EUR. Even as late as March 2008, Volkswagen was worth under 200 EUR. But a short squeeze has a mind of its own, and by October 2008, Volkswagen was briefly worth over 1000 EUR, an increase of 10x in less than two years, and 5x in a few months. This patently ridiculous price, brought about exclusively because of the mechanics of shorting and delivering shares, caused consternation with the German regulator BaFin. That led to a host of rather extraordinary and arbitrary decisions by the German futures exchange concerning the makeup of their benchmark index the DAX (among other interesting consequences). A complete impossibility, but it happened.

The Chief Unpegs

One of the consequences of the 2008 financial crisis was a general reevaluation of the creditworthiness of a variety of entities, in particular of countries. The reevaluation was important in Europe, whose member countries had (with a few exceptions) joined in a currency union (the Euro) by 2002. Of course, each country still had significant control over its own finances and fiscal policy, so there was some measure of tension between the various members of the currency union. Large, well-functioning Germany shared (and still does) a currency with the more profligate and inefficient Greece, and the hope was that the closer economic union would bring these peripheral European economies more in line with the workhorses of the continent (Germany, France) over time.

The crisis of 2008 put the lie to those hopes. General sentiment was that the Euro was a doomed project, and its former status as a safe haven steadily eroded thereafter. Worldwide, investors began to pull money out of Euro-denominated sovereign debt. The logical result was a steady devaluation of the Euro relative to other developed-nation currencies. This caused tension in Switzerland in particular, being surrounded on all sides by Euro-nations with whom they were trading partners. Switzerland's currency, the Swiss franc (CHF, or "chief") had long been considered a safe-haven currency by the world's investment community. Much of the EUR-denominated sales went into CHF-denominated purchases in one form or other. Switzerland's export industries (a significant part of the Swiss economy) in particular began to suffer as the cost of their exported goods rose while the EUR kept dropping relative to the CHF.

The Swiss National Bank (SNB) responded to this by declaring in no uncertain terms on August 3, 2011, that "the Swiss franc is massively overvalued." This sort of declaration by a central bank often has the effect of notifying investors of the direction the political winds are blowing, and investors generally heed those warnings. However, in this case, it had little effect. The EUR kept dropping relative to the CHF. Again, on August 17, 2011, the SNB issued a statement calling its own currency massively overvalued and threatened to take further steps to halt the appreciation.

It's comparatively rare for a national bank to loudly and publicly complain that their currency is overvalued and for that complaint not to have much of an effect. This is because the central bank of a currency has the power to print money at will, so if devaluation is a goal, it's one that's easily achieved. Just flood the country with newly printed money. And so, on September 6, 2011, the SNB drew a line in the sand and declared that the EUR would not be allowed to drop below 1.20 per CHF.

The peg remained for years. Any time that the SNB saw the EUR/CHF rate ticking above 1.20, it would begin selling CHF and buying EUR (and any other currencies it saw fit) in order to reduce the value of the CHF. Over those four years, the world grew accustomed to the peg. Sometimes the EUR would tick above 1.20, sometimes it would hit the 1.20 limit, but over time this became the way of things for EUR/CHF. An average day in the EUR/CHF saw moves on the order of 0.03%. The SNB repeated its proclamations about the importance of the peg, and there was no reason to doubt them. After all, they could always print money if they wanted to decrease the value of the CHF. Even on January 12, 2015, the vice chairman of the SNB went on television and declared, "We are convinced that the minimum exchange rate must remain the cornerstone of our monetary policy."

But things were secretly becoming untenable for the SNB. They kept buying foreign currencies, and by early 2015 the SNB held foreign reserves of 70% of their GDP. The European Central Bank (ECB), meanwhile, had announced the possibility of further quantitative easing measures designed to stimulate the European economy (printing money under a different guise), with the inevitable result of putting further downward pressure on the EUR. Could the SNB withstand the onslaught of the ECB purposely devaluing the EUR?

The SNB decided to stop trying. On January 15 2015, they quietly removed the peg, and in one day the EUR dropped 17% almost immediately. Looking at the sizes of the price moves in the previous three years, this represented a ~500 standard deviation move in the EUR/CHF, an event so unlikely (when looking only at recent historical data) that it would be likelier to win the lottery every day for a week. But of course, it wasn't *that* unlikely. Nonetheless, a variety of Swiss foreign-exchange (FX) trading firms, who enabled retail traders to put on large FX positions with extremely high leverage (up 100x the capital invested), promptly announced bankruptcy the very same day. Their business model of high leverage and few limits was predicated on the CHF only being capable of small moves versus the EUR. Once the large move happened, there was nothing these FX trading firms could do. Relying on something being impossible, when it is actually quite possible, is a poor business plan at any time but particularly when a battle between central bankers is involved.

Summary and Looking Ahead

- The mental tools you use to learn about the world—an understanding of what's possible and the idea of induction—are quite problematic when applied to random, feedback-driven systems like financial markets.
- Markets where participants rely on the non-occurrence of not-impossible things induce those not-impossible things to actually happen, no matter how seemingly unlikely.
- The interplay between small probabilities and small correlations means that, again, seemingly unlikely events can be made much more likely through even small changes in their correlations.
- Crazy things happen in financial markets all the time. And they will continue to happen.

In the next chapter, we'll turn our attention back to our own behaviors. Specifically, I try to look at what goes into creating and maintaining a successful trading operation. It turns out that aligning the incentives of everyone is by far the most important job, and you'll also see how and why creating such alignment is so incredibly difficult.

References

Reuters. (2008). Retrieved from https://www.reuters.com/article/us-volkswagen/short-sellers-make-vw-the-worlds-priciest-firm-idUSTRE49 R3I920081028.

Black, F. A., and Scholes, M. (1973). "The Pricing of Options and Corporate Liabilities." *Journal of Political Economy* 81, No. 3, pp. 637–654.

Carlson, M. (2006). *A Brief History of the 1987 Stock Market Crash.* Retrieved from https://www.federalreserve.gov/pubs/feds/2007/ 200713/200713pap.pdf.

Cartwright, E. (2018). *Behavioral Economics*, 3rd ed. Routledge.

FRED. (2018). Retrieved from FRED Economic Data, https://fred .stlouisfed.org/series/CSUSHPISA.

Gorton, G. (2010). *Slapped by the Invisible Hand: The Panic of 2007.* Oxford University Press.

Kment, B. (2017, March 21). "Varieties of Modality." Retrieved from Stanford Encyclopedia of Philosophy, Edward N. Zalta (ed.), https:// plato.stanford.edu/archives/spr2017/entries/modality-varieties/.

Lewis, M. (2011). *The Big Short: Inside the Doomsday Machine.* W. W. Norton and Company.

Munroe, R. (n.d.). Retrieved from XKCD, http://xkcd.com/1391.

Pearl, J. (2018). *The Book of Why.* New York: Basic Books.

SEC. (2008, June 19). *SEC Halts Short Selling of Financial Stocks to Protect Investors and Markets.* Retrieved from https://www.sec.gov/news/ press/2008/2008-211.htm.

Taleb, N. N. (2012). *Skin in the Game.* New York.

C H A P T E R

Alignment

The Ballad of Victor Niederhoffer

Among the most interesting characters in modern finance is Victor Niederhoffer. A former squash player and academic with a penchant for Ayn Rand, his investing career began in the 1970s. By the 1980s he was a partner of the famous investor George Soros, and until the fall of 1997 Niederhoffer's hedge fund Niederhoffer Investments had returned significantly above the market for many years in a row. However, just as his book was hitting the press in 1997, some bad bets in Thailand had Niederhoffer's fund under stress.

On October 27, 1997, the US market dropped 7.2%, a large but not especially catastrophic drop by historical standards. This drop was nonetheless more than Niederhoffer's fund could handle and it forced the shuttering and liquidation of the fund. Victor Niederhoffer had blown out.

Ever resilient, he started trading again in 1998, mortgaging his house in order to find the capital for the new Wimbledon Fund. By 2002 he was again managing money for other clients under the name Matador Fund. Again, his returns were excellent, always returning more than 40% per year. Disaster would again strike 10 years after the first blowout. Some odd equity moves in the summer of 2007 caused an incredible 75% decline in the value of the Matador Fund. The fund shut down. Niederhoffer had blown out again.

This chapter will look at the incentives that lead to trading that is likely to cause blowouts. I'll also look at the sociological structures that lead investors to repeatedly invest in managers who have a demonstrated tendency to take perhaps-unnecessary risks with client money.

> Working to align everyone's interests is time well spent.

Roles

Running even a small trading operation is no easy task. There are a lot of moving parts, and the parts interact in complex ways. Running a larger operation is even more difficult. In this chapter, I'm going to examine these parts and interactions, and try to tease out some useful ways of thinking about the organization of trading firms. It turns out that much of what you'll learn applies to virtually any high-performance organization.

What are the components needed to build a trading operation? Obviously, you can't do without good traders, and those traders need some capital with which to trade. But building a sustainable, world-class organization requires more than these important components.

Capital

First and foremost, trading requires capital (money). As I discussed in Chapter 3, at a very minimum your counterparties will demand that you put up capital as collateral for the trades you're going to do. But the capital needs of a trading firm encompass more than the regulatory or market-based requirements needed to trade. The capital base of a firm, and its makeup, constitutes the main tangible asset of a trading firm and represents the most direct measure of the health, capability, and performance of the firm.

In particular, you need to look at the source of capital: who funded the organization? The most important distinction here is whether the entities putting up the capital are involved in the day-to-day operations of the firm. That is, is the source of capital internal or external to the firm? You'll see in what follows why this is an important distinction for a variety of reasons.

Labor

Trading is a labor-intensive pursuit. This is not true for all ways of interacting in financial markets. Warren Buffett famously does very little in his small Omaha office other than read newspapers and drink Cherry Coke. While this tale sounds a bit too folksy to be believed (surely running a firm with half a trillion dollars in assets is more than a part-time job), it is conceivable for long-term investment to be a capital-intensive but low-labor sort of endeavor.

Trading, however, is labor intensive. The job of developing trades, studying them, running them, trading them, adjusting their parameters intraday if need be, and keeping an eye on the bigger picture, certainly isn't a part-time job. The marginal value of a good trader as opposed to a mediocre one is typically high, and this disparity has only increased with technology. As you'll see in Chapter 10, technology is a force multiplier. This means that over time the difference in value between a 90th-percentile trader and a 60th-percentile trader increases. This is what has led to the arms race for talent that you see in modern hiring markets.

Technology

Very few trades in modern financial markets can be run with a pen and paper and good horse sense. Modern models typically need computers to instantiate them, and also to store and manage the data needed to study them and improve them. Computers are needed for all the bookkeeping and firm management in just about any busy trading operation. The collection of physical hardware and the software that runs on it (the highest value of which is typically custom-built) constitutes the technology value of the trading firm.

In fact, there is interesting recent research about corporations (Bessen, 2018) that suggests that the edge larger corporations have over smaller competitors in a given sector is largely driven by superiority in information technology (IT). By making IT a core competency, even if the business isn't directly technology-based, corporations can erect first-mover advantages based on the ability to manage logistics and highly complex processes. Making technology a first-class component of the business means new entrants first have to invest heavily in acquiring such abilities before being able to compete with established, skilled participants.

Relationships

Trading doesn't happen in a vacuum, as you know. It requires interacting with a wide variety of other entities: brokers, lenders, exchanges, regulators, and others. A trading firm that has good, productive relationships with these entities has something of significant value. These relationships can help facilitate the development of the business, improving and optimizing current trading, and will of course help with the recruitment and retention of key employees.

Good relationships are something that's hard to value, but relatively easy to recognize. Taking a page from the book *Getting to Yes* (Fisher, 1991), you can extrapolate the idea of mutual advantage in negotiation to a more long-term concept. The key to a good long-term relationship is the idea that both sides are better off for having the relationship. I'll discuss later how to develop and maintain such productive relationships in business.

The Power and Limitations of Self-Interest

The key question I tackle in this chapter is how to get good alignment among the various roles of an organization. I'll mostly stick to discussing trading operations, but as you'll see, the ideas developed apply broadly. In fact, the importance of aligning interests is the focus of this chapter's rule.

> Working to align everyone's interests is time well spent.

This rule may seem like a trivial one, but getting everyone's interests pointing in the same direction is more difficult than it may seem. As an example, I'm going to examine the relationship between fund managers and their investors. Canonically, the investors provide the capital and get paid with profits, whereas the fund manager provides the labor and gets paid with a salary. This example will show, however, that if the person with the capital isn't the same as the person doing the labor, this arrangement can lead to some suboptimal incentives.

A Common Situation

Arthur is a wealthy retiree, looking for investments that secure him a steady flow of income. If he hires someone to manage his capital (to trade it and so forth) on a fixed salary, the latter's primary incentive to do a good job is to keep getting paid a salary.[1] In particular, the only incentive the fund manager has to maximize profits for Arthur is the possible threat that he'll replace the manager with someone else. But how strong is this incentive? Consider:

- It's well known that most people are hesitant to move their investments from one manager to another. Status-quo bias is strong.
- It's easy for a manager to explain away or obfuscate mediocre results, either by choosing debatable benchmarks or because most investments are inherently high-variance affairs. It will take a lot for Arthur to become convinced his investment manager is doing a bad job.

You can safely conclude that the "the client might leave" incentive isn't a strong one. In the meantime, the manager will be incentivized to find other clients, since labor economies of scale in investment management are strong. It's not twice as much work to run a $200 million fund as it is to run a $100 million fund, after all.

In essence, from a purely economic perspective the investment manager will be incentivized to do the minimum necessary to avoid getting fired while simultaneously expanding his base of clients. This is an example of an *agency problem*: the interests of Arthur the investor are not well aligned to those of the investment manager. While a well-intentioned and principled investment adviser may work hard and go the extra mile, typically it isn't wise to rely exclusively on the goodness of someone's heart in matters of money.

I'm always astounded by the amount of money that is extracted from retirees and investors by banks and brokerage houses. A few years ago, my mother, now retired, moved back from England to Canada and as a result transferred her banking and investment accounts back to Canada. Ever the dutiful son, I talked to her about how that transfer was going. She was happy, telling me she had found a nice young investment adviser to help her out at the bank. Something didn't sound quite right, so I asked her to investigate the fees she was paying.

(continued)

The next week she reported back, relieved. There was no cost to either buy or sell the funds in which she was invested. I told her that wasn't quite the question I had asked. I got her to pore through the fund prospectus (everyone has to do this at least once, I think) to look for words like "fund-management fee." Unsurprisingly, we find out that this fund, which tracks the TSE200 index, charged 1.9% per year for doing so. It doesn't sound like much until you realize that you can buy into funds that do the exact same job but charge only 0.3% per year!

I also got her to examine her statements line by line because I suspected there was something else. Sure enough, there it was, buried in small print, one line among many: advisory fee 3% per year. It's hard to describe the rage I felt at hearing that my mom's bank was charging her 3% of assets *per year* for the benefit of their advice, advice that was to invest in a *terrible* high-cost fund. All in all, she was incinerating 4.6% per year that she didn't need to be. It took a few weeks but she finally got set up with a self-directed retirement plan where the costs were minimized, with bank employees dragging their feet the whole way. If this book does anything for you, let it be this: study your bank and investment statements. I bet you're paying more fees than you think, and certainly more fees than you should!

Adding an Incentive

How can Arthur incentivize the investment manager to do a good job? The most obvious solution is to give him a percentage of the profits. If he gives the manager 20% of profits, then the latter has a financial incentive to generate profits. And from Arthur's perspective, 80% of something large is certainly better than 100% of something small.

This sort of reasoning, among other deregulatory factors, led to the creation of the hedge fund industry. Hedge fund managers typically get paid a percentage of assets under management (AUM) and also a percentage of profits. Historically these numbers hovered in the range of 2% of assets and 20% of profits, though the numbers have come down in the last decade as the Arthurs of the world realize the majority of hedge funds don't outperform their benchmarks by enough to justify these high fees. No matter the specific percentages, the question remains: does this profit incentive solve our agency problem?

Let's do a thought experiment to try to answer the question. Consider the manager who has to choose between two different investments:

1. A guaranteed profit of 5%, or
2. A simple coin flip for 50% of the assets under management. Heads, the fund returns 50% on the year. Tails, it loses half its value.

Clearly Arthur would rather choose the first investment (since its expected value is higher and its variance is lower). Notice, however, that the manager makes a lot more with the second investment. The profit share for the manager in the first case is 1%. In the second investment, either:

- The fund loses 50% if the coin comes up tails. In this case the manager makes nothing.
- The fund makes 50% if the coin comes up heads, in which case the manager makes 10%.

On average, the fund manager makes 5% with the second investment. Since the manager doesn't share in the losses when they occur, he is incentivized to take high-variance gambles in the hopes of making a big profit when profits do end up occurring. This heads-we-win, tails-you-lose sort of incentive structure was extremely common in the hedge fund world even up to the early 2000s. It's worth briefly looking at how this patently crazy state of affairs could have come about.

Winners of Coin-Flipping Tournaments

Imagine you start off with a set of 16,384 hedge fund managers. In a simplified model, assume that all of them choose investment 2 in the above example, and let's further assume the coins they all flip are independent.[2] After the first year, on average, 8,192 fund managers will have made 50%, and 8,192 will have lost 50%. The half that lost will close up shop, with many of them immediately planning new funds to try their luck again. But what about those who won?

They get to play the next year, where again half win and half lose. After 10 years of this coin-flipping tournament, you're left on average with 16 fund managers who have an unblemished record of making 50% per year. These managers, billionaires by now, will be feted by the finance establishment, will be wined and dined by brokers, will collect expensive modern art, and will be interviewed in soft-focus profiles by middlebrow weekend magazines. "What makes these men tick?" the articles will ask, since these fund managers are invariably men. People will want to know the secret of their incredible investment prowess and, as you learned at length in Chapter 5 about biases, they will have developed excellent "systems of thought" to explain their unique edge. These explanations will never center on their incredible luck in winning the 10-year coin-flipping competition in which they've engaged.

By this point, these phenomenal fund managers write their investment contracts in such a way that they contain onerous fees and odd and restrictive redemption rules. For the investor, so much the better. That way only the truly committed and knowledgeable investors will win the contest to provide the star manager with their capital. Imagine the value of being able to say, at gala dinners and charity auctions, that you're invested with the superstar fund manager du jour.

Profit-only or profit-heavy incentives lasted for decades in the financial world until investors, burned multiple times, began to demand better treatment.

High-Water Marks

By now, the variance-incentivizing issue with profit-only fee structures is well known. One solution that has gained popularity in the last decade is the enactment of high-water-mark provisions. Suppose a fund takes a loss in a given year. The high-water provision stipulates that the manager cannot take any future profit incentives until the fund again reaches the value it had before the loss had been incurred. This disincentivizes risky behavior to some extent.

This solution is not without its problems, however. For one, the high-water-mark only disincentivizes risky behavior that could lead to losses. If the manager has a choice between a safe 5% investment or one that has a half chance of either a 0% return or a half chance of a 10% return, the fund manager still has an incentive to take the riskier investment. Because of the tournament nature of fund management asset acquisition, making decisions that bring attention (and hence new assets under management) is still attractive to the manager even if those decisions are not in the investor's best risk-adjusted interest.

Furthermore, managers whose funds are in a high-water mark restriction due to previous losses have lost their incentive to labor to recover the losses. Much better to close the fund entirely, return the capital to investors, and subsequently start a new fund that, by virtue of being new, will not have any high-water-mark restrictions. Many fund managers availed themselves of this option after the steep losses of 2008–2009.

An Unavoidable Tension

Other ideas have been proposed for the hedge fund manager fee model that attempt to fix these issues. The solutions attempt, quite directly, to further align the incentives of the investors (the capital) with those of the managers (the labor). I'm going to argue that fixing these problems must involve a fundamental reevaluation of the relationship between labor and capital. In essence, the only real solution is to collapse the distinction between the two. By making the fund manager an active and large part of the capital base, interests are automatically aligned because the same person is acting in both roles. Short of a schizophrenic fund manager, the incentives are automatically aligned.

Agency Issues in Other Areas

The problem that Arthur has with his investment manager isn't specific to finance. Economics has a broad class of literature dealing with what they term the *principal-agent problem.* Perhaps the most well-studied example of an agent acting in their own interests, as opposed to those of their clients concerns real-estate agents. In a very well-designed study (Rutherford, 2005), it was determined that when real-estate agents sell their own homes, they manage to extract nearly 5% higher prices than when they're acting on behalf of their clients. Why is this the case?

Real-estate agent fees are typically a fixed fraction of the sale price of the home (5%, for example). If an agent can quickly sell a home for $500,000, they make $25,000. If they work for months, perhaps five times harder, they could sell it for $550,000 and thus make $27,500. In the meantime, all that extra work could have gone to selling four more separate houses, each with a $25,000 commission. The most expedient and financially rewarding approach for a real-estate agent is to convince the client to accept a bid (if they represent the seller) or to pay the asking price (if they represent the buyer) in order to complete the sale. The key is to turn houses over: that's how real-estate agents make money. Grinding over small improvements certainly advantages the client, but it's not the way to riches for the agent.

Incentive Structures That Work

The difference between the payoffs of owners (capital) and traders (labor) is a fundamental one, and while you can create incentive schemes to minimize agency problems, you cannot eliminate them entirely. So, what can you do to create incentive structures that do align the interests of the various parties?

Traders with Edge

In Chapter 5, I discussed edge without really examining the sociology of the people who find, develop, and trade these profitable strategies. Where did they gain the knowledge and skills to successfully do such a difficult job?

With exceedingly few exceptions, these profitable traders learned from other profitable traders. They also invariably rely on infrastructure (technology and relationships) that takes time and effort to construct, and that requires the skills of others (technologists, operations, legal, and compliance personnel, etc.) to run. Autodidacts in trading are like jailhouse lawyers: for every person who's truly discovered and developed a successful strategy sui generis, there is an army of people who either significantly undervalued the teaching that others provided, or they are deluding themselves about the profitability of their trading.

Given this long and difficult process of learning how to trade profitably, why would such a person then employ their rare abilities to enrich someone else? I can think of two main reasons:

1. *Insufficient capital:* If the strategies the trader can profitably run require more capital than she has then she will need to look for external investment to capitalize the trade.

2. *Structural restrictions:* Some trades only are available to certain market participants, such as regulated investment banks or other large entities. Complex over-the-counter derivative trading, for example, frequently requires a big name and its attendant big balance sheet to be profitable.

Let's examine each in turn.

Insufficient Capital

If the issue is insufficient capital, then the incentive for the profitable trader is to take just enough capital to be able to run the trading, then hopefully make enough profit over time in order to be sufficiently capitalized themselves. At that point, any additional capital they have (the capital from the original investors) becomes a constraint. Company structures that allow the investment of external capital generally come with significantly more restrictive laws and regulations. If a successful trader can avoid these restrictions while still maintaining sufficient capital from their own capital base, then over time they will prefer to do so. The result is that successful traders, once they're shown to be successful, will seek to eliminate external capital investments.

Consider this same situation from the other side of the coin: that of the investor. Generally, the only choice is to invest in poorly capitalized traders they believe are profitable ones, in spite of limited evidence that they are successful. Making matters worse, the investor needs to deal with the phenomenon of Batesian mimicry. In the animal world, Batesian mimics are animals who evolve to mimic the appearance of another animal, usually a more dangerous one, in an effort to obtain for themselves the protection that such a dangerous appearance confers without having to go to the expense (evolutionarily) of becoming dangerous. For example, various snakes mimic the band pattern of the highly venomous coral snake, but they themselves are not venomous. Predators stay away from these mimics, believing them to be coral snakes, and the mimics don't even have to evolve expensive venom glands and self-protections against their own venom.

In an insightful blog post, Eric Falkenstein (2010) draws a parallel between the phenomenon of mimics in the wild and a plausible explanation of economic business cycles. For these purposes, you can draw a similar parallel with traders who are advertising themselves to prospective investors. Because of intellectual property protection, traders who truly have edge will tend to avoid publicizing the source of their edge. They will rightly obfuscate and only say as much as is necessary to obtain the investment. Similarly, traders with no edge will mimic this parsimonious approach to providing information. No trader with edge would publicize their edge after all. The result is that Arthur is left with a very difficult decision in determining which traders do indeed have edge.

Even if Arthur successfully navigates this mimicry minefield and ends up investing in a successful trader, his reward is for the trader to work as hard as possible to make his investment unnecessary.

Structural Restrictions

Traders with edge who need large structures to support their trades face a similar situation. They will tend to rent out their services to the name firm (a large investment bank or established hedge fund, for example) only as long as they need to in order to obtain enough capital to either leave for a better opportunity or start their own competitor, usually with fellow friends and co-workers about whom they have excellent private knowledge with regard to their profitability. In the end, the large firm is in the same shoes as the investor: if a successful trader becomes successful enough, you won't have access to that person for very long.

Aligned Monetary Structures

Given what we've seen so far, we're left with an unavoidable conclusion: the only way for successful traders (laborers) to have good incentive alignment with investors (capital) is for them to be one and the same. And this idea applies not just to formal investor/manager relationships. The power of this idea generalizes across all of finance.

Imagine someone tells you about a can't-miss profitable trade. Perhaps on CNBC, a book like this one, a website, or a penny-stock newsletter. Do you believe them? If you've been paying attention so far, you should be thinking something along the lines of "Why would they tell me their trade instead of doing it themselves?"

Unless you happen to be a very unique investor, perhaps one with a personal connection to the information-teller, and the trade requires your uniqueness in some way, by default you should think, "They wouldn't." People just don't broadcast profitable trades for someone else to do. Fortunately, financial education in the modern world has mostly gotten to a point that the average retail investor understands this. While these siren calls of quick profits will always attract a certain percentage of would-be Greek mariners, most of us can identify them as the self-interested appeals they invariably are.

Now imagine someone tells you they're a profitable investment manager, one with edge, and that you should place your capital in their hands to invest for you. They're not telling you their trade, and in fact they're being quite cagey about the details of their edge. But they seem reputable, they work for a reputable retail brokerage or investment management firm, and they do wear a suit. The line of thought developed in this chapter should have you asking yourselves the same question: "Why would they manage my money for edge, when they could be managing their own?" If they are indeed managing their own in the exact same way they would be managing yours, you need to ask how much of their income comes from service labor (the fees they're charging you) versus their trading labor (their own inherent profitability).

This line of thinking hasn't fully penetrated the retail investor zeitgeist. While the rise of index-tracking mutual funds and ETFs indicates that a progressively greater portion of the investing public is beginning to understand, this is still a story that needs to be spread more broadly. In fact, the continued rise of hedge funds, and their democratization, indicates that progress in this direction is halting and subject to reversals.

In summary, the profitable trades that exist in the world are either (a) the ones you're intimately involved in running, or (b) the ones that are inaccessible to you. There is no (c). And what's funny about the situation in trading is that, if we were discussing just about any other industry, the very notion of a (c) would be laughable. Imagine if someone who's good at manufacturing cars came to you and said: "Hey, I'm a profitable car-maker. If you like, I'll let you take all the profit from my car-making skill in exchange for a small fee for me." You would rightly suspect they're trying to pull one over on you. So why is the situation different in trading?

Incentives within a Firm

By now you might think that I believe monetary incentives are the only incentive aligners worth thinking about. This is far from the case: no successful organization can rely exclusively on monetary alignment for its success. What I've discussed so far is merely a recognition that when monetary incentives *are* misaligned, very few nonmonetary incentives can successfully battle that misalignment, and certainly not for very long. Having seen a variety of incentives at work both within trading and in my previous career in engineering, it's clear there are many other things you can do in constructing a firm and its culture that help maintain alignment of interests within it.

Pay Structures

We've seen that traders need to have enough of their capital in the firm, and for the trader's capital to be enough of the firm that they're appropriately motivated. In fact, this is a general point that isn't specific to trading firms at all. The people at the sharp end of any business need to have a compensation structure that reflects that position. In a sales-centric organization, the sales people should have strongly incentive-based pay, for example. But does this mean that anyone who works for a firm should be similarly compensated? Consider some difficulties with this idea:

- *Logistics:* Employees are hired and leave with regularity. Having the capital structure of the firm tied to these moves is poor risk management, at the very least. Those with capital in the firm, owners, shouldn't be changing their composition very much, and certainly not as frequently as normal employment periods and cycles would require.
- *Employee risk:* Not everyone who wants a job as an office admin, for example, is going to want to have to invest a significant portion of their wealth with their employer, nor are they going to want a significant portion of their pay to come as profit shares.
- *Employer risk:* Hiring someone and paying them a fraction of profits adds unreliability to the relationship. If the firm had a bad month, will the admin accept not being paid that month? Owners with significant equity stakes should be well-capitalized enough to withstand such variation, but lower-level employees are unlikely to be as resilient to variations in pay.
- *Mimicry, again:* Batesian mimicry arguments again tell us that prospective employees will have a hard job figuring out if their prospective employer is profitable or not. An unwillingness to pay a salary would mark out a prospective employer as

someone who (a) doesn't believe enough in their profitability to be willing to pay a fixed salary, and (b) is also skeptical enough of their profitability that they're willing to give up a fraction of the profits merely to gain an employee.

These arguments explain from first principles why any profit-seeking enterprise will want to pay its employees a fixed salary. Paying employees a salary instead of a fraction of profits may seem obvious, but looking at the question with fresh eyes lets you understand why such an arrangement should be favored. It also lets you more clearly think about the question of bonuses.

How big a fraction of an employee's total pay should come in the form of a regular salary and how much should be paid the form of a performance-based bonus? The answer varies by the kind of job the employee holds, and as you'll see, the most important consideration is: how close are they to the sharp end of the firm?

- General office staff should receive relatively small fractions of pay as performance bonuses. Their job is generic to nearly all white-collar work, and so the differential value at a specific firm compared to some other sort of firm is small. Office staff can have high value and hence high pay (for example, a manager of a large facility), so this isn't an argument against high pay for such staff. The argument is that the nonspecificity or distance from the profitability of the firm, argues for a small bonus fraction.
- Operational and financial support staff (accounting, HR, etc.) should have higher performance pay fractions, since their work requires more business-specific knowledge and skills. Nonetheless, much of this skill is portable across related domains (legal, regulatory, accounting, etc.), so the bonus fraction shouldn't be particularly high.
- Technical staff (programmers, network engineers, etc.) are a more difficult case. Typical programmers, no matter how skilled, lie closer to the generalist end of the spectrum: their skills could be used in any number of other fields. However, some technical staff have deep and specific expertise in business-related technologies and so their pay structure should reflect this.
- So, who should have large fractions of their pay come in the form of performance bonuses? Simply those employees who

are, in a sense, training to become owners of firms themselves. Their job is directly to make the money for the firm, and as such their pay should reflect this reality. As we've seen in the previous example, a trader who gets paid a salary and no bonus has incentives that are misaligned with those of the firm paying them to do that job. But the same can be said of other roles in other businesses.

As I've said, the idea of asking the question "How close are they to the core work of the firm?" generalizes well as a way of determining how much pay should be performance-based. For example, life insurance is a product that is famously sold, not bought. People don't go out of their way to buy life insurance and so these companies need a small army of salesmen to go out and find clients. This is the sharp end of the life insurance business, so it makes sense that life insurance salesmen should have highly variable pay structures. This idea also explains why large companies' upper management and C-suite pay comes largely in the form of performance pay: it aligns the interests of these individuals with those of the company (typically, the shareholders).

> When I started my career as a trader, I got assigned as a junior to a senior trader. Given the dynamic at work, by a few weeks into the job I was pretty sure that he wasn't one of the main owners of the firm. In fact, it wasn't all that obvious who they were. So I asked my senior, "Who are the owners of the firm?" He chuckled and told me to guess, and I grinded away to come up with a list. Needless to say, my list wasn't very good. But over time, I came to see that failure as a good thing.
>
> You shouldn't take this to mean that confusion over the ownership structure of a private firm means there isn't a clear reporting structure. The latter is critically important in any business. But when you see just about every senior person acting as though they too were the owners of the firm, the degree of alignment that results makes you think that way too. When everyone's on the same team, coming to work every day feels that much better.

Silos

There are a variety of structural decisions you can make in the creation of a firm that affect the incentive structure of its employees.

One of the most important of these is the question of internal intellectual property (IP) and other barriers: how strong and tight should they be? There are many factors that affect this decision, and I'll touch on a few of these here.

- *How important is IP to the organization?* This is the most important question that needs to be answered. If a group's intellectual property (a) is extremely important to success and (b) is easily extracted or copied, then this argues in favor of strong barriers or silos. Conversely, if much of the intellectual property is ephemeral or stored in the minds of the employees, there is little value to siloing the group.
- *How much employee turnover is there?* In companies with high turnover, even a small fraction of employees leaving with important IP argues in favor of strong silos. Conversely, companies with low employee turnover can afford significantly weaker intra-company IP protections, and in fact they can benefit greatly from this cross-pollination of ideas.
- *How standard or "normal" is the business?* For firms with steady and stable businesses, the cost of silos is comparatively small. There is little benefit from the sort of cross-business idea sharing that is essential in businesses where markets are changing rapidly. In the latter situation, sequestering good ideas in one small area of a company carries a high cost, since those good ideas could be used elsewhere to improve.
- *What are employee expectations?* Consider prospective employees of a defense contractor. Their expectation of the nature of the work environment is undoubtedly going to involve strong silos and information protections. Conversely, someone entering a nonprofit organization will expect a much more open structure. These expectations are important since mismatches between expectations and reality lead to frustration and poor alignment.

Culture and Consistency

It's possible to run successful trading businesses with very different cultures. Some are very hierarchical, siloed, and regimented, others are more open. In the end what makes the difference, and what creates good incentive alignment, is consistency in the application of the cultural values of the firm, whatever they may be. Let's think about the characteristics we've looked at already:

- A strongly hierarchical firm must have its managers provide subordinates with clear, consistent instruction. Leaving instructions vague or subject to interpretation creates confusion and frustration: "Why can't they just tell me what they want?"
- Conversely, an open, collaborative, consensus-based culture requires managers to spend time soliciting ideas and feedback from subordinates and other co-workers. Everyone must feel invested in the decision-making process. The result of overly strong management directives leaves everyone asking, "Why can't they listen to what I have to say?"
- Someone whose performance pay fraction is small cannot be required to exercise significant autonomy in determining their duties or approach to their job. Low performance pay fraction attracts people who value the security of "clocking in and clocking out" without needing to worry about themselves defining the job they do.
- People who receive high performance pay fractions cannot be expected to rigidly follow the directions they are given. Performance pay only makes sense when someone has the autonomy and ability to decide for themselves how to do the job, and indeed what job needs doing.

Aligning the culture of a firm to the nature of the business is an essential component of starting and maintaining a successful business. Regardless of what culture is desired, the key is to create consistency across the business. One of the most powerful methods of creating this consistency is to create and evangelize a set of corporate principles that reflect the culture that's desired.

The idea of a set of corporate or organizational principles is rightfully derided in many circles. Consider Google's famous "Don't be evil." This noble-sounding principle manages to simultaneously be devoid of any actual useful content, and also damages the culture of the firm:

- Very few people, perhaps only sociopaths, would consider their frequent actions (such as a job) to be evil. Most of us are conditioned to think that evil is something others do, not ourselves, so it doesn't function very well as a brake on our own behavior.

- Who defines "evil"? Philosophers and theologians have spent thousands of years defining, discussing, and debating the subject of evil, with very little in the way of consensus so far. It's unlikely that a tech company has happened upon a universally acceptable definition that can be used to guide corporate behavior.
- Given the absence of a universal definition, you're left with a situation where employees can use the principle as a tool to attack political enemies within the organization. If you can successfully label the actions of another as evil, you've won the rhetorical and moral battle, whether or not such a victory was deserved on the merits.

In order to be useful, principles cannot be so general as to be vacuous. They have to be able to specifically guide behavior in desired directions. "Great customer service at any cost" is a difficult principle to actually enact: should a customer service agent charter a helicopter to pick up and replace a defective pair of shoes? Better something like "When in doubt, err on the side of giving customers what they want." The nuance is that most of the time, you do what you are trained to do, but in questionable situations the principle guides the employee in a useful direction.

It's important for leaders to actually enact the principles in their daily actions. It's particularly important to refer to principles when explaining and defending decisions. This creates good alignment with the people affected by the decisions: employees, partners, customers. By continually reinforcing the use of organizational principles, leaders embed the culture in the minds of employees and the principles become more than empty words intoned at a yearly meeting.

Summary and Looking Ahead

- Good incentive alignment is incredibly hard to achieve in the financial world.
- In the end, true alignment can only happen by collapsing the distinction between capital (the people with the money) and labor (the people doing the work).

- Creating a company culture with good alignment requires you to pay attention to the details of everyone's motivation, and in particular how close they are to the money.

In the next chapter, I'm going to move from the most human-centric ideas to the most machine-centric. What is the role of technology in trading, and how do you manage the incredible ongoing changes in the technological landscape?

References

Bessen, J. (2018, June). *The Policy Challenge of Artificial Intelligence.* Retrieved from https://www.competitionpolicyinternational.com/wp-content/uploads/2018/06/CPI-Bessen.pdf.

Falkenstein, E. (2010). *A Batesian mimicry explanation of business cycles.* Retrieved from Falkenblog, https://falkenblog.blogspot.com/2010/07/batesian-mimicry-explanation-of.html.

Fisher, R. a. (1991). *Getting to Yes: Negotiating Agreement Without Giving In.* Penguin Books.

Rutherford, R. T. (2005). "Conflicts between Principals and Agents: Evidence from Residential Brokerage." *Journal of Financial Economics* 76, pp. 627–665.

CHAPTER 10

Technology

Shifts and Shocks in Human Competences

Zog was a hunter-gatherer 12,000 years ago in what is now southern France. Life was difficult for him, especially in the winter. But what was hard about it? What was Zog good at that permitted him to survive? You might think that he had to be a good hunter, or perhaps a good gatherer. Those were indeed valuable skills, but they were easily learned. The issue is that even a skilled precivilized human like Zog generally can't survive *alone* in the wild. Humans can't digest raw meat or most plants, and compared to animals we're slow, weak and fragile. In Zog's preagricultural era, the real difference between success and failure came from political skills. Zog had to have good ties to his family and kin group. He had to find a good niche within it, and this basically determined his chances of survival and success.

Zog's descendants eventually developed the technology and social structures to be able to live in larger, denser, and more permanent agricultural settlements. With that change in structure came changes in the skills necessary to survive. Zog's village-dwelling descendant Shem now had an incentive to specialize in learning specific skills: those of a warrior, farmer, priest, or administrator, for example. He still needed good political skills, but having a good life once civilization happened required even more cognitive skill than it did before the agricultural revolution.

The skills that Shem developed were tangible and concrete: they involved learning *how to* do something specific and valuable, in his case farming. As development progressed, those skills became more and more specialized. By the time we meet Jacques in the Middle

Ages, an average person could have a reasonable, average existence (for the standards of the time) by becoming, in his case, a chandler. Jacques the chandler was someone who specialized in the fabrication and management of wax, candles, and soap. This required years of apprenticeship and an even higher cognitive demand than for Shem's time.

This state of affairs continued until sometime around the middle of the sixteenth century in England and Holland, when a true middle class began to emerge, and with it the value of more general cognitive skills. Beginning around then until around the end of the Industrial Revolution, the value of being able to read went from something reserved for the aristocracy to something at first useful then nearly essential to the success of the average person. By the end of the nineteenth century, it was very difficult for Jacques's descendant Barry to secure a comfortable middle-class life without being able to read. The cognitive requirements for an "average" life had increased again, which meant the invention of compulsory education for children.

A similar transition occurred more recently. For most of human history it was possible to be successful even if you were functionally innumerate. An inability to add, subtract, multiply, and divide numbers wasn't an impediment to almost any profession or trade. Society remained in this mode until around the 1970s, after which it became progressively more difficult to find good employment without a decent competence in mathematics. Blue-collar jobs that required little in the way of mathematical knowledge began to be replaced by automation, and the "normal" jobs of the past disappeared. The average job in advanced economies became a white-collar job in an office, one where being innumerate is a significant handicap. Schools adapted, placing more focus on basic mathematical skills in addition to reading and writing.

It's worth noting that innumeracy is not a default state of affairs, and it isn't inevitable if school is absent. Many studies demonstrate that even "unschooled" people with little or no formal education, are capable of complex mathematical feats when their job and situation requires them. Psychologist Sylvia Scribner studied a dairy factory in Baltimore in the 1980s (Scribner, April 1987), and found such abilities among the workers. Loading milk into milk crates and partitioning these crates into efficient loads for transportation involved complex math: "equivalent to shifting between different base systems of numbers." Those unschooled workers performed concrete but complex mathematical feats with few mistakes.

Similar studies exist among street children in Brazil. These children sell peanuts and coconuts, and the need to calculate a total and make change requires arithmetic with decimals that even educated adults find difficult or at least annoying. However, when presented with similar problems in a more abstract school setting, these children performed poorly.

The evidence appears to be that what school teaches you, with respect to numeracy, isn't necessarily the ability to add and subtract successfully. People with little or no formal schooling can manage it when their lives require it. What school teaches you about math is its power as a tool of *abstraction*. It teaches the idea that math is something that can be applied generally, to any useful situation, and not merely for counting coconuts or peanuts. This idea of abstraction in fact underlies the transition I'll discuss next.

Over the last decade or so, the evidence has become quite strong that the cognitive demands of an average job are seeing another rapid increase. In Erik Brynjolfsson and Andrew McAfee's *The Second Machine Age* (Brynjolfsson and McAfee, 2016), you learn about the ways in which increasingly intelligent machines have begun to replace the labor of white-collar workers. Whereas in the past machines replaced the *physical* labor of people, the growing sophistication of information technologies means that more and more *cognitive* tasks are being done by computers directly. As a result, those jobs that endure necessarily involve close interaction with computers.

Even entry-level retail jobs require familiarity with complex point-of-sale and inventory-management systems. And as the level of cognitive demand increases for a job, the amount of computer interaction, and the level of that interaction, also increases. An average office job requires good familiarity with tools such as Excel and Word, at a minimum. Furthermore, these jobs often require independent research skills that thirty years ago would only have been required in either academic settings or highly selective professions. We're all consumers, distillers, and repackagers of information and knowledge now.

At the top of the cognitive-demand pyramid, extensive skill with managing data and information is steadily becoming an important and non-negotiable aspect of many high-wage jobs. This opinionated history now bends back toward the realm of trading, although nearly all of what follows applies quite readily to most highly demanding modern professions. Gone are the days when a trader with good horse sense, intuition, and personality was able to compete with those who have access to data and know how to wield it.

> If you don't master technology and data, you're losing to someone who does.

Data, Data Everywhere

Why has facility with technology, specifically computer technology, become such an important component of the modern labor economy? Quite simply, it's because of data. Reliable numbers are hard to come by, but many informed observers estimate that more than 90% of all the data the world has ever generated has been generated in the last two years. And this exponential (literally, for once) increase in the amount of data available shows no signs of slowing down.

Within that raw data, the information exhaust of the modern economy, lies the potential for more deeply understanding just about every aspect it. As you've seen in preceding chapters, the human mind's ability to understand and make sense of complex phenomena is tempered by the cognitive biases with which we're all afflicted. Overconfidence bias, confirmation bias, and many others put a strong limit on the degree to which we can truly understand complexity. And, with the continued increase in economic interconnectedness, this complexity continues to rise. The only way to tame this complexity, and to understand things better, is to look at the data directly, and for everyone to become statisticians and scientists.

The extreme competitiveness of financial markets has already made it the canary in the economic coal mine. The value of information, in particular information that no one else possesses, has been known for centuries. This may be best exemplified by the perhaps apocryphal story of Nathan Rothschild. The story goes that, in the early nineteenth century, Rothschild had an army of couriers to provide him with news of the battle of Waterloo before anyone else received it. As a result of this advanced knowledge, he was able to trade British government bonds with private information about the outcome of the battle, and hence trade profitably.

The modern importance of information, however, has relatively little to do with how private that information is, and a lot more to do with how to process it. As I've said, the world is awash in data and most of that data, especially in financial market settings, is public and therefore available to whoever is interested in it. For this reason, the scarce resource (the high-value skill) is to be able to find the needle of insight and true knowledge in the haystack of relatively worthless data.

The Value of Data

Given the sea of data that's available, you need to understand what data is valuable, and why. Finding a needle in a haystack is no doubt easier if you know where in the haystack to look. I'll take as an example, as always, a modern trading operation with good access to technology, quantitatively inclined traders, researchers, and developers, and data. If you want to find good edges, build good models, and run good strategies, what sort of data do you want to look at?

Perhaps counterintuitively, it turns out the best place to look is at the end. What this means is that you first want to answer the question "What is the output of the process I'm building?" In the case of a trading operation, the result of the process is a strategy that does trades. The data exhaust of this process is, directly, information about orders and trades. Thus, information about past orders and trades is the most valuable sort of information you can provide to the process.

This feedback-like idea is so universal that it manages to rise to the level of a general principle. The most valuable data as inputs to a process are past outputs of the same (or sufficiently similar) processes. You see this principle at work everywhere data is used to gain insight or make decisions:

- The most important sort of data for a company selling a new product is sales information about previous similar products (Roberge, 2015).
- The most valuable information about employees and how they will perform in the future is data about their past abilities and behavior (Mathis, 2013).

- If you want to know how an ecosystem will respond to the reintroduction of a missing predator, the best information comes from the results of similar reintroductions in the past (Peglar, 2018).

It's easy to see the connection to the inductive hypothesis I discussed in Chapter 8. But in this case, you can say something more specific about induction from the past about the future. The question of what data to look for embodies a notion of locality: what is most relevant for A is information that is causally *local* (in the sense of proximal, or close) to A.

In this principle about data there is also a strong connection to some established ideas in the world of machine learning (ML). The science of creating computer algorithms to extract information from data has grown significantly in importance in the last decade or two, with the rise of modern deep learning ideas. Yet in spite of the incredible improvements in performance in a variety of historically human-dominated fields (image recognition, speech recognition, game-playing, etc.), the most important scarce resource remains the availability of sufficient amounts of high-quality labeled datasets upon which to train these modern ML models. In particular, the need to have humans do the job of manually labeling tens or hundreds of millions of images for an image recognizer limits the ability of these systems to be adapted and improved over time. Finding ways of having systems do prediction without requiring human labels is a very active area of research.

Among the most promising of these areas is the subfield of reinforcement learning. As described by one of its founders, Rich Sutton (Sutton, 2017), the idea of reinforcement learning is to have the system be an active participant in the process of transforming input into output. That is, the output depends causally on the operation of the system, so it's impossible to learn a useful system without modeling its own interaction with the environment. In the context of the similarity rule, the connection is to an idea called temporal-difference (TD) learning.

The insight of TD learning is the following: in order to eliminate the need for a system to have human-labeled examples, you make the system predict its own future input. If a system can successfully predict its own future input, the idea goes, it will have extracted from the data the necessary information to make such predictions. This extracted information is, by definition, useful since it tells you something about the future that you didn't know before. But, crucially, no external intervention was necessary to tell the system which aspects of the future are important. Interestingly, some of the most promising modern theories of human cognition (known as the predictive processing model) are based on very similar future-prediction foundations (Clark, 2015).

Defining "Same"

Sharp-eyed readers may have noticed that, in the above discussion about the most useful data being past outputs of similar systems, I haven't defined what I mean by "similar systems." This seems crucially important since the definition of the rule makes similarity the essential characteristic upon which you're judging the usefulness of data. For example, if you're designing a new trading strategy, what counts as a relevant historical strategy you can use as a point of comparison?

If you're merely making an adjustment to an existing strategy, then the answer is easy. The current strategy's results are the most useful and relevant data in judging the performance of the adjustments to this strategy. However, if you're dealing with a wholly new strategy, then relevant points of comparison aren't necessarily easy to find. As with many difficult questions that you've seen in previous chapters, the answer is human experience. Data is powerful and has revolutionized the way in which trading firms do business, but the process of understanding *which* data is relevant is still an area where humans dominate automated mechanisms. The reason has to do with what humans are good at, as compared to what machines are good at. And combining the best of what humans do with the best of what machines do ends up yielding the most powerful results of all.

Humans Competences versus Machine Competences

If you examine closely the sorts of problems where machines now dominate humans, you can discern some universal characteristics.

Let's take a wide view, and look at historical situations where machines have replaced humans in the economy:

- *Farming:* One hundred years ago, the majority of the world's population farmed for its livelihood. In the US, for example, the number of farmers peaked in 1900 at 12 million but currently sits below 1 million (Roser, n.d.). This happened as the US population more than tripled.
- *Factory work:* Machines continue to increase their fraction of value-add in nearly all manufacturing operations. This is a process that began nearly 200 years ago and shows no signs of stopping. So much so that when the process happens in the reverse direction, on the rare occasions it does, it becomes newsworthy for mainstream news outlets.
- *Transportation:* The palletization and containerization revolution in intermodal shipping has decimated the ranks of stevedores and dockworkers (Levinson, 2016). Similarly, railroads in 1947 carried 655 billion ton-miles of freight and employed 1.35 million workers. In 2014, the numbers were 1850 billion ton-miles and 187,000 workers. That's a factor of 20 in decreased employment per ton-mile shipped.
- *Routine data processing:* There was a time when corporations employed armies of clerks to do filing, and armies of secretaries to do typing. These jobs disappeared almost entirely by the 1990s and show no signs of returning.

What sorts of characteristics make these jobs amenable to automation? You can identify a partial list:

- *Repetitiveness:* Jobs that can be transformed into something that can be repeated reliably benefit greatly from automation.
- *Speed:* Jobs where raw throughput or low latency matter a lot are excellent candidates for automation.
- *Reliability:* Jobs where natural and ineradicable human variation yields a poorer product have a strong incentive to automate processes.
- *Many examples:* Situations where building a machine that can replace many workers are more automation-prone than those where the number of people replaced is limited.

Conversely, you can identify characteristics of jobs where machines have, at least so far, made few inroads:

- *Uniqueness:* Jobs that critically depend on the contributions of a specific person, such as art and music, are difficult to automate.
- *Emotion-centric:* It's difficult to automate jobs that require empathy, motivation, or other uniquely human emotions. Examples include psychologists and personal trainers.
- *Creativity and insight:* There are few machines coming for the jobs of Nobel-worthy researchers, as yet.

What Makes a Human Trader Valuable?

Given the classification of the characteristics of jobs that suit machines as compared to humans, you can now examine the job of a trader to see where it lies on the spectrum of machine-replaceability. There are many breathless articles about the death of the manual human trader, and it is true that trading floors and pits have all but eliminated open-outcry trading in the last 20 years. Nevertheless, there are many markets where manual trading still takes place, especially in developing or frontier markets. It's just that this trading occurs in a computer-hosted market, instead of one managed entirely by humans.

The role of a trader is multifaceted, so the question of machine-replaceability becomes one of asking which parts of the job of a trader have been supplanted by machines. Given the above list of characteristics, it's clear that the aspects that are repetitive and require speed and reliability have been eliminated from most traders' job description. No one is writing manual trade tickets, then manually stamping them, nor are there market makers who manually manage the order book of even lightly traded securities. Those functions are easily automated and they have been.

Even higher-level functions, like manual trade execution, are aspects of trading that few professional traders engage in anymore. The speed and precision required to avoid losing money relative to even a simple trading algorithm are now beyond even the most skilled keyboardist. So, what's left for a trader to do? The answer, it turns out, is pretty much everything else.

The high-value aspects of trading remain the same as ever: understanding the value of securities, their relationships to other securities, the mechanics of supply and demand, and the ability to skillfully play the game (in the game-theoretic sense of the word) of trading. Of course, the use of those skills has changed significantly in nature in the last 20 years, and it's this aspect that's most interesting in the context of the role of technology in trading. Deeply understanding securities is as valuable as ever, but the way you seek to understand them has changed.

Consider a typical situation in a semiliquid stock: a large mutual fund has decided to divest itself of its holdings in the stock. Their position is large enough that naively putting out large offers would have significant price impact, so the mutual fund needs to trade out of its position carefully and discreetly in order to minimize this impact. Thirty years ago, a skilled trader working for the hedge fund would have had a variety of options: she could call around to friends of hers, those at other large institutions with whom she had good relationships, to see if they'd be interested in buying up the fund's position. If she got lucky, she could transact a large block trade this way and have relatively little impact on the stock price. If not, she could parcel out the trade into somewhat smaller blocks and *work* the position over a few days or even weeks.

All the while, the skilled market maker would attempt to discern the order flow in the stock. By looking carefully at the orders coming in, their sizes, their timing, their source, a sharp market maker could perhaps see in the first day or two that there is out-of-the-ordinary selling activity in the stock, and rightly suspect that there is more selling where that came from. By adjusting his market down, the market maker avoids getting run over by the large trading activity of the mutual fund.

Thirty years later, the situation is exactly the same but the mechanics are completely different. The mutual fund trader's connections don't exist in the same way they did before, since the clubby everyone-knows-everyone nature of old-line equity markets has long since disappeared. However, new options have emerged: the fund's trader could post a dark offer in a dark pool, a trading venue where bids and offers aren't posted visibly. If someone comes in trying to buy, again in the dark, the two will transact without necessarily notifying anyone else in the market. All the while, the skilled trader is intimately aware of the algorithmic trading systems available to her, developed either in-house or provided by the fund's brokers. These algorithmic systems, or *algos,* have many parameters to tune performance, and the skilled fund trader has run enough statistical studies on past trading to understand which parameter settings will be optimal for this situation. She knows to which market venues to route her orders, she knows what times of day and days of the week are best, and how to hide the signal of her large order.

Conversely, the modern market maker doesn't manually post two-sided markets. He has machines co-located at the exchange (the better to minimize delays in information transmission and reception), running trading systems that have millions of lines of code inside them. Traders and researchers have run endless simulations, A/B tests, and parameter optimizations to tune the parameters (possibly numbering in the tens of millions) of these systems. The goal is to do the same thing as thirty years prior: avoid getting run over by a large order, and to discern in all the noise of trading the tiny signal of a large order. But at this point, the gut instinct and feel of a traditional trader have been almost entirely replaced by advanced statistical, technological and game theoretic approaches to the same problem. To quote Slim Charles in *The Wire,* "Game's the same. Just got more fierce."

A Whole Greater than the Sum of the Parts

The "humans versus machines" question is, like many dichotomies I've discussed in this book, a false one. Humans without machines are left naked in modern markets, but machines without human oversight represent risks that almost no sensible trader would be willing to take. The essential question becomes how to put together a super-trader that takes advantage of the largely complementary skills of skilled humans and of machines.

Given what you've seen already, the answer is easy to state, albeit difficult to implement.

- The main task of human traders in modern developed markets is to try to understand them in such a way that the conclusions drawn are statistically valid. This requires extensive skill and training in statistics, programming, logical reasoning, machine learning, game theory, and related fields.

- The main task of machines is to implement the edges and models developed and validated by humans. By maximizing the amount of repetitive, speed-sensitive work that machines perform, you offload these tasks from humans who are disadvantaged at them as compared to machines.
- Machines are still quite bad at understanding context. Context represents all the variables to a trade that aren't encoded in a machine's model of the world. Changes in context can be anything from a sudden market outage to the military invasion of a country. Well-trained humans are good at understanding this sort of context without needing a large dataset to do so, but machines are largely hopeless at reliably dealing with situations for which they haven't been built. As you saw in Chapter 9, "impossible" things do occur regularly in financial markets.

There are pitfalls with this conceptually clean division of labor. For one, traders who have never manually traded a share or manually pored through market data to understand the behavior of a market will find it hard to develop intuitions upon which to base statistical analyses and studies. There remains very little substitute for the knowledge developed by manually replicating the tasks that machines perform so effortlessly. As an educational exercise, this sort of going-back-in-time is essential.

On the other end of the spectrum, it's relatively easy to rest on your laurels and decide a priori that some variable or context cannot profitably be placed within a machine's model of the world. In fact, human creativity knows few limits when properly incentivized, and many seemingly hard-to-define intuition-based variables can indeed be systematized enough to be studied and integrated into machine models and trading systems. It's this effort to do so that represents the cutting edge of the human-machine hybrid that's so successful in modern markets.

Software Engineering

Given the importance of computers and the software they run, it's important to discuss how to build such software successfully. Software engineering is largely the work of managing complexity, and much of that complexity ends up being sociological as much as technological.

Developing Large Software Systems

All but the most basic trading systems require a software effort that spans the work of multiple people, from two to hundreds of developers. Organizing such an effort, and managing it successfully, is a large discipline of study in the world of computer science. Analyzing what goes into writing high-reliability enterprise-scale software successfully is beyond the scope of this book, but I can highlight certain ideas that may have gotten relatively little treatment in the existing literature.

Many books and methods developed for writing good large software systems are quite prescriptive and didactic. Paradigms have proliferated as software has successively entered more sectors of the economy. The waterfall model, the spiral model, and more recently agile development have a large number of adherents. Methodologies within those paradigms, such as Kanban and scrum, have also proliferated. Many discussions on Reddit and Hackernews end up taking on the nature of a holy war between adherents of the various sects and factions.

What you learn in studying the various approaches is that different paradigms offer different benefits and drawbacks in their implementation. There is no one approach that rises head and shoulders above the others. So how are you going to choose between these methods of organizing a large-scale software effort? Given the evident success that can be achieved by a variety of approaches, you can conclude that it actually doesn't much matter. What matters more than the specifics of the software engineering paradigm, or the framework used to implement it, is the sociology of its implementation.

Having a development workforce that understands, at a deep and intuitive level, how the firm intends to develop software, and for the workforce to buy into the approach, are by far the most important predictors of success. Whether or not an agile paradigm works for a given firm, for example, depends much more on having everyone understand, accept, and thrive in the paradigm than the specifics of how it's implemented. And the key to achieving this sort of alignment largely goes back to training. When hiring new software developers for any organization, training must include not just the details of specific projects, development tools, and languages used, but also the philosophical and sociological approach to development that's been implemented at the firm. Without such nontechnical training, no amount of technical training can paper over the gap.

Debugging

I want to make a special mention, when discussing software development, of the skill of debugging (Agans, 2006). Debugging is the act of finding errors in systems, most frequently software systems. These errors are behavior that's undesired by the developers or users of the system. When looking at the education of software developers in particular, debugging is by far the most important concrete skill that is essentially never taught explicitly, or at best is taught poorly.

Much time is spent teaching computer architecture, computer languages, how to architect large software systems, and other related skills. But the skills required to actually make those systems work, and work well, represent a gaping hole in nearly every educational curriculum for software developers. The reason for this is simple: debugging isn't a clean academic discipline suitable for in-class educational approaches. Debugging is learned by doing, much like in those medieval trades I described at the outset of the chapter. Those trades were learned through a method of apprenticeship, and this method of learning has largely disappeared from the curricula of university-educated people.

Apprenticeship is still practiced today for trades such as plumbing, construction, and other highly manual fields. But the implicit assumption in our educational system is that if someone has the mental capacity and inclination to put themselves through a highly selective university program, then they must have the ability to learn just about anything on their own. Some skills, however, resist almost anyone's efforts at self-learning. Or at least, neither a self-directed nor a classroom approach can impart the skill of debugging effectively.

To make matters worse, most workplaces don't put a priority on teaching new hires, especially new graduates, the concrete skills of debugging that make their work product more effective. For the most part, companies aren't organized that way: new hires get assigned some small project, they progress at some pace, and over time they are given more responsibility. There is little room, given the usual tight schedules and competitive business environment, for a senior and experienced developer to sit and spend time debugging a problem with a more junior developer. Even less frequently does the senior developer have a syllabus to specifically address and develop the skill of debugging problems. Experience has shown that companies that do invest in this sort of apprentice-like training in debugging reap benefits over the long term that more than outweigh their cost, often by orders of magnitude.

I've been writing software since I was eight years old. The idea of making a machine do exactly what I wanted captured my imagination then and it has yet to let go. And some of the most frustrating times in my life have happened when I couldn't figure out why some piece of software I had written wasn't working. I had a bug, and I couldn't find it. I never did get any formal training in how to debug problems, and as a result I was honestly pretty bad at it for a long time.

Over time I got better at debugging by finding the bugs in my own debugging *process*. I often went too fast, skipping over essential steps with unwarranted assumptions. Or I didn't look carefully at the results of my debugging experiments, missing critically important details. As I reminded myself of these tendencies, I learned to avoid them, and I got better at debugging. Everyone's process has bugs, and getting better involves finding the bugs in *your* process. Learn about yourself, about your failure modes and tendencies, and squash those process bugs!

Technical Debt and Depreciation

One of the main issues in producing robust production-quality software concerns updating the codebase over time. Questions surrounding how and when to make local patches as compared to deep architectural updates are especially difficult, particularly when those decisions have to be made under some sort of time or resource constraint. When you make the expedient decision to do a small local patch or change, one that is suboptimal compared to doing a "proper" re-architecture of the system, you can say that a sort of "debt" is created in the system.

The term *technical debt* was first coined by Ward Cunningham in a 1992 paper (Cunningham, 1992). Although the paper is short and mostly concerns itself with specific technologies used at the time (the Smalltalk programming language, for example) the concept of technical debt has, over the last 25 years, taken on a much more prominent role in discussions of software engineering. And the idea it embodies, that updates to software have a natural and unavoidable disorder-increasing property, is one I'll examine in detail.

You can think of a working piece of software as the result of a complex optimization process over a very multivariate space of possibilities, one whose fitness landscape is exceedingly nonconvex and in fact discontinuous. Quite a mouthful, but for the less mathematically inclined, this means that a functional and useful piece of software has a few interesting characteristics:

- There is an almost uncountably large number of ways of changing the code. Any one-letter substitution, any one-letter insertion or deletion, or transposition, already encompass possibly billions of possible changes in a multi-million-line codebase. The two-letter changes number in quadrillions. Even restricting yourself to semantic changes (i.e. ones that are meaningful) still gives you an uncountable number of possible "directions" in which to go.
- Small changes to the code are overwhelmingly likely to make the product worse. As a simple example again, even a one-character change to the source code can render the product impossible even to compile into a functioning, let alone correct, executable program. Restricting yourself again to semantic changes, the vast majority of changes make programs worse, not better.

Given this brute state of affairs, it's perhaps shocking that software can even be created, changed, or improved at all. It's important to lay this out as a baseline to describe the difficulty of what you're attempting: to create a technical and social system that allows and in fact encourages the production of good software. It should now be less surprising that software engineering is a difficult discipline indeed.

You can now think about technical debt in its proper context. The nature of changes to software are such that, in order to make a change that improves the state of affairs (either by fixing a bug, by changing functionality, or by creating new functionality), it's likely that a lot of significant changes will have to be made. The distance (in terms of editing the code, then compiling, testing and deploying it) between a current operational piece of code and a successive one is large indeed. Given any reasonable constraints on either time or resources, and given the difficulty of moving far from the current codebase to a new and better point, development teams are strongly incentivized to find good-enough solutions that are nearby to the current codebase. In less technical language, coders find it nearly irresistible to implement *kludges*: fixes that get the job done in the sense of satisfying the narrow testable requirements, but that aren't in a real sense "better" than what came before.

Over time, as the accretion of kludges proceeds, each one narrowly satisfying the requirements of the day, you're left with a codebase that is significantly worse, when viewed globally. Code becomes brittle: small changes become harder to implement without breaking existing functionality, and creating large amounts of new functionality becomes all but impossible. The notion of technical debt attempts to use a financial analogy to describe this process: by implementing a kludge, the programmer has mortgaged his future against the requirements of today. And that suboptimal decision will have to be undone, or "repaid" in the future.

As a notion, technical debt is quite useful. It teaches you that no small-but-useful change is free: it must eventually be paid for in terms of doing the larger architectural change that brings the codebase back to a good state. However, I've found that the notion of technical debt rarely goes past the level of analogy. And it turns out you can do significantly better at managing large software projects by taking the analogy even further and actually financializing technical decisions.

Taking Technical Debt Seriously

At first blush, the mere idea of technical debt in actual dollars and cents seems not only difficult, verging on impossible, but also somewhat pointless. Yet I'll argue that doing so is essential. After all, what is the point (in a profit-making enterprise such as trading) of writing all this software other than to make money for the firm? But how, exactly?

A lot of software engineering research to date has been devoted to solving the problem of finding technical debt in a given code base. Numerous products exist on the market that advertise themselves capable of identifying debt. How do they do this? Most operate by implementing *static analysis* tools that look for code that violates specified rules, then try to price out the cost of fixing these violations. The rules are based on generally understood software best-practices. For example, one best-practice is that a code base should not contain duplicated code. Such code duplication is certainly wasteful, but in the worst case it's a potential bug hazard since there is an opportunity for divergent implementations of the same functionality. A "debt finding" tool can identify such duplications and warn the user to eliminate the debt by collapsing the duplicates. Another form of static analysis focuses on so-called *cyclomatic complexity*, which is a measure of the number of paths through a piece of code (McCabe, December 1976). The best practice is to minimize complexity, so code with unusually high complexity is a candidate for repair when it is identified by static analysis tools.

Such tools can be useful, especially in situations where the code base has been inherited or it has aged to the point where the technical staff maintaining the project has lost first-hand knowledge of the problem areas. However, as highlighted in these examples, static analysis tools can only identify hazards. They can't tell you to what extent these have actually resulted in time wasted by engineering staff. You need a way to directly measure the impact of debt on engineering efficiency.

Technical debt expresses itself in two distinct ways: (a) in bugs that are attributable to architectural flaws, and (b) in the incremental cost required to develop new features. To measure technical debt, you need to measure both. What makes technical debt particularly nefarious is that both (a) and (b) are usually buried so deeply in the daily activities of the developers that they will not reveal themselves unless there is a concerted effort by developers and managers.

Let's consider the first technical debt manifestation, defined as bugs that are attributable to architectural flaws. All modern software companies have bug tracking systems. It is possible to mine the data in order to extract a debt estimate directly from the bug database. What is needed, however, is to perform a root cause analysis of each bug and to answer a critical question: is the bug (i.e. defect) the direct result of legacy architectural flaws or is it a "new" defect? This question might seem somewhat arbitrary or puzzling at first, but developers can soon get used to this kind of analysis. For example, suppose that the software code base had a function that was duplicated in two places. As you saw earlier, such coding is generally a bad practice and an example of technical debt. Suppose further that a new feature was implemented that modified one (but not the other) copy of the function. This caused a bug, which was filed and fixed. Clearly, the time spent to update the second function was a form of waste directly attributable to technical debt. Working through the bug list in this fashion can actually produce a good estimate of the number of bugs attributable to architectural flaws.

The second debt manifestation, defined as the incremental increase in new feature cost, is more difficult to measure. In essence, it requires an analysis at design time. Suppose a new feature is requested and the developers determine that there is no simple way to implement the feature without significant re-architecture of the code. This is a hint that the existing software base is architecturally weak and indebted. Developers sometimes make the decision to implement the feature in a "quick and dirty" way that adds more debt. This decision, the decision to move forward with an expedient solution, commonly happens without enough management oversight. However, a software organization can train its people to capture these decisions (say in a design review) and add them to a "log" of technical debt. In other words, by far the best way to capture a price estimate on the technical debt is exactly at the time it is being introduced. If the developer decides to implement the feature the "right" way, then it will indeed take more time. That incremental cost can be added to the debt log as well. The key is to do it at design time.

Finally, a way of identifying this "feature debt cost" is by careful examination of the test costs associated with feature development. Specifically, software companies will almost always perform a *feature regression test* before promoting a new feature to their released codebase. Regression testing involves checking that new functionality doesn't break old functionality. This can be a very useful canary in the coal mine. By measuring the number of regression test failures, you can get an indication of technical debt. For example, in an ideal system with no debt, adding new features should not cause older features to break (assuming the new feature was well-tested to begin with). If creating a new feature causes an old feature to break, the cost associated with diagnosing and fixing the old feature is of a sort of "debt payment."

Although these debt measurements are much more hidden in the real world, the good news is that most software operations have existing processes and checkpoints they can leverage. For example, agile scrum prescribes a monthly retrospection, which is an opportunity to do root cause analysis of bugs. Other approaches have similar examination periods. Moreover, most companies have procedures for performing design reviews of new features. This presents an opportunity to ask the developer if they are taking shortcuts or adding new debt in the interest of expediency. Finally, turning bug counts and incremental feature costs into dollars is a matter of having engineers estimate time spent on these things. Once the right processes are in place, it is not difficult to sustain these practices.

Summary and Looking Ahead

- Competence with handling information technology is now a non-negotiable element of the modern workplace.
- For more cognitively demanding jobs, learning how to deal with and extract useful knowledge from data is similarly non-negotiable.
- Humans and machines are good at complementary tasks. Figuring out how to optimize the man-machine symbiosis is the best way to extract the most value from both.
- Writing software properly is as much a sociological challenge as a technical one. By focusing more on the former, technically-minded organizations will improve dramatically at the latter.

In the next chapter—the last one—I put the whole story together. Drawing from all the lessons you've learned, the laws of trading, you can come to an understanding of what trading is, the promise of mastery and understanding that it brings, and the deep humility that must remain at its core.

References

Agans, D. (2006). *Debugging: The 9 Indispensable Rules for Finding Even the Most Elusive Software and Hardware Problems*. New York: AMACOM.

Brynjolfsson, E., and McAfee, A. (2016). *The Second Machine Age: Work, Progress, and Prosperity in a Time of Brilliant Technologies*. New York: W. W. Norton & Company.

Clark, A. (2015). *Surfing Uncertainty: Prediction, Action, and the Embodied Mind*. New York: Oxford University Press.

Cunningham, W. (1992). The WyCash Portfolio Management System. Retrieved from c2.com, http://c2.com/doc/oopsla92.html.

Levinson, M. (2016). *The Box: How the Shipping Container Made the World Smaller and the World Economy Bigger*, 2nd ed. Princeton, NJ: Princeton University Press.

Mathis, R. et al. (2013). *Human Resource Management*, 14th ed. Cincinnati: South-Western College Publishing.

McCabe, T. J. (December 1976). "A Complexity Measure." *IEEE Transactions on Software Engineering*, 308–320.

Peglar, T. (2018, July 9). 1995 Reintroduction of Wolves in Yellowstone. Retrieved from Yellowstone Park, https://www.yellowstonepark .com/park/yellowstone-wolves-reintroduction.

Roberge, M. (2015). *The Sales Acceleration Formula: Using Data, Technology, and Inbound Selling to go from $0 to $100 Million*. Hoboken, NJ: John Wiley & Sons.

Roser, M. (n.d.). Employment in Agriculture. Retrieved from Our World in Data, https://ourworldindata.org/employment-in-agriculture.

Scribner, S. (April 1987). *Head and Hand: An Action Approach to Thinking*. Arlington, VA: Eastern Psychological Association.

Sutton, R. a. (2017). *Reinforcement Learning: An Introduction*. Cambridge, MA: MIT Press.

CHAPTER 11

Adaptation

Every living creature in the world today is alive because its parents were successful at reproducing. You are the result of a literal life-or-death struggle won by those who came before you. Somewhere along the line, a small mouselike creature grabbed that last walnut before the winter; he survived, his brother froze to death, and millions of years later you're alive because of that parent's success. We're all winners merely by virtue of having been born! This process of adaptation and selection has made us phenomenally good at surviving, and it's a good thing, too, because everyone we compete with is similarly so endowed. It ain't easy out there.

You may have noticed that the story I've been building in this book is that markets have many of the same properties that characterize biological systems. There are complex feedback loops, a competitive landscape of variation and selection, and even the appearance of intentionality. In the previous chapters, you've looked at trading from a number of perspectives. Each of these chapters approaches this biological analogy from a different angle, but here I will synthesize these viewpoints into a coherent view of adaptation and evolution in trading.

As I said at the outset, trading is a complex activity, but one with a fundamentally simple goal. That goal, assuming you don't fall into traps and cognitive byways, is to make sustainable profits. In my career I've found that, in teaching the mindset necessary to trade successfully over the long term, the viewpoint of adaptation and evolution ends up resonating most strongly with the greatest number of people. It is that viewpoint I develop in this, the final chapter of the book.

> If you're not getting better, you're getting worse.

Natural Selection

In the standard Darwinian telling, natural selection is a biological mechanism that requires two main components in order to operate:

- A source of variation in the characteristics of organisms (or the units of selection)
- Differential reproductive fitness as a result of that variation

With these two components acting together over a long enough time scale, and over a varied enough fitness landscape, the mechanism of natural selection explains the entire panoply of living organisms that populate the earth (Dawkins, 2016). And what a panoply it is: from extremophilic bacteria living in scalding and acidic waters, their lives nothing like anything else we know, to quaking aspen tree systems where a single individual can span multiple acres of land, to our own lowly human condition. While financial markets don't have nearly the grandeur and spectacle of the Earth's biome, the very same selection mechanism applies to the development, and yes even evolution, of the world's markets. I will therefore examine the characteristics of natural selection, and in turn show how they apply in financial markets.

Units of Selection

Biological natural selection operates at multiple levels of the biological hierarchy: gene, cell, organism, group, and perhaps more controversially, at higher taxonomic levels. There are biologists who stress, for example, the importance of gene-level selection. Others stress the importance of organism-level selection. These philosophical differences have led to some acrimonious debates in the past, and it's not my place to weigh in on them here. Nonetheless, it's undeniable that as an explanatory mechanism, viewing selection at multiple levels of hierarchy is a useful and productive paradigm for doing biology. In a similar vein, financial markets have natural selection operating at many different levels of hierarchy:

- *Individual:* Not everyone who starts at a financial firm ends up with a successful career, after all. But even the most famous flameouts and blowouts (Victor Niederhoffer and John Meriwether are two prominent examples) nonetheless achieved a measure of success before their eventual fall. And even today, spectacular "disasters" like Michael Milken lead happy and successful lives. But the vast majority of people who have unwillingly left the world of trading have done so quietly and without fanfare. The selection pressure I'm talking about here is largely the culling of those who couldn't find a foothold in the business, for whatever reason. The people who remain and thrive in trading today are the survivors of this selection process.
- *Group:* Groups of individuals (trading desks and business units, for example) can live and die collectively. Investment banks and trading firms start and shutter trading desks and groups regularly, even if the people themselves are good employees and traders, and even if the markets in which they operate are growing and thriving. The people who populate those groups can often find other niches and groups within the larger organization. Groups that continue and endure over time do so by surviving this group-level selective pressure.
- *Firm:* This is perhaps the strongest level at which selection operates. The list of famous and failed firms is long and ever-growing. In late 2007, who would have thought Lehman Brothers would be wiped off the face of the earth a scant 11 months later? LTCM, Knight Capital, and many other funds and trading firms similarly have been bankrupted or absorbed at steep discounts. Even exchanges and trading venues themselves are not immune, as with the example of BATS Global Markets in the aftermath of its failed self-IPO. Only the strongest and most adaptable firms survive the constant churn of competition in modern financial markets.
- *Market:* Many formerly thriving markets themselves also wither and die. After all, there is very little trading in whale oil futures anymore.

What's interesting is that natural selection is operating at all of these levels simultaneously. Individuals who get hired into a group may succeed or fail, but that probability is affected by the success of the group in question. It's important to note that the arrow of causation runs in both directions: relatively unsuccessful groups are less likely to hire quality employees, and those mediocre employees cause, over time, even worse performance from the groups that hired them. The converse is also true, of course.

The same argument works with the interaction of groups and firms, and of firms and markets. As an example, there were once many great trading firms with excellent traders who specialized in the sort of open-outcry trading that has now almost entirely disappeared from modern financial markets. These traders were left in a market that was drying up, and no matter how successful the trader and firm, it's difficult to survive the elimination of your entire market.

Sources of Variation

In biological natural selection and hence evolution, the canonical source of variation is the random mutation of the DNA that encodes an organism's genome. In fact, biologists now understand that this is only one of many sources of variation. In particular, as they've sequenced the DNA of more and more species and individuals, they've learned that genes (trait-producing segments of DNA) can transfer "horizontally" across individuals and species, outside of the usual reproductive mechanism (Quammen, 2018).

In a similar manner, you can examine the sources of variation operating in financial markets. Viewing things from this evolutionary paradigm, you can see a lot of sources of variation:

- *Ex-nihilo brilliant idea*: Although rare, sometimes people or groups do have a brilliant new idea that no one has thought of yet, and that has no immediate antecedents. ETFs, for example, were an invention that emerged from little more than the creativity of a few traders and salesmen in the early 1990s (Gastineau, 2002). But these Eureka-like "flashes of brilliance" are rare, and most novel developments are of a different sort.
- *Porting a trade to another market*: This is among the most common sources of variation in financial markets. There is no

shame in imitation if that imitation is profitable. Many good new trades are merely the realization that an existing trade could be applied in some new country, market, or product.

- *Combining two trades*: As discussed in Chapter 5, edges can emerge in various ways. It's frequently the case that you realize two or more trades that appear independent of each other are in fact versions of a more general phenomenon. By synthesizing the two, you create a new trade that combines the best of the component trades.

- *Regulatory changes*: Trades and markets can come into being by changes in regulatory regimes. Foreign exchange markets didn't exist in any significant form until after the market changes brought about by the US's de-facto withdrawal from the Bretton-Woods currency system in 1971 (Lowenstein, 2011). Contract-for-difference trades in the UK, for example, are a result of the changes in the early 1990s in how stamp tax is assessed and collected. Likewise, carbon-credit trading became a big business nearly overnight when the Kyoto Protocol came into force and set out a mechanism for trading carbon emission rights directly.

- *Newly available data*: It's very common that exchanges and other trading venues, in a search for more revenue, create and market products that provide more detailed and informative views of the activity on those exchanges. Many exchanges, particularly those in Nordic countries for example, provide information on the entity on both sides of a trade, partially de-anonymizing that market's activities. This data enables trades and edges that would be impossible to implement without it.

- *Trades enabling other trades*: The development and spread of a new trade can enable the follow-on creation of other trades that work based on the existence of the first. The creation of index futures and their use in hedging has created a need for arbitrageurs that maintain the necessary relationships between the future, the underlying basket of stocks, and any ETFs that may exist. Similarly, the securitization of mortgages and their consequent trading on financial markets has made possible a variety of credit derivative trades that rely on the securitization process.

- *Size and liquidity*: Increasing the scale of trading in a market frequently enables new sorts of trades. As liquidity increases, the ability to trade out of positions more quickly and cheaply allows traders to hold more and larger positions. This can allow for more economies of scale, making viable those trades that wouldn't have been so in smaller or more illiquid markets.

- *Negotiation and relationship-building*: Many new trades occur because of fortuitous conversations between clients and their bankers or brokers. "What we'd really like to do is X," begins the conversation from the client side. The service provider, always trying to help and gather more fees and commissions, didn't realize clients wanted X, but is incentivized to work out how to make that trade happen. Portfolio margining, for example, probably emerged from this sort of conversation between market makers and their clearing firms.

Differential Reproductive Fitness

What does reproduction mean in the context of financial markets? Again, you can look at the units of selection to see how reproduction can work:

- *Individual*: Short of two traders getting together and having super-trader babies, reproduction at this level seems like a bit of a stretch. That said, excellent traders who are also excellent teachers do, in an important sense, reproduce themselves by teaching their skills and knowledge to others.

- *Groups*: Groups certainly combine and separate in a manner much like the reproductive processes of unicellular organisms like bacteria. Groups that achieve enough size and success to warrant splitting them into multiple parts can be said to be reproducing. Similarly, bringing two groups together can frequently create new ideas and approaches that are only possible because of the merger of the groups' existing ideas and approaches.

- *Firms*: Companies both merge and split regularly. Famously, Fairchild Semiconductor and Hewlett-Packard birthed, in one way or another, nearly all of the successful tech companies that populate Silicon Valley today. Individuals and groups within these organizations struck out on their own, taking good ideas and good ways of organizing their work from these powerhouses of innovation. Similarly, former employees of Newport Partners and DE Shaw have gone on to found some of the largest and most successful trading firms in the world. In fact, Jeff Bezos, founder of Amazon and now the richest man in the world, got his start at DE Shaw. Mergers also occur, as with the merger of Getco and Knight Capital in 2013, for example.

You've seen in previous chapters, especially in Chapter 5, the results of all of this adaptation and reproduction, of repeated success and failure. The entities that do manage to survive in modern, mature financial markets are tough indeed. They've thrived in an extremely competitive and hostile environment. Markets aren't perfectly efficient and never will be, of course: there is an ineradicable amount of inefficiency that must remain for trading firms to be willing to trade at all. However, the minimum level of skill, the table stakes of trading in today's markets, continue to rise. Markets may not be perfectly efficient, but they are *adaptive* (Lo, 2017).

Getting Better

The adaptive and evolutionary nature of financial markets means that staying in business and thriving over time requires improvement. Doing what's worked in the past is no guarantee of future success, and indeed an approach that emphasizes that sort of stasis is a virtual guarantee of failure. So, how are you to structure your efforts such that you give primacy to this chapter's rule? Let's begin by revisiting, with a view toward "getting better," the lessons from the previous chapters.

Ten Visions of Adapting and Getting Better

1. In Chapter 1, I began by looking at the idea of motivation. You studied the importance of knowing yourself first before venturing forth into the world of trading. Self-knowledge and motivation can be seen as the cornerstones of a long-term career in trading. Without them, you cannot hope to maintain the effort necessary to continually improve over time, even in the face of setbacks and difficulties.

2. The second rule shows why maintaining that motivation is so difficult. The fundamental nature of trading is adverse selection, and as a result of it you'll always be dissatisfied with the trades you've done. Getting better in a world ruled by adverse selection requires a constant push to win the battle of information asymmetry. In an adaptive market, the marginal trader is always improving. Being better than the marginal trader means staying above water in an ever-rising ocean of skill.

3. The chapter on risk teaches that because capital is a finite resource, you have to evaluate carefully the risks you're willing to take, even if the trades you do are profitable ones. Evaluating these risks is an exercise in never-ending vigilance, and much of what "improving at trading" means in practice is improving your understanding of the risks to which your trades expose you.

4. In Chapter 4, you get a first look at the idea of liquidity. The liquidity of the markets in which you trade defines the sorts of trades that are possible there. Over time, the liquidity parameters of markets change, sometimes dramatically. Adapting and getting better, in this context, means understanding how liquidity shifts affect your trading, and it means acting in anticipation of those changes.

5. No trading firm can be successful without edge, as you learn in Chapter 5. Those edges represent things you understand and can do that others cannot. Markets adapt over time, as you know, and thus over time the circle of things that you know that others don't shrinks. Similarly, over time there are fewer things you're uniquely able to do that others cannot. Adapting and improving requires a near-obsessive focus on improving edges and finding new ones.

6. The discussion in Chapter 6 on models sheds light on the concrete process of improving over the course of time. Trades lose profitability over time, either due to the edge or the model becoming stale. Only by understanding deeply the process by which this happens, and by being able to tell which of the two is the source of the decay, can you improve your existing trades.

7. The relationship between costs and improvement is subtle, as you learn in Chapter 7. Over time, the visible costs of a trade generally decrease as economic development (especially in technology) drives them down. On its face, this is good for a trading firm. And yet, decreased visible cost also drives down the barrier to entry for competitors. This increased competition can easily drive up invisible costs, meaning that the balance of costs of a trade changes throughout its lifetime. Adapting means understanding and anticipating these cost shifts.

8. Chapter 8 teaches that philosophical issues do arise in thinking about the nature of trading. In particular, some deeply counterintuitive behavior results when a process evolves based on feedback. The historical accidents I examined show the process of adaptation and evolution in action, and you learned some lessons about the mindset necessary to adapt successfully to seemingly impossible turns of events.

9. By contrast, Chapter 9 delves into some of the most concrete and human ideas for building a structure that withstands and thrives in such a competitive world as trading. Misaligned incentives are, over time, a cancer that eats away at organizations and prevents the sort of nimbleness and adaptability necessary for survival. By thinking carefully about these incentives, you can create organizations that thrive in difficult markets.

10. Finally, in Chapter 10 I look at the evolution of human competences and the threat and opportunity represented by modern technology. The world is now awash in data, so learning how to take advantage of the information dissolved in the sea of data is one of the most important ways you can successfully adapt and evolve.

You should think of these different visions as just that: a variety of perspectives on the same fundamental fact. Without considering the necessity of improvement as the important core of building a successful trading operation, you're left doomed to short-lived success at best. Long-term sustainable profitability requires adaptation, lots of it and all the time.

Improving at an Individual Level

You can also study the idea of improvement and adaptation as it relates to the levels of hierarchy I've already discussed. Doing so gives a more detailed view of the sort of mindset required to implement an improvement-centric approach at these levels.

At the individual level, there is no shortage of popular books, seminars, and training programs that purport to teach the famous "growth mindset" (Dweck, 2006). And, as can be expected with a new paradigm that jumps into the collective consciousness, the idea of the growth mindset is not without its detractors. The details of these debates, fortunately, aren't particularly important here. But it is worth noting that in the context of trading and other competitive pursuits, many of the usual exhortations related to the growth mindset (praise effort not talent, failing is learning, view challenges as opportunities) are at best only mildly useful. After all, no amount of effort or failing/learning will transform me into the next 100 meter sprinting champion. There is an inescapable lack of athletic talent that prevents such a transformation, no matter my mindset. In trading, similarly, without important technical skills and a relatively high minimum raw IQ, no amount of effort will transform a well-intentioned, hardworking but marginal trader into a world-class one. That said, the ideas contained in some of this growth-mindset research do provide a starting point for discussing individual-level adaptation and improvement.

One useful idea you can extract from growth-mindset thinking is that of motivation. Fundamentally, being able to improve at your job over the long term is indeed a matter of desire more than anything else. By its nature, trading presents difficulties and challenges, and taxes you in ways that can be discouraging even for the most motivated. And it's this internal motivation, as I discussed in Chapter 1, that must be present in order to surmount the inevitable difficulties over the long term. External motivation can work, for a time, but the exclusive or near-exclusive reliance on external motivators like money, promotions, and prestige can only take you so far.

More concretely, in trading and similar fields, one of the most useful sources of information about where to improve is finding and being sensitive to situations that don't make sense. Among the best predictors of success in creative fields such as research science or trading is the development of a sixth sense or feeling about "things that don't quite fit." It could be an experimental result that didn't quite yield the expected result, or a trading strategy that doesn't quite do what you expected. In the context of the pressures and constraints present in a typical job situation, it's overwhelmingly easy to ignore these odd situations and to proceed as planned. Paradoxically, some of the best trading ideas and new strategies I've been privy to had their genesis in someone noticing something a little off. Instead of ignoring it or shelving it for later, the odd situation was instead explored and studied. And once that happened, like following the thread in a tangled yarn, you began to learn, unravel, and understand things you didn't expect existed.

Of course, going overboard in this direction is counterproductive. Following every little surprising result or odd occurrence would paralyze you with too many wild geese to chase. The task, in order to learn to be good at improving, is to develop a good feel or taste for the sorts of odd things that are worth digging into and spending time investigating. This is greatly facilitated, of course, by having a group culture that encourages the right amount of these sorts of "will probably amount to nothing" investigations.

The most interesting thread I ever unraveled in my career was the German tax-dividend trade I described in Chapter 5. No one I worked with had ever heard of it, and I probably wouldn't know about it today if it hadn't been for some odd trades I noticed one day in short-dated options on large German companies. Options that are struck far from the current stock price rarely trade, let alone ones that are struck at 0.01 EUR. And yet I saw that thousands of 0.01-strike calls were trading at levels that didn't make a lot of sense. I also knew there were other more natural ways to make the bets that these options traders were putting on. Something smelled fishy.

These options trades didn't affect any of the work I was doing, but they seemed odd enough to merit more digging.

Over the next few weeks, I found other examples of large German companies with similar odd trading around dividend time. We called in

(continued)

some of our brokers to try to explain what was going on, and over time the full extent of this tax-dividend trade became clear. And boy did the smell get worse. Our brokers were wary of telling us too much about it, since they knew it was a sketchy trade and they didn't want us piling into that business. There was never any chance of us doing these trades given their questionable ethics, but learning about these forces did let us make much better markets in other products that were affected by these trades.

Improving as a Group

I've already implicitly defined a *group* as a relatively self-contained set of individuals, working together on a common project. In particular, let's further assume that all members of the group know one another. Practically, this puts a strong upper limit on the possible size of any group, and this limit is known in the anthropological literature as Dunbar's number (Gladwell, 2002). Beyond this number (somewhere between 50 and 150, depending on the situation), the use and maintenance of social ties as the main mechanism for organization begins to break down. The social ties become too weak to sustain cohesion. Thus, in what follows, I'll assume that group size remains comfortably below this magic limit.

As I alluded to in the previous section, group dynamics strongly define how adaptation-friendly a group of people can be. One particular aspect that affects this adaptation ability is the degree and strength of any hierarchy that's present. Historically, groups in corporate settings were defined by a relatively rigid and strongly hierarchical system of organization. This approach was largely pioneered by Frederick Taylor and became known as Taylorism after his famous 1911 monograph (Taylor, 1911). In the inevitable backlash that followed, beginning in the early 1970s, many modern companies that emerged from this stifling environment went far in the other direction, especially those companies headquartered on the West Coast of the United States.

I argued in Chapter 10 that a wide range of strengths of hierarchy can be made to work, but they must be responsive to the nature of the work in question. Highly creative groups in very fluid markets and businesses require a less heavyweight organizational structure than groups that operate in more rigid markets with more emphasis on efficiency. In the former, improvement typically comes more from ideas that are outside of the norm or current operating procedure. In the latter, improvements are much likelier to be incremental in nature. The organizational structure defines the sorts of new ideas and improvement that are likely to result in the typical case.

One example where groups improved through the selective weakening of hierarchical structures is in the management of aircrews in passenger airliners. On December 28, 1978, United Airlines flight 173 was scheduled to fly from JFK airport in New York to Portland, Oregon. This flight never made it to Portland and crashed in the suburbs of Portland due to lack of fuel. In the NTSB investigation that followed, it was determined that problems began because, upon approach to Portland, a loud thump was heard when deploying the landing gear. The landing attempt was aborted, and the plane circled Portland for an hour attempting to determine the source of the noise, and whether there was indeed a problem that prevented landing. During this time, neither of the two pilots or the flight engineer monitored the fuel levels. The result was that, once the plane was on final approach, both engines flamed out due to a lack of fuel. The plane crashed 6 miles from the airport.

The NTSB report on the crash recommended that airlines provide training in "flight deck resource management, with particular emphasis on participative management for captains and assertiveness training for other cockpit crewmembers" (NTSB, 1979). In essence, the idea is to explicitly weaken the hierarchy where the captain of the plane has full command and, due to seniority, doesn't pay enough attention to the ideas and information coming from more junior members. By weakening this hierarchy, small groups of pilots can perform better. And indeed, widespread training in crew resource management (LeSage, Dyar, & Evans, 2009) has led to improvements in communication and a reduction in incidents, a reduction that is directly attributable to this training (Beaubien & Baker, 2002).

Useful changes in the other direction can also be important in other contexts. In situations where not enough hierarchy obtains, the introduction of a more structured approach can prove effective as well. This has been the experience of hospital surgical units that have adopted a checklist-based method of managing the complexity of an operating room (Gawande, 2011). By removing some fluidity and arbitrariness, these groups manage their work more efficiently and productively.

Improving as a Firm

By contrast to the definition of a group, I'll define a firm as a society of groups—that is, a larger organization where members don't necessarily know everyone else. As such, the most useful operative level at which to view this scale of organization is in the interaction between groups, as opposed to the interactions between individuals. It's worth noting that many actual firms, the small ones, are more usefully viewed as groups. In this telling, organizations need to have at least a few hundred members before the ideas in this section can be most usefully applied.

Improvement at the firm level must consist of improvement in the organization of the groups that make up the firm. Adaptation at this scale of organization involves the creation of groups and the elimination and merging of groups in order to maximize their suitability to their tasks. But these undertakings are relatively heavyweight and aren't nearly as common a source of improvement as the more everyday and prosaic process of improving the communication and interaction between groups.

Once organizations reach a scale where people can no longer rely on personal connections or relationships in order to interact productively (since the average person only knows a small fraction of the people with whom they might interact), firms need to install a different mechanism to mediate those interactions across groups. The long-term success of a firm is intimately tied to the success in implementing a functional and efficient mechanism for these interactions. Again, the nature of the business of the firm constrains and guides the sorts of mechanisms that are best to implement.

Another useful resource for studying the design of firm-level structures is found in the military. Organizations responsible for national defense can have little tolerance for suboptimal processes and results. As a result, military tacticians, theorists, and other thinkers have, over millennia, developed some of the most leading-edge accounts of how to successfully organize large numbers of people in pursuit of a goal. It was Alexander the Great's organizational skill, as much as his tactical skill, that won him famous battles in the fourth century BC. And a century later, the same can be said of Hannibal of Carthage as he successfully prosecuted the Punic Wars with a significant disadvantage in territory and men.

Perhaps the first important semi-modern work on the subject was Carl von Clausewitz's *Vom Kriege* (On War). Though subject to as much interpretation as any other important work from a different age, you can nonetheless discern useful management principles that are still applicable today. In particular, von Clausewitz stresses the importance and value of strong emotional and political motivation, especially if you're the defender. As you saw in Chapter 7, large incumbents (such as Kodak) with seemingly strong positions can be easily overtaken by more-motivated and nimble competitors, even if the latter lack the resources of the former.

In an even more recent and highly influential strain of thought, known as the "Revolution in Military Affairs," theorists argue that technological progress defines the speed at which doctrines, strategies, and tactics must change and adapt in response to that progress. In *Leading Change* (Burr, 1998), the author argues that sustaining military performance and responsiveness is only possible by transforming the organization into one that considers learning and adaptation a fundamentally important skill. This idea very closely mirrors the argument in this chapter. Organizations that don't learn will not remain competitive in any undertaking with aggressive and constantly improving opponents.

Productively Viewing Your Place in the World

If readers have been internalizing the lessons of this chapter, at this point they may feel disheartened by the picture I've painted of competitive endeavors. The inescapable need to adapt, or otherwise to wither away and die, can feel like an overwhelming and oppressive reality from which there is no escape. And it is true that, short of finding something else to do, there is no escape from natural selection in competitive environments, whether for an antelope or a trading firm.

Notwithstanding this reality, it may surprise you that you can view it in a positive light. In fact, the seeds of this more-optimistic viewpoint have been sown throughout the book. The argument is, like many others in the book, somewhat paradoxical and perhaps subtle. But I'm convinced that accepting this reality of never-ending competition and ceaseless adaptation, and finding within it your own calling to greatness, is the most important gift this book can bestow.

A Trader and His Trades

Consider my friend Mark, an equities trader in New York at a world-class proprietary trading firm. Over the years, he's created and developed some successful trading strategies, and today is going to be a day much like any other. A typical morning consists of:

- Reading general news headlines to get a sense of what's important in the world.
- Reading a bit more deeply some relevant financial news.
- Reading stories that relate specifically to the products he's trading.
- Talking to his counterpart in London: understanding how their shared strategies have performed on the day so far, what's been interesting, etc.
- In the meantime, his assistant has checked the trading summaries from the day before, started up the premarket automated systems, and perhaps preliminarily adjusted some parameters in the strategies.
- Mark and his fellow traders and assistants get a sense of their risk exposures, adjust edges a bit more, perhaps they do some light pre-market trading, and they wait for the opening bell at 9:30am.

He takes one last deep breath before the market opens, secure in the knowledge that:

- He operates in perhaps the most competitive human undertaking on earth.
- His competitors have, in aggregate, gotten just a little bit better than yesterday.
- His job, to do profitable trades, has gotten a bit more difficult than it was yesterday. People will figure out his trades, the ones he's spent so much effort developing, and those trades will decay over time.

- Tomorrow will be more difficult than today, and the day after more difficult still, and on until the day he decides to retire from the business. There is no respite and there are no pauses to the inexorable adaptation of markets.

It's easy to view Mark's job as a soul-destroying, almost Sisyphean effort. And indeed, it's this ceaseless competition that does, over time, break the will of many market participants. But I will argue in what follows that the best traders view their situation with very much the opposite perspective: as a liberating and redemptive force.

I first need to address the idea that the trades Mark has developed, through dint of hard work and constant improvement, are *his* in any meaningful way. It's certainly true that our legal system very explicitly considers trading strategies as intellectual property. And trading firms do indeed sue each other with regularity for stealing strategies or code from each other. But as a matter of worldview, in particular the emotional and psychological attachment that results from viewing trades as property, this idea is not very useful.

In particular, given the inevitable fact that profitable trades will decay and disappear over time, attaching yourself to them and considering them "yours" is bound to cause frustration. It's much more productive to view your trades as discoveries than possessions. Isaac Newton discovered the law of universal gravitation, but in no way should we consider that law to be owned by him, even when he was alive. Trades are much more like discoveries in science than they are a boat or a sandwich. They are things that you've understood, or can do, that others cannot. Understandings and abilities cannot reasonably be considered property, and so trades shouldn't either. And when a trade starts to decay, psychologically it's much easier to deal with the event if you view it as "hmm, someone else figured out what I figured out" rather than "hmm, someone stole my trade."

Having done away with the idea that trades are "yours," I now return to the question of what Mark's job is really about. Presumably Mark makes a good living as a trader. But why is that? Is it because he's good at running profitable trades? Put another way, if you replaced Mark with a well-trained trader who could run the trades, would that person deserve Mark's income? Understanding adaptation as you now do, you should see the answer is a resounding no.

In many team sports, modern methods of evaluating player skill attempt to compare players to a hypothetical world where that person is replaced with an average or marginal player (Value Over Replacement Player, Wins Above Replacement, etc.). By doing so, you identify how much that player is worth. Similarly, in trading you can talk about the value of the "seat." If you replaced Mark with the marginal trader in the market, how much money would that person make? It's probably more than zero since the strategies Mark and his team have developed likely make money even if they're not managed perfectly optimally. But over time as these strategies decay, the replacement trader will go back to being a zero-profitability trader.

Over the long-term, the value that Mark provides is defined almost entirely by his ability to create, develop, and execute those profitable trading strategies. This is the crux of the argument: given that this creative process is the essence of what Mark is good at, what the world is willing to pay Mark to do, why should he bemoan the competitive and adaptive processes that make his trades less profitable over time?

For someone whose value derives from this creative process, what worse hell could there be than to be consigned to maintain forever some trades he created long ago? In this hypothetical world where trades don't decay, the logical profit-maximizing thing would be to continue to push the buttons, over and over again, on his past creations. And since those trades don't ever become unprofitable (again, in this hypothetical world), he has little incentive to find new ones. The unique and valuable skills that Mark possesses would be left unused, collecting mental dust somewhere in his brain.

Profitable traders are some of the most intelligent, driven, perceptive, and adaptable people on earth. To relegate such a person to a life of maintenance and literally trading on past glories sounds and is soul-destroying. The essence of trading, the thing that makes it such an interesting and stimulating undertaking, is this very process of adaptation and competition. Channeling again the work of Abraham Maslow, true self-actualization comes from doing what you were meant to do. For a profitable trader, that means creating and developing new things, not maintaining old things. It calls to mind John F. Kennedy's speech in 1962 in support of the Apollo moon program: "We choose to go to the moon ... not because [it is] easy, but because [it is] hard."

A Trader and the World

By happy coincidence, coming full circle to the book's introduction, the world gains immensely from Mark doing his job. By understanding the world better, and expressing that understanding through trading, prices become more accurate, the world allocates scarce resources more efficiently, and the engine of human progress continues to run. As it happens, my friend Mark trades US pink sheet stocks, specifically making markets in American Depositary Receipts (ADRs). These ADRs, you may recall, are US-listed versions of foreign stocks. In Mark's case, the ADRs are those of emerging Asian and African markets.

ADRs exist for a variety of reasons, but among the most important is the desire of American investors to invest in companies that are not based in the US. If a US-based person wants to invest in Nigeria, for example, the task ahead of them is formidable:

- Find a broker that provides connectivity and clearing services for the Nigerian Stock Exchange (NSE) in Lagos.
- Transfer US funds to that broker and effect a foreign-exchange transaction into Nigerian naira.
- Obtain NSE market data in order to place an order during times the market is open (5am Eastern to 11am Eastern).
- Comply with all relevant Nigerian laws for foreign investors, including tax and profit-repatriation laws.
- If the US investor is a fund or other investment vehicle, ensure that the Nigerian investment complies with all SEC and FINRA regulations, and also complies with the fund's own rules and covenants.

In practice these steps are so onerous that historically, only the very largest and most well-organized US investment firms would be willing to go through them. The result of these various impediments was that, before ADRs, US investors who wanted to invest in foreign businesses had no practical means to do so and those businesses in turn couldn't access the large pools of capital available in the US.

If, however, that Nigerian stock had a US ADR, the situation changes considerably. All the US brokers have connectivity to US markets, no foreign exchange transaction needs to take place, market data and trading hours are convenient for US investors, and it's significantly easier to comply with all the relevant laws, regulations, and covenants. What happens when a trader like Mark decides to make markets in ADRs is that the US investor offloads all those pesky issues onto the shoulders of Mark, a professional whose job it is to deal with those issues. The existence of ADRs, and the willingness of Mark to make markets in those ADRs, results in a movement of capital whose beneficial results are difficult to overstate.

The story of international financial markets in the last 25 years is largely the story of emerging and frontier markets opening their doors to foreign investment. You can imagine a great dam, which was blocking the flow of capital from rich to poor countries, slowly getting chipped away. Through the dogged efforts of people like Mark, finding ways to profitably provide markets in the stocks of these countries to US investors, capital finds its way to profitable investments. As I said at the outset, trading is not a zero-sum game. Investors in developed countries get better returns from these new emerging-market investments, and these countries get access to capital that brings up their standard of living over time.

That is the true story of trading, and it's a story well worth telling.

References

Beaubien, J. M., and Baker, D. P. (2002). *Airline Pilots' Perception of and Experiences in Crew Resource Management (CRM) Training*. American Institutes for Research.

Burr, M. R. (1998). "Leading Change: The Military as a Learning Organization." Australian Army.

Dawkins, R. (2016). *The Ancestor's Tale: A Pilgrimage to the Dawn of Evolution*, rev. ed. Wilmington, MA: Mariner Books.

Dweck, C. (2006). *Mindset: The New Psychology of Success*. New York: Ballantine Books.

Gastineau, G. (2002). The Exchange-Traded Funds Manual. Hoboken NJ: John Wiley & Sons.

Gawande, A. (2011). *The Checklist Manifesto*. New York: Picador.

Gladwell, M. (2002). *The Tipping Point: How Little Things Can Make a Big Difference*. New York: Back Bay Books.

LeSage, P., Dyar, J. T., & Evans, B. (2009). *Crew Resource Management: Principles and Practice*. Burlington, MA: Jones & Bartlett Learning.

Lo, A. (2017). *Adaptive Markets: Financial Evolution at the Speed of Thought.* Princeton, NJ: Princeton University Press.

Lowenstein, R. (2011, August 4). The Nixon Shock. Retrieved from Bloomberg Businessweek, https://www.bloomberg.com/news/articles/2011-08-04/the-nixon-shock.

NTSB. (1979). *United Air Lines, Inc. McDonnell-Douglas DC-8-61, N8082U Portland, Oregon: December 28, 1978.* Washington DC: National Transportation Safety Board.

Quammen, D. (2018). *The Tangled Tree: A Radical New History of Life.* New York: Simon & Schuster.

Taylor, F. (1911). *The Principles of Scientific Management.* New York: Harper & Brothers.

Notes

Introduction:

1. STOCK: A share of stock is a piece of the equity (E) of a firm. The fundamental accounting identity tells us that the assets (A) of a firm need to be balanced against the debt or liabilities (L) and equity (E) of the firm. A = L + E. In fact, the dichotomy between liabilities and equity is a false one. There is merely an order of seniority that tells us who gets paid if a company goes bankrupt. In most countries, employee salaries have the first claim, then secured debt holders, then unsecured debt holders, then senior or preferred equity, and thereafter, finally, common equity (shares of stock). Thus, the shares of a company are in fact the least-senior, last-to-get-paid, riskiest tranche of the capital structure of a firm. Which makes it at best curious that it's the most common asset class into which average people invest their retirement savings.

2. COMMODITIES: Commodities are standardized physical things, and it is this standardization that is the key to commoditization. A sheaf of wheat may be a physical thing, but it's not a commodity until it has been classified, adjusted, collected into a standard amount, and located in one of a few standard locations.

3. As with most universal claims about financial markets, there are exceptions. In fact, there can be rare instances during stock tender offers where buying two identical-seeming shares of stock actually yields two different financial outcomes.

4. Crude oil in fact has two main "standard" contracts: (a) West Texas Intermediate crude oil delivered at a set of tanks in Cushing, Oklahoma, at a set of prearranged dates. The satellite view of the area just south of Cushing shows how large an industry this is. (b) Brent crude oil delivered at one of four terminals on the North Sea, again at a certain set of dates.

5. RETAIL: Retail is a generic term that encompasses all nonprofessional trading activity in financial markets. Almost always, unless you are getting paid a salary (by someone else) to trade, you are a retail trader. As a group, it's clear that retail traders are not profitable, and so

261

historically the term has been used by industry participants to denote someone pays higher costs than professionals, and against whom it's safer to trade.

6. **PENSION FUND:** A pension fund is a (typically) large pool of money that invests in markets in order to provide its investors with retirement income. Unlike the investors of a mutual fund, a pension fund doesn't simply pass through the investment results of the fund to the investor. The investors have typically negotiated a defined benefit with the pension manager: a steady, well-defined, income no matter (in principle) what the investment results have been. In fact, pension fund investors typically fall into a wide range of ages, with the current contributions of working investors funding the current retirements of older retired investors.

   Needless to say, with all this time-shifting of cash-flows and variance of investment outcomes, pension funds are fine-until-they're-not sorts of investment vehicles. Which is why, predictably, governments typically insure them so that a badly run pension fund doesn't leave its investors without a retirement income. Even more predictably, misaligned incentives and questionable management are endemic features of the pension fund world.

7. **HEDGE FUND:** Few categories of market participants are as misunderstood as hedge funds. Even the name is a misnomer, some of the time. It is hard to see where Bill Ackman and his fund Pershing Square is doing any hedging. Perhaps the most accurate (but sadly unhelpful) definition of a hedge fund is a pool of capital that can trade whatever it wants, in whatever manner it wants.

8. **INVESTMENT BANK:** A recently maligned market participant, the investment bank's job is to provide financing, advice, and connections for client companies. This includes arranging loans, bringing them public, consulting, and just about any other activity for which companies would be willing to pay fees. Investment banks have become the essential middleman of the modern market economy. Historically, these banks were quite different from commercial banks that held either explicit or implicit government guarantees, but the crisis of 2007–2008 taught the world that these investment banks have, if anything, even stronger implicit backing from governments. This is ostensibly due to their systemic importance in the economy, but the regulator/investment bank revolving door of employment likely doesn't hurt either.

9. **MARKET MAKER:** A market maker's job is to always be willing to both buy and sell the securities in which they make markets. Market makers don't have fundamental opinions about the securities they trade; they simply want to carefully manage inventory and collect the bid/ask

spread between the price at which they buy and the price at which they sell.

10. INVESTOR: In the traditional categorization of participants, investors are those individuals or organizations who buy a security and hold it for a long time. They attempt to profit by shrewdly selecting which securities to buy and, in principle, trade rarely and slowly. The canonical example of an investor is Warren Buffett.

11. SPECULATOR: The speculator attempts to profit by understanding medium-term movements of securities better than others. Typically, they seek out securities that have news or uncertainty surrounding them, and frequently bet on the direction in which the uncertainty will resolve itself. Someone buying AAPL, say in anticipation of good earnings, is speculating on the earnings report and once the news event occurs, she will close out of the position. Many other strategies—for example, merger arbitrage—more properly fall under this definition.

12. HEDGER: A hedger is someone who is active in a security in order to reduce or eliminate a market risk incurred elsewhere. If a speculator wants to bet on AAPL earnings by buying AAPL stock, she has also incurred broad market risk that she could hedge by selling a broad market security such as the SPY ETF.

13. INDEXER: The indexer's goal is to match the performance of some market index, typically a broad-based one such as the S&P 500 or the Russell 2000. The indexer's goal is to trade in order to minimize tracking error, i.e. the difference between the performance of the portfolio and the index it is tracking. Passive mutual fund investors are indexers, as are those who buy and hold broad market ETFs such as SPY or EEM.

14. SWAPS: Swaps are simply an agreement between two counterparties to exchange cash flows based on the prices of some underlying securities.

15. SPY: SPY is a US-listed ETF that holds a basket of stocks intended to track the S&P 500 index. This index is of the largest and most important publicly traded companies in the US.

16. BROKER: A broker provides connectivity (and usually financing) for clients to transact in financial markets. The broker's fee is a commission in the case of trading fees, and interest in the case of financing. Brokers frequently provide other services such as research and stock lending.

17. ARBITRAGE: The formal definition of arbitrage is simply "riskless profit." As with most two-word definitions, it's not particularly helpful. For one, it's hard to conceive of a real-world situation where riskless profit is truly on offer. Even pocketing found money on the street has some amount of scam-victim risk attached to it. It's more useful to think of arbitrage as attempting to identify the regularity about the world (whether legal, regulatory, social, or statistical) upon which a trade

relies in order to be profitable. The result is that an arbitrage trade is the act of making two versions of the same thing have the same price.

While seemingly uncontroversial and altogether good for the world, arbitrage has a somewhat checkered history. Consider the 1964 movie *Goldfinger*, where the world's most resourceful superspy is tasked with investigating the nefarious and vaguely Germanic Auric Goldfinger. The evil mastermind's suspected crime? Arbitraging the price of gold between London and Pakistan. Arbitrageurs being so thoroughly and irredeemably evil, it's perhaps unsurprising that it was later discovered Mr. Goldfinger planned to corner the market in gold by detonating a nuclear bomb in Fort Knox.

Chapter 1:

1. CAPITAL: Capital is simply the amount of money an entity has. However, in practice that definition is nearly useless. Over time, the world has developed ever more complicated ways of measuring "how much money one has," and the measurement can be more art than science. Consider measuring the capital of a typical homeowner. We can look at the money in her checking accounts, and perhaps savings accounts too. Whether to include retirement accounts is a slightly difficult question, since withdrawal penalties and tax issues could factor in. What about the equity in the house? How should that be measured? Should we consider the value of the house assuming a quick sale today, or the expected value when the house gets sold? How do we discount that value? What about the mortgage(s)? If such a common situation is complicated, consider trying to determine how much capital JPMorgan has. In fact, it's flat-out impossible to do so, even to a broad accuracy of a few billion dollars. This fact should be somewhat sobering, considering that capital is the cornerstone of our economic system.

2. EXPECTED VALUE: If we play a game where we roll a 6-sided die and I give you a dollar per pip on the result, then your expected value is 3.5: One sixth of the time you get 1, 2, 3, 4, 5 and 6 dollars, so on average you expect to get 3.5 dollars.

3. Which is more likely: (a) the Golden State Warriors will be behind after the first quarter but will win the game, or (b) the Golden State Warriors will be behind after the first quarter. In many studies with questions like these, people consistently rate (a) more probable than (b), even though (a) is a *subset* of (b)!

4. RISK: There are at least as many definitions of risk as there are people walking the earth. Even if we restrict ourselves to the small fraction of reasonably coherent accounts of risk, we're still left with a lot of ways of thinking about it. In this book, for the most part the sense is that

the risks of a situation for someone (an actor or agent) are the set of negative possible outcomes in that situation, and their associated probabilities. We can intelligibly talk about both perceived risks (from the perspective of the actor) or actual risks (which may contain outcomes that neither the actor nor indeed anyone else perceived).

Chapter 2:

1. A market maker's job is always to be willing to both buy and sell the securities in which they make markets. Market makers don't have fundamental opinions about the securities they trade; they simply want to carefully manage inventory and collect the bid/ask spread between the price at which they buy and the price at which they sell.
2. Quoting a stock is the act of making a two-sided market in it. There are four numbers that make up a quote: a bid (buy) price and size (number of shares), and an offer (ask, sell) price and size. For example, a quote of (100) 10.50 – 10.55 (200) means a bid (willingness to buy) for 100 shares at a price of 10.50, and a simultaneous offer (willingness to sell) 200 shares at 10.55. When the bid and ask sizes are the same (a frequent occurrence), this is usually abbreviated as 10.50 – 10.55 (200x).
3. An example is the story of luminiferous aether, a completely undetected and undetectable substance that purported to explain how light could travel in a vacuum.
4. The Bloomberg terminal is the industry-standard mechanism for getting information about markets and the products that trade on them. For better or worse, you could consider it the Facebook of financial markets: no one loves it, but no one can do without it.
5. In principle, the investment bank should want to make the company's owners happy, since they are the ones who are paying their bills. In practice, they're more likely to want to make the management of the company (CEO, CFO) happy, since (a) they're the ones the bank deals with, and (b) the C-suite being the revolving door that it is, a bank is likelier to get repeat business from the same manager than the same company.
6. If each share is worth $40 and 10 rights entitle the holder to buy one share for $20, then each right is worth ($40 − $20)/10 = $2.

Chapter 3:

1. Junk refers to high-risk, high-yield debt. The *spread* to highly rated (AAA) debt denotes how risky the world thinks junk is *relative* to the risk of AAA debt.

2. The idea of selling money sounds confusing, but it really isn't. If you bought a pair of shoes for $80, then you could also think of it as selling 80 United States dollars. You just happened to be paid for your dollars in shoes.

3. Reg T is not the only margin regulation that applies in the US. Looser margin requirements are available to certain US entities, generally professional traders or people with enough capital (equity) to qualify for *portfolio margining.*

4. If the stock is currently trading at $10 and the possible outcomes are $5 or $25, then the probability of good news is 25%: 75% * $5 + 25% * $25 = $10, the current value of the stock. Ensuring relationships like these are maintained is the job of the (questionably named) risk arbitrageur.

5. There is much debate about the role of position-marking in the mortgage crisis of 2007–2009. On one hand, regulators and other external agencies have strongly argued in favor of mark-to-market, i.e. that banks and related entities declare the value of their illiquid securities to be the last price at which the security traded. Marking to market, it has been argued, forces banks to use a price that is derived from a concrete transaction, instead of marking positions to some complex and untradeable model (known as mark-to-model).

   On the other hand, during crises and stressed market conditions, mark-to-market can exacerbate the crisis by setting up a chain reaction of forced sales. If some bank has paper losses on some security caused by some very low mark, they may well be forced to sell other assets to cover the margin requirements on those assets. These sales will depress the prices of other assets, causing a chain reaction that could have been avoided if the banks hadn't been forced to mark to market.

   It is clear that both extremes are unhelpful: marking to market can cause crises to worsen, but at the same time some discipline in reporting profits and losses needs to be enforced by the actual market prices of securities. Defining and policing reasonable rules on these matters is quite difficult in practice.

6. Short selling is the act of selling stock one doesn't own. In order sell something we don't own, we first need to borrow it.

7. A recent example is the 2012 renationalization of YPF by the Argentine government. The Spanish oil giant Repsol held a large stake in YPF and suffered losses that, depending on whose numbers one believes, amounted to over $5 billion. An Argentine minority shareholder, Petersen Group, happened to be well connected politically and ended up with a significantly better outcome.

8. When you buy a vanilla option, you can hedge by hedging the delta (stock risk) of the option. In practice, this means selling shares when the market moves up and buying shares when the market moves down.

The process of hedging a long option is the same thing, synthetically, as selling an option. If you do exactly the same thing (selling on the offer, buying on the bid) without having bought an option to begin with, then you're simply (synthetically) selling an option, albeit in an elaborate way.

Chapter 4:

1. ADR: An ADR is an American Depositary Receipt, a tradeable instrument that represents a promise of exchangeability with shares in a foreign country (ordinary shares). Sanofi ADRs are promises by a depositary bank (BNY Mellon) to provide Sanofi shares in Paris when the ADRs are tendered to them (plus a fee, of course). Arbitrageurs and market makers relate the prices of the ADR and the ordinary shares through this share exchange process.
2. In fact, retail traders have access to an extra source of liquidity that's not available to professionals. Equities market makers compete to trade against them and they do this by entering into agreements with retail brokerages. The brokerages route the orders directly to those market makers, bypassing the lit markets entirely. The retail customer gets a small price improvement, and the market maker gets to trade against less informed orders.

Chapter 5:

1. When the US Treasury issues bonds, the most recent issuance is known as the on-the-run issuance. The on-the-run bonds are the most liquidly traded ones, whereas off-the-run bonds have lower trading volumes and liquidity. It can happen for the prices of the two to diverge. Over the long term, there should be little difference in price between a US Treasury bond maturing in 30 years and one maturing in 29.9 years, so if the prices get too far apart one could bet on them reconverging. Of course, we know that the market can stay crazy longer than you can stay solvent, so this trade is not without risks. Long Term Capital Management famously blew up in 1998 in part because of this trade.

Chapter 7:

1. Historically, the deposit for glass bottles in most US states was 5 cents. In Michigan, however, the deposit was 10 cents. This led to many people trying to figure out ways of buying bottles in 5-cent states, redeeming the deposit in Michigan, and pocketing the 5-cent profit.

2. The terms "fundamental" and "speculative" are put into quotes to indicate that there are no hard-and-fast definitions of market participants that clearly place someone in one camp or the other. In practice, the definition ends up being more political than anything else. Frequently, if the trader lives in Chicago or New York, then they're a speculator no matter the specifics of the trading being done.
3. You can, in fact, formalize the idea of information leakage quite precisely. By using the ideas of information theory and a few standard assumptions about how markets react to trading, you can develop a well-founded mathematical theory that answers questions like "How much is 1 bit of information about the future worth?" Such a theory is beyond the scope of this book, but the mathematically minded reader can probably connect the dots.
4. LTCM ended up holding such large positions that its losses represented a systemic threat to the world financial system. In the end, a Federal Reserve–backed rescue fund had to be set up to inject capital into the various entities that stood to suffer catastrophic losses on the money lent to LTCM. Disaster was only narrowly averted.

Chapter 8:

1. Many philosophers also defend a separate notion of possibility called metaphysical possibility, which deals with possibility in conceivable universes, possibly ones with different physical laws. Again, this distinction has quite a fascinating intellectual history. Nonetheless, for my purposes the claimed distinction between metaphysical and logical possibility is too fine to be worth drawing.
2. I'm ignoring the importance of the government mortgage companies (Fannie Mae, Freddie Mac, Ginnie Mae, etc.). Their story is also long and fascinating, but is beyond the scope of this book. The effect of these entities in the mortgage markets doesn't affect the story I'm telling.
3. NINJA loan: An informal acronym denoting "no income, no job, no assets". These are loans (mortgages in this case) issued by bypassing the usual borrower creditworthiness process.
4. Interest-only ARM: An adjustable-rate mortgage where the borrower pays only interest and no principal for a period of time. After this period, the rate adjusts and the borrower must also begin paying down the principal. These mortgages only make financial sense if there is a strong expectation of an increase in the value of the home, such that selling it after the ARM period expires yields a profit.
5. If such systems are independent, then the number of failures per year follows a Poisson distribution.

6. The correlation coefficient is a mathematical measure of the relatedness of two random variables. It spans from -1 (indicating perfect anti-correlation) through 0 (uncorrelated) to 1 (perfectly correlated).
7. A reasonable theory about this is that, when people are asked to come up with party-attendance probabilities, they think of all the possible reasons that they might not make it, say ten of them, and realize that only one of them has any reasonable chance of happening. Hence, 10% of the time they won't make it. Of course, this is terrible reasoning if that one "small" thing that would prevent party-attendance has a large probability of happening.
8. Vanilla option: a normal call or put, that is the right but not the obligation to buy or sell, respectively, the underlying instrument. Options contracts can get significantly more complex than this, and Black-Scholes hedging argument does not necessarily apply to those exotic contracts.

Chapter 9:

1. Salaried investment managers are in fact rare. Much more common is for the manager to get paid a fixed percentage of the assets under management (AUM). This serves as a strong incentive to find new clients, not to maximize profitability.
2. They're actually not independent, but this correlation between coins doesn't change the story enough to matter.

Index

401(k) plan, usage, 68

A/B testing plan, 137
Activist investor, pressure, 28
Adaptation, 239, 245–247
Addiction by Design (Schüll), 5
Adverse selection, 21, 30–39,
    94, 147
Agency issues, 205–206
Agency problem, 201
Akerlof, George, 35
Alignment, 197
Amazon, rise/effect, 90–91
American Depositary Receipts
    (ADRs), 74, 257, 267
Anderson, Chris, 90
Annualized volatility, 117
Annuities, 84
Anti-inductive behavior, 177–181
Apple, 111–112
Apprenticeship, practicing, 230
Arbitrage, 34, 263–264
Assets under management (AUM),
    44, 202–203, 269
AT&T, 159
Auctions, 35–36

Banks, actions/loans, 32, 178
Barker, A.L., 24
Barter system, 42
Batesian mimicry, 207, 210–211
BATS Global Markets, self-IPO
    (failure), 241
Bayesian belief, updating, 24

Bayesian reasoning, 23–24, 98
Bayesian updating, 28
Bayes, Thomas, 23, 24, 26
Behavior, step-change, 134
Beliefs, 24–26, 98–99
Bell Labs, 158–161
Benchmarks, selection, 201
Bentham, Jeremy, 63
Berkshire Hathaway, 72
Biased interpretation, 99
Biased recall, 99
Biased search, 98–99
Biases, 15, 67, 97–101, 103, 201, 220
Black-box strategies, 125
Black box trading, 101
Black, Fischer, 187
Black Monday (1987), 189
Black Scholes formula, 188–189
Black-Scholes-Merton (BSM)
    options pricing model,
    generative model (example),
    116–117
Bloomberg terminal, 28–29, 265
Bogle, Jack, 163
Bonds, 74, 151, 178
Boredom, 4–5
Borrowers (money lending), MBSs
    (usage), 180–181
Bottom-up risk, 55–58
Box, George, 136
Bretton Woods currency system, US
    withdrawal, 243
Brokerage fees (visible linear
    costs), 144–145

Brokers, 84, 257, 263
Brynjolfsson, Erik, 219
Buffett, Warren, 27, 64, 73, 198
Business, 27
    business-related technologies,
        expertise, 211
    normalcy, 213

Calibration exercise, 185–186
Calls, 79–81
Capacity, 141
Capital, 41–46, 200–201, 205–208
    amount, 77
    capital-intensive business,
        funding, 33
    definition, 264
    loss, 63
    personal value, 63
    reduction, 180
    requirement, 44, 106, 198
    risk, 56
Capital goods, company purchase,
    148
Carroll, Lewis, 167
Cars, 86, 89–90
Cash, borrowing, 42
Cash infusion, 33
Catastrophic risk, 63–65
Change-point, 133
Christensen, Clayton, 161
Churchill, Winston, 57
Clearing costs (visible linear costs),
    144
Clearinghouses, problems, 51
Cognitive biases, 67
Cognitive demands, 219–220
Coin-flipping tournaments,
    203–204
Collateral, 43–44
Commodities, 146, 261
Common shares, issuance, 32
Common stock, derivatives, 79–80
Communication risk, 57
Computers, usage, 124

Concrete probabilities, 184–185
Confidence, 24, 125
Confirmation bias, 98–99, 220
Consensus-based culture, 214
Context (understanding),
        machines (problems), 228
Contracts, 85–86
Corporate actions, 43
Correlation coefficient, 269
Correlations, 179–184
Costs, 43, 141, 143–161
    improvement, relationship, 247
    structure, reduction, 178
    underestimation, 162–163
Counterparty risk, 50–51
Creativity, 102–103
Credit card payment protection, 65
Credit-default swap (CDS),
        contract, 53–54
Crude oil, standard contracts, 261
Cum-cum trade, 109
Cum-ex trade, 109
Cunningham, Ward, 231
Curve-fitting, 119
Cyclomatic complexity, 234

Daily percentage returns, plotting,
    61
Data, 123–132, 220–228
    availability, 243
    processing, machine
        replacement example, 224
Debt, 87, 231–236
    junk debt, comparison, 41
Debugging, 125, 230–231
Decision making, 2–3, 15, 214
Default correlation, 180
Deferred pay, 88
Dentsu IPO, 189–190
Depreciation, 149, 231–233
Derivatives, 78, 187
Derivatives contracts, 54, 146
DE Shaw, 151, 245

Development
  production, contrast, 131–132
  workforce, impact, 229–230
Diagonal cloud, meaning, 61
Differential reproductive fitness,
  244–245
"Disruption Machine, The"
  (Lepore), 157
Disruptive innovation, 157
Dividends, 43, 108
Downside risk, 47
Driving, perception, 98
Dunbar's number, 250
Dunning-Kruger effect, 3, 98

Earnings announcement, 80
eBay, adverse selection (usage),
  35–37
Economic business cycles,
  explanation, 207–208
Ecosystem, 222
Edges, 5, 93–101, 106–113, 162
  changes, 135
  defining, 94–95
  expression, model (usage), 115,
    121
  impact, 246
  reliability/robustness, 123
  source, identification, 149
  strategies, 135–136
  usage, 111–113, 206–207
Efficient market hypothesis (EMH),
  impact, 94
Emerging market, trading, 56
Emotional reactions, studies, 4
Employees, 210–213, 221
  company hiring, 37
  pressures, impact, 37–38
Employers, risk, 210
Engines, failure (correlation), 183
Enron, bankruptcy, 68
Equal profits/losses, value, 63

Equipment (visible nonlinear cost),
  145
European Central Bank (ECB),
  34–35, 193
Evil, defining, 215
Exchange fees (visible linear costs),
  144
Exchange technical issues, 50
Exchange-traded funds (ETFs), 45,
  73, 107, 162–163, 209
Exchange-traded securities,
  trading, 51
Execution risk, 56
Ex-nihilo idea, 242
Exotic market, trading, 149
Exotic mortgage structures, usage,
  181
Expected value, definition, 264
Experimentation, encouragement,
  106
Explain-away effect, 179
Exploratory research, failure
  (impact), 161
External motivators,
  counterproductivity, 18
External technical environment,
  change, 135

Factory work, machine replacement
  example, 224
Failure
  impact, 161
  probability/rate, 182–183
Falkenstein, Eric, 207–208
Farming, machine replacement
  example, 224
Fear, trading emotion, 3–4
Feature debt cost, identification,
  235
Feedback, 170–177, 189
  mechanisms, 46, 174
  process, impact, 180–181
Fiduciary responsibility, absence, 84

Fifth Third Bancorp (FITB), 76–81, 83
Financial crises, occurrence, 30
Financial crisis (2007-2008), 180–181, 192
Financial gain, 12
Financial Industry Regulatory Authority (FINRA), 71, 257
Financial markets, 154, 170–172
    adverse selection, usage, 30–34
    competitiveness, 100–101, 127
    historical episodes, 187–194
    natural selection, 241
    technology, usage, 199
    trading, 52
Financial risk, 50
Financial services, marketing strategies, 12–13
Financial stocks, exposure, 82
Financing (visible linear costs), 144
Firms, 252–253
    culture, damage, 214–215
    employees, compensation difficulties, 210–211
    incentives, usage, 209–215
    involvement, 241, 244–245
    success, edge (usage), 246
Flash Crash (2010), 101–102
Force multiplier, 199
Free Solo (documentary), 8
Frequentist statistics, birth, 23–24
Fundamental, term (usage), 268
Funds
    losses/fees, 202, 203
    trading, 107

Galton, Francis, 23
Gates, Bill, 64
Gaussian distribution, 133
Generative models, 118–119, 137
German tax dividend trade, 108–111, 249–250
Getting to Yes (Fisher), 200

Global financial markets, competitiveness, 110
Goodhart's law, 46, 68, 69, 136
Government mortgage companies, importance (ignoring), 268
Grabel, John, 7
Gradual changes, 135–136
Great Recession (2008-2009), 101–102
Greed, trading emotion, 3–4
Griffin, Albert, 93–94
Groups, improvement/ involvement, 241, 244, 250–252
Grove, Andy, 57
Growth mindset, 248

Habit, formation, 14–15
Hardware, usage, 124–125
Hedge funds, 174, 202, 205, 262
Hedges, 59–63, 67–68
Hedging, 42, 45–46, 65, 150, 187
Herding, 150–154
Heterogeneity, 75–76, 154
Heteroskedasticity, 127
Hierarchical firm, subordinate instruction, 214
Hierarchy, level, 241
Higher-order reasoning, 29
High-frequency trading, example, 121–122
High-water marks, 204–205
Hindsight bias/usage, 15–16
Historical data, 123, 133–134
Historical probabilities, 81
Hit-miss ratios, identification, 149
Homes (houses), financing/dates/purchases, 87, 181
Honnold, Alex, 8, 46
Hour Between Dog and Wolf, The (Coates), 4
Housing, 86–87

Humans, 217–220, 223–228,
247
biases, mitigation, 102
capital, requirement, 163
model-building machines, 136
productivity, 253–258
safety considerations, 182
Hyperparameters, 130

Idea Factory, The (Gertner), 158
Illiquid options, trading, 51
Illusory superiority, 97
Image recognition network, 126
Implied volatility, 117–118
Impossible events, creation,
191–192
Improvement, costs (relationship),
247
Incentives, 202–204, 206–215
Indexer, definition, 263
Index funds, rise, 162–163
Index-tracking mutual funds, rise,
209
Individuals,
improvement/involvement,
241, 244, 248–249
Induction, importance, 170
Inductive hypothesis (IH), 169–170
Industrial Revolution, reading
(importance), 218
Information
aggregation, 26
asymmetry, 21–22, 36
incorporation, 25
short-lived information, reliance,
148
Information technology (IT),
superiority, 199
Initial public offerings (IPOs),
30–32
Innovation, 143, 157–161
Innovator's Dilemma, The
(Christensen), 156

Insider information, 57
Inspectability, 125–126
Institutional self-knowledge, 112
Instruments, variety, 152
Insurance, 65–66, 187–189
adverse selection, 39
buyers, quotes, 39
rates, change, 68
Intellectual property (IP),
importance, 213
Intellectual validation, 10–12
Intelligence quotient
(IQ), 97
Interest-only (IO) ARMs, 181, 268
Interest rate risk, 74
Interest rate swap contracts,
variation, 74
Interfaces, cleanliness, 126
Intermediation layer, 27
Internal technical environment,
change, 135
Interviewers, employee
qualification, 38
Interviewing, process, 38
Intuition-based variables,
systematization, 228
Investments, 201, 203–205
advisers, 84
banks, 31, 262
Investors, money (extraction),
201–202
Invisible linear costs, 147–150
Invisible nonlinear costs, 150–161
Iterative improvement, 125
Iterative testing, 104

Japan Airlines (JAL), problems,
93–95
Japan, Dentsu IPO, 189–190
Jobs, 17–18, 37–39, 88–89
automation, impact, 224
description, embellishment, 38
machines, impact (absence), 225

Jobs (*continued*)
  offers, 38, 66–67
  pressures/constraints, 249
Junk debt/definition, 41, 265

Kahneman, Daniel, 2
Kanban (methodology), 229
Keep Your Identity Small (Graham),
  13–14
Kelly, Mervin, 159, 161
Kennedy, John F., 256
Kludges, implementation, 233
Knew-it-all-along symptom, 15
Knight Capital, 132, 241, 245
Knowledge, 22
  overestimation, 3
Kodak, bankruptcy, 156–157, 253

Labor, intensiveness, 198–199
Leading Change (Burr), 253
Legal costs (visible nonlinear cost),
  145
Legal risk, 52
Leland, Hayne, 188
Leland O'Brien Rubinstein
    Associates (LOR), initiation,
    188
Lepore, Jill, 157
Leverage, 154, 194
Levine, Matt, 54
Linear costs, 143–145, 147–150
Linearity (cost characteristic), 143
Linear scaling, impact, 143
Liquidity, 71–91, 154, 244
  customer demand, 107
  idea, 246
  risk, 51, 55–56, 147
  source, retail trader access, 267
Loans, 84–85
Logical possibility, 167–168
Long illiquid high-yield bonds, 151
Long Russian government debt, 151
Long tail, concept, 90

Long Term Capital Management
    (LTCM), 151, 153, 241, 268
Long-term holding, sale, 176
Long-term strategy, usage, 148
Low-probability events, correlations
    (relationship), 179–180

MacAlpine, Wayne, 94–94
Machine learning (ML) models,
  222
Machines, 223–228
Management, 84, 214
Margin, 43, 56, 77, 78, 144, 175
Marginal traders, importance,
  95–96
Market crash (1987), 47, 187–189
Market maker, 34–35, 262–263, 265
  co-located machines, 227
  reaction, 189
  rights, shorting, 33
  supply and demand knowledge,
    28
Market risk, 50, 53–55
  evaluation, 58–59
  reports, 58
  varieties, 59–63
Markets, 100, 104–107, 170
  anti-inductive behavior, 177–181
  data (visible nonlinear cost), 145
  futures, 45
  heterogeneity, 154
  impact, estimation, 77
  liquidity, 91, 154
  market-friction-induced
    illiquidity, 88
  movements, 45, 189
  participants, 54, 72, 134
  prices, movement, 127
  random number generators, 104
  society, relationship, 26–27
  trading, 51–52
  two-sided market, refusal, 76
  value, underestimation, 26

Maslow, Abraham, 112, 256
Matador Fund, value (decline), 197
Max drawdown, 46
McAfee, Andrew, 219
Mean reversion, 154, 172–174
Medium-complexity model, 130
Memberships, 85–86
Mental biases, 103
Mental tasks, 98
Merchandise, sales, 36–37
Mergers, 57, 245
Meriwether, John, 241
Merton, Robert, 151
Meta-model, creation, 125, 130
Meta-rational reason, 169–170
Metrics, usage, 76–77
Milken, Michael, 241
Modeling effort, 128
Model risk, 51
Models, 115, 120–126, 130–139, 162
  defining, 116–118
  domain, 119
  hyperparameters, 130
  impact, 246
  options models, 120
  parameters, 12
  scariness, 118–119
  software, usage, 124–125
  usability, 123
  validity/value, 147
  variation, expectation, 133–134
  world simplification, 116–120
Models, building, 122
  data management, relationship, 126–132
  process, 131
  psychology/sociology, 116
Modular design, requirement, 125
Momentum strategy, 172
Monetary structures, alignment, 208–209

Money, making/pledge, 2, 44–46
Mortgage-back securities (MBSs), 177–178, 180–181
Mortgages, 87, 177–178
  crisis (2007-2009), position-marking role, 266
  markets, crisis (impact), 181
  mortgage-to-mortgage default correlation, 180
  securitization, 243
Motivation, 1, 11–13, 245–246, 248
Motivation and Personality (Maslow), 112
Move-out dates, move-in dates (alignment), 87
Mutual funds, 84

National best offer (NBBO), 75
National Longitudinal Survey of Youth, dataset, 7
Natural hedges, 67–68
Natural selection, 240–245
Negative feedback, 171
Negotiation, 244
Network topology changes, 135
News, impact, 49
Newton, Isaac, 255
Niederhoffer, Victor, 81, 197, 241
Nigerian Stock Exchange (NSE) market data, 257
NINJA loans, 181, 268
Noncompete clauses, 88
Nondisclosure agreements, 88
Nondisparagement clauses, 88
Non-instantaneous transactions, cost, 90
Nonlinear costs, 143, 145–146, 150–161
Novel risks, 59

Okazaki, Akira, 93
On-the-run bonds, off-the-run treasury bonds (relationship), 107

Operational risk, 51
Operations staff, performance pay
    fractions, 211
Opportunity cost, 43, 86, 155–158
Options, 176, 187
    models, 120
    sale, 60
    strike price, 117
Organization, intellectual property
    (importance), 213
Out-of-sample (OOS)
    performance, 130
Out of the money call,
    consideration, 80
Outperformance, 45, 59–62
Overconfidence bias, 97–98,
    100–101, 220
Overdraft protection, 66
Ownership, problems, 109

Paradigms, proliferation, 229
Paranoia, usefulness, 67–68
Participative management,
    emphasis, 251
Pattern recognition, 105
Pay structures, 210–213
Pension fund, 173, 262
People, hiring/models,
    137–138
Performance, 211–212
    changes, 135
    pay fractions, 211, 214
Persistence, impact, 103
Personal edge, 112–113
Personal value, 63
Phenomenological models, 119,
    137
Phone contracts, 86
Physical labor, replacement, 219
Physical possibility, 168–169
Pierce, John, 160
Political instability, 50
Political risk, 56

Political turmoil, victims, 56
Portfolio insurance (PI), 187–189
Portfolio margins, 83
Position-marking, role, 266
Positive feedback, 171, 175
Possibility, 167–169
    evaluation techniques, 184–186
Potential energy, release, 171
Power of Habit, The (Duhigg), 14
Practicality, impact, 106
Precommitment, 14–18
Predictive Processing Model, 138
Principal, 50, 205
Probabilities, 2, 182–185
Productivity, 253–258
Profit, 203–204
    maximization, 12, 256
    yield, 53
Profitability, 13, 146, 162
Profit-and-loss (P&L), 48, 110, 133,
    148, 175
Programming interfaces, 135
Program trading, 189
Prospective employees, selection
    pressure, 37–38
PTT Limited (Thailand), 55
Public exchanges, shares trading,
    30–31
Puts, sale, 81

Qualitative assessments, 59
Qualitative review, 105
Quantitative easing, measures, 193
Quantitative review, 103–105

Rabbani, Abed, 7
Rand, Ayn, 197
Randomness, impact, 133
Rare events, behavior, 184
Rational inquiry, baseline rule, 177
Regression, 62
Regulation, change, 243
Regulation NMS, 75

Regulation T (Reg T), 43, 77, 79, 266
Regulatory costs (visible nonlinear cost), 145
Reinforcement learning, idea, 222
Relationship-building, 145, 244
Relationship manager, 71
Rent (visible nonlinear cost), 145
Rental contracts, writing, 87
Replication, crisis, 104
Reputational risk, 48, 52
Residential real estate, returns, 87
Resources, allocation, 148–149, 155–156
Resources, fungibility, 156
Retail, definition, 261–262
Retail Liquidity Program (RLP), 132
Retirees, money (extraction), 201–202
Retirements savings, vehicles, 84
Return requirements, assumption, 24–25
"Revolution in Military Affairs," 253
Rights, 32–34, 57
Rights to inventions, 88–89
Risk, 41, 58–68, 197
  compensation, 48
  counterparty risk, 50–51
  definition, 42, 46–52, 264–265
  downside risk, 47
  evaluation, 53–59
  financial risk, 50
  hedging, relationship, 45–46
  instruction, 246
  limits, 24, 49
  liquidity, relationship, 76–83, 147
  management, 182
  measure, 46, 48–50, 53
  measurement, 53–59
  mismeasure, VaR (relationship), 47–48
  plan, 52–53
  reputational risk, 48, 52
  risk taking, emotional reactions (studies), 4
  seeking, 6–9
  setpoints, 8
  systems, 58–59
  tolerance, 7–8
  types, 50–52
  understanding, 53
  volatility risk, 60
Robustness (models), 123–124
Rothschild, Nathan, 220–221
Rubinstein, Mark, 188
Russia, economy (stability), 151

SAC Capital, brokerage fees, 144
Salary (visible nonlinear cost), 145
Sales-centric organization, incentives, 210
Sales information, 221
Same, defining, 223
Scariness, disagreements, 119–120
Scholes, Myron, 151, 187
Schüll, Natasha, 5
Scrum (methodology), 229
Search results, 98–99
Second Machine Age, The (Brynjolfsson/McAfee), 219
Sector, performance, 59–60
Securities, 75, 107, 152
Securities and Exchange Commission (SEC) regulations, Nigerian investment compliance, 257
Securities Investor Protection Corporation (SIPC) guarantees, 84
Segmentation, 161
Selection, 240–245
Selective perception, 67
Self-financing portfolios, 42–44
Self-image, size (change), 14–15

Self-improvement, precommitment
     (usage), 18
Self-insurance, 66
Self-interest, power/limitations,
     200–206
Self-knowledge, 12–13, 16–18, 112,
     185, 245
Self-labeling, importance, 14
Self-organized feedback systems,
     170
Series A funding, 66
Shareholders, rights (exercise), 32
Shares, 77–78
     ex-rights, 33
Short equity volatility, 151
Short-lived information, reliance,
     148
Short low-yield high-quality bonds,
     151
Short selling, action, 266
Silos, 212–213
Single-stock future (SSF), 78–79
Six Sigma event, 133
Skewness, 46
Skills, development, 217–218
Social Security, insurance product,
     65
Society, markets (relationship),
     26–27
Software, 124–125, 135
     code, change, 232
     development, cost estimation, 67
     engineering, 228–230
Soros, George, 197
South African rand (ZAR)
     valuation, 22–25, 28–29
Special trades, 28–30
Specificity, 77
Speculative, term (usage), 268
Speculative traders, influence, 146
Speculator, definition, 263
Spinoffs, 57
Spread to cross, 76

SPY, 60–62, 73
     definition, 263
     purchase, 76, 82
     puts, purchase/sale, 83
Squeeze, 175–176
Standard deviation, 46, 97
Static analysis tools,
     implementation, 233–234
Statistical regularities, 137–138
Statisticians, fight, 23–24
Status-quo bias, 201
Stochastic markets, 170
Stock Exchange of Thailand (SET),
     trades, 55
Stocks, 28, 49, 52–53, 261
     market, consideration, 173–174
     price, increase, 32
     quotation, 22–23, 265
     selection, problems, 44–45
     split, 57
     trading, 107, 266
     volatility risk, 60
Store sales/specials, adverse
     selection (usage), 36–37
Stories, 96–97, 101–106, 147
Strategy performance, randomness
     (impact), 133
Stratification, 161
Stress event, 154
Structural precommitment, 16
Structural restrictions, 207,
     208
Structure, building, 247
Structured products (SPs), 84
Supply and demand, market maker
     knowledge, 28
Sutton, Rich, 222
Swaps, definition, 263
Swiss franc (CHF), safety (loss),
     192–193
Swiss National Bank (SNB),
     response, 192–193

Tail exponent, 46
Taleb, Nassim, 186
"Talking your book"
    (phenomenon), 174–175
Tax rates, difference, 108–109
Taylor, Frederick, 250
Technical debt, 231–236
Technical staff, performance-based
    bonus, 211
Technological disruptions,
    157–158
Technological risk, 51–52
Technology, usage, 199, 217
Temporal-difference (TD)
    learning, 222
Tenacity, reward, 103
Theories of everything, 120
"Theory of Human Motivation, A"
    (Maslow), 112
Thinking, Fast and Slow
    (Kahneman), 2
Thorp, Ed, 151
Ticket charges (visible linear costs),
    144
Top-down risk, 53–54
Trade depreciation, insight, 150
Traders, 225–227, 254–258
    edge, usage, 206–207
    pay structures, 210–213
Trades, 174–175, 207–209, 242–243
    calm, 29–30
    collateralization, 44
    depreciation, 147, 148, 150
    discoveries/possessions, 255
    landscape, 161–163
    market-based requirements, 198
    mean-reversion trade, 154
    metrics, usage, 76–77
    ownership, 163–164
    regulatory requirements, 198
    undercapitalization, 45
    undertaking, 56
    worsening, 110

Trading, 1–12, 22–28, 198–200
    activity cost, 142–143
    algorithm, usage, 225
    businesses, culture/
        consistency, 213–215
    firm (success), edge (impact),
        246
    high-frequency trading, example,
        121–122
    high-value aspects, 226
    normal mode, 174
    positions, stress, 58–59
    price increases, 31
    profitability, 96
    reinvention, 58
    strategies, 101, 121
    stress/risk, 30
Trading in the Zone (Douglas), 6
Transportation, machine
    replacement example, 224
Trustworthiness, impact, 62
TSE200 index, tracking, 202

UBS Warburg, shares (sale), 190
Uncertainty, experience,
    186–187
United Kingdom, contract-for-
    difference trades, 243
United States
    corporate bonds, market, 152
    funds, transfer, 257
    short sale ban, 191
    Treasury, bonds (issuance), 267
Universal gravitation, law
    (Newton), 118
Unknown unknowns, 156–158
Updated beliefs, usage, 24–25
Utilities, 3, 63–65, 87
Utility function, convexity, 64
Utilons, 63

Value at risk (VaR), 46–48
Vanilla option, 266–267, 269

Variation, sources, 242–244
Venture capital, impact,
    102–103
Viniar, David, 119
Visibility (cost characteristic), 143
Visible linear costs, 144–145
Visible nonlinear costs,
    145–146
Volatility, 60, 117–118
Volkswagen AG, size (increase),
    191–192
Vom Kriege (von Clausewitz), 253
von Clausewitz, Carl, 253

Water-mark restrictions, 205
Wealth, 2, 63–64
Wearing a position, 51
Wetware, usage, 124–125
When Genius Failed (Lowenstein),
    151

Whitman, Walt, 164
Wimbledon Fund, 197
Winner's curse, adverse selection
    (usage), 35–36
Workers, incentives/inventions, 38,
    88–89
Workforce, education (investment),
    161
World
    change, 134
    models, 136–137
    simplifications, 116–120
Worst-case scenarios, 67
Worth, public signal, 26

XLF, 61–62, 76, 81–83

"You," 13–15
YPF, renationalization, 266

Zone, 5–6